An Introduction to Ontology

An Introduction to Ontology

Nikk Effingham

polity

First published in 2013 by Polity Press

Polity Press
65 Bridge Street
Cambridge CB2 1UR, UK

Polity Press
350 Main Street
Malden, MA 02148, USA

ISBN-13: 978-0-7456-5254-2
ISBN-13: 978-0-7456-5255-9(pb)

A catalogue record for this book is available from the British Library.

Typeset in 10.5 on 12 pt Palatino
by Toppan Best-set Premedia Limited
Printed and bound in Great Britain by MPG Books Group Limited, Bodmin, Cornwall

The publisher has used its best endeavours to ensure that the URLs for external websites referred to in this book are correct and active at the time of going to press. However, the publisher has no responsibility for the websites and can make no guarantee that a site will remain live or that the content is or will remain appropriate.

Every effort has been made to trace all copyright holders, but if any have been inadvertently overlooked the publisher will be pleased to include any necessary credits in any subsequent reprint or edition.

For further information on Polity, visit our website: www.politybooks.com

Contents

Acknowledgements

I'd like to take this chance to thank Richard Woodward and Al Wilson for looking over some/all of this book manuscript; those students from Glasgow and Birmingham who studied on the metaphysics course that helped this book evolve; the staff at Starbucks who always made sure I was supplied with the requisite liquid materials to get the work done (in particular Abi Owen who always keenly asked how many words I was on); and Iain Law, Jussi Suikkanen and Heather Widdows for mostly everything else.

Preface

How this book is arranged

This book is an introductory guide to contemporary ontology in the analytic philosophical tradition, dealing mainly with questions about what things exist, and what those things are like. Except for the first chapter, each chapter examines a different category of entity and the ontological questions surrounding them. However, in ontology, the methodology is itself a prime suspect as a cause of many of the problems. Indeed, recently it has come under renewed scrutiny as philosophers debate exactly how we are meant to answer ontological questions. So every topic-based chapter (except chapter 9) also introduces a different methodological issue for your consideration; in each chapter you'll get to see how that methodological principle is meant to work with regard to the category in question, giving you the chance to see it in action.

Chapter 1 is a straightforward introduction to the basics of ontology for those who either don't know what it is, or they know what it is but fear that it doesn't make any sense. Chapter 2 then introduces the Quinean theory of ontological commitment, as well as the notion of theory choice (i.e., how we determine which theory is correct and by what standard such a choice is made), illustrating how these pieces of methodology function by examining the ontology of holes. Chapter 3 turns to the ontology of properties, including questions not just about whether they exist or not but what they are like if they do exist. During the course of that chapter, we introduce the idea of metaphysical explanation and the role it might play in settling ontological questions. Chapter 4 examines whether numbers exist. We also introduce 'Meinongianism': that there's a difference between what exists and what there is. Chapter 5 turns to modality – questions about possibility and necessity – and introduces possible worlds. We get to see another theory concerning ontological commitment – fictionalism – and how that works with regards to possible worlds. Chapter 6 examines whether space (or spacetime) exists. We examine at this stage how scientific theories can feed into metaphysical reasoning. Chapter 7 examines the ontology of things that exist at other times, e.g., whether dinosaurs or Napoleon exist. We also introduce another methodological tool – the theory of truthmaking – and see how that works with regard to the ontology of time. Chapter 8 examines mereology: the study of parts and wholes. We will look at what composite objects there are, e.g., are there tables, chairs, mountains or goats? If not, how is it that we think there are? In that chapter, we shall examine Neo-Carnapianism, a theory which, if true, would deflate ontological questions to merely being confusions about language. Chapter 9 introduces questions about persistence and whether there are things like statues and people. Finally, in chapter 10, we finish off by deploying a variety of issues from previous chapters to a specific ontological question: whether there are works of music. In that chapter, I end by talking about whether we can distinguish between what exists and what fundamentally exists, and how such a distinction would play a role in practising ontology.

Certainly, if you have never studied ontology, some of the above will sound like a foreign language. Have no fear! Whilst much of ontology sounds initially esoteric, this book will slowly take you through each theory, and each piece of methodology, explaining exactly what is involved and how best to understand it.

What this book assumes

This book is written for philosophy undergraduates but should be suitable for the intellectually sophisticated who are not studying undergraduate courses. Whilst it assumes some passing acquaintance with philosophical theories, all metaphysical and ontological theories will be introduced in detail. What it *does* assume is the ability to understand first-order predicate logic – not the ability to do proofs or truth-tables, but just the ability to read and understand sequents in standard first-order logic.

The symbols I will be using are:

∀	universal quantifier
∃	existential quantifier
→	material conditional ('if . . . then')
¬	negation ('not')
&	conjunction ('and')
∨	inclusive disjunction ('or')
a, b, c . . .	names
x, y, z . . .	variables
P, Q, R . . .	propositions

Those not acquainted with these symbols will be able to find good introductions in a variety of places. I highly recommend Paul Tomassi's *Logic* or, if you want something shorter, Joe Morrison's *Logic*. However, the level of logical aptitude required is only limited. As long as you can translate things like 'All balls are round', 'Nikk Effingham is a philosopher' and 'Some raven is a bird', you'll find nothing to worry you here.

What this book leaves unsaid

In many ways, this book is a tissue of lies. It is not a definitive guide to every area of ontology for it is written primarily as a textbook for undergraduates. In light of this, accuracy rightly gives way to pedagogical demands. When reading this book, you should bear in mind how much of what it deals with is contentious, and how what I am offering you are theories for your consideration, not set-in-stone truths dictated to you by some imaginary philosophical establishment. With that in mind, I have not prefaced every sentence with 'Some philosophers believe . . .' or 'It is arguable that . . .' or other phrases to make clear the tendentious nature of the material. To do so would be unduly annoying for you. So bear in mind that for every theory, every position, every argument (heck, every assertion!) contained in this book, there is a serious philosopher somewhere who denies it. Frankly, I find some of the positions you'll find in later chapters utterly ludicrous and have had to grit my teeth and force myself to neutrally state the theories as best as possible. But this is a textbook, not a polemic, and it's a pedagogical requirement that I present to you these theories as best as I think is possible for you to mull over yourself. Similarly, the vast majority of principles and generalizations I state have innumerable exceptions and tweaks that have been ignored for the sake of brevity – I am sure you'll encounter many such details as you engage in your independent research and come to see that this introduction glosses over many niceties (which might well prove important to you!). And this is all okay, for the main part of any philosophy course is contained *not* in your reading this book but in your own independent research and the independent development of the thoughts and theories presented here. So just bear in mind how you should be reluctant to treat everything this book says as (even intended to being!) the last word on the topic at hand.

1

The Basics

Ontology

Crudely, ontology, at least in the context of metaphysics, is the study of what things exist. Obviously, this stands in need of some clarification. For instance, physicists set out to find out what things exist (are there black holes; Higgs-Boson particles; superstrings?) As too do biologists (what insects are there; what antibodies; what plants?) As too do archaeologists (does the lost city of El Dorado exist?); property speculators (is there any radon gas under such-and-such a house?); oil speculators (how much oil is there under the Arctic?); stamp collectors (what stamps are there?); and UFO watchers (are there any aliens?) 'Are these people', you might ask, 'doing what you call ontology? Isn't ontology something that *everyone* does?' Of course, the answer is no – ontology is not something that everyone does, and the physicist, biologist, stamp collector and UFO watcher are not engaging in ontology even though they all have a vested interest in finding out what things exist. This is because the ontologist is not interested in the existence of any old things. You will not find ontologists rummaging around your wardrobe, scribbling down on a scrap of paper what things they find in there as they build their 'list of all things that exist'. Whilst humorous, and whilst it would give me an excuse to rummage around other people's private belongings without having to live out my childhood dream of being a private investigator, this is not what ontologists do at all. Indeed, there is virtually no fieldwork whatsoever, for ontologists are – unlike the physicist, biologist, UFO watcher etc. – interested in far more *general* questions about what exists. All of the examples cited above (subatomic particles, insects, antibodies, buildings, build-ups of gas, stamps and aliens) are examples of **material objects**. The ontologist generally accepts the existence of such material objects (but will, as we shall see in chapters 8 and 9, vary over the details). But this doesn't even come close to exhausting the things that ontologists are interested in. Far from it! For they are not just interested in material objects, but interested in whether there are more things besides. By this, we *don't* mean whether there are *im*material objects, like angels, God and the Devil (although some ontologists *may* be interested in that as well if they have an interest in the philosophy of religion), but whether there are things like numbers, properties, events, works of music, etc.

Let's illustrate this with an example. A historian may tell us that, on 1 July 1916, 19,420 British soldiers died during the first day of the Battle of the Somme. Imagine the historian gave an ontologist detailed reports concerning what happened, and what went on, explaining what people were there, how much ammunition each side had, what terrain featured in the battle, and so on. The ontologist will probably agree that all of these things existed – they're material objects and, with little exception, ontologists believe in material objects. But, they may ask, in addition to the material objects (the guns, the mud piles, the people involved, etc.), were there *also* things like **events**? In other words, if you listed everything that existed, would you write down not just all of the guns, the mud piles, the people and so on but also scribble at the bottom 'The Battle of the Somme'? Or 'the event of Private John Smith missing his target with his rifle'? Or any of the numerous events that took place during the Battle of the Somme? Or would you *not* stick those things on the list? Would you say such things *didn't* exist, and that, in listing all of the material objects (the people, the guns, the geographic features, etc.), you'd have exhaustively listed everything that there was?

There are also more things than events to worry about. The Somme is a place. Do you have to put 'The Somme' on the list – that is, do **places** exist? Or consider this: many people were shot and were in pain. They had the **property** of being in pain. So do we have to add to the list of things that exist 'the property of being in pain'? Or what about the fact that 19,420 people were killed? Does that mean that we need to add in **numbers**? Knowing full well that the number of people who were killed was 19,420, after listing all the material objects, properties and events that existed, do we stick down 'the number 19,420' on the list of all things that exist? Do we stick down *every* number (for surely if one number exists, all of them do)? We can even ask about the trenches. After all, isn't a trench a hole in the ground – it's a lack of earth that makes a trench and surely that lack, that absence, isn't a thing in itself? Or do the tunes that the soldiers whistled during the day (however few and far between they may have been) get put on the list? And why stop the questions there! It's possible that Private John Smith died during the battle even though he survived. So do **possibilities** exist? Do we have to add to our list of objects (and events, and absences, and numbers, and tunes, etc.) the possibilities that could have played out instead?

It is *these* kinds of questions that ontologists are interested in. They examine these broader, more general questions about what things there are. Each of the later chapters will deal with a specific category of things, in order: holes; properties; numbers; possibilities (and possible worlds); places (or regions, as we'll call them); objects from other times; objects in general; and works of music. For this chapter, though, we'll keep with elucidating how these kinds of questions even make sense. They are, after all, pretty esoteric sounding, and it's not obvious that finding out whether there are numbers or not (etc.) is a worthwhile, or even intelligible, task. So let's turn to examining some reasons for thinking that these questions are intelligible and intellectually worthwhile.

Abstract versus concrete

Start by introducing some basic terminology. Ontologists generally split things into two categories: the **abstract** things and the **concrete** things. When we say 'concrete', we don't mean things made of cement – more than mere buildings get to be concrete in the ontologist's use of the word. The concrete things are those things like particles, people, buildings, planets, goats, stamps, etc. 'Concrete', then, generally includes everything that is inside space and time, and usually extends to things like events and places. Indeed, if there are such things, people generally think that ghosts, God, and the Devil (i.e., immaterial things) are concrete. The concrete things (what we can call 'concreta') are the focus of the second half of this book.

Abstract things are things like the numbers, properties, possibilities, facts or propositions. Unlike the concreta, you won't find

abstracta anywhere. The number 4 isn't down the back of your
sofa, the proposition that $2 + 2 = 4$ isn't in Washington, the property
being in pain can't be found and picked up, taken home and sold
on eBay (note that we italicize the names of properties). However,
they might nonetheless exist (if you think it weird that things that
aren't anywhere nevertheless get to exist, I discuss this more below).
So the abstracta are, crudely, those things which are not in space
and time. They are sometimes said to be in **platonic heaven**, and
if you read around the subject I'm sure you'll come across that
phrase. Plato believed that our world was just a sub-standard
version of Heaven, whilst Heaven contained all of the 'Forms'. The
Forms were what things share when they have something in
common. For instance, we are all human and so there is a Form
corresponding to what it is to be human, and so all humans partici-
pate in these Forms (this is closely allied to the debate about properties that we shall discuss in chapter 3). Plato believed that they were
abstract entities, and it has become common to say that they are 'in'
platonic heaven (where 'in' is meant to be read figuratively, for they
are abstract and so not really 'in' or 'out' of anything). So using the
term isn't to endorse the existence of a heavenly realm, but is
just a shorthand way of saying that something is abstract, and not
in space and time.

This is a *very* rough idea of what these terms mean, and when
reading the literature you have to take what I've just said with a
full tablespoon of salt rather than just a pinch. For instance, there
is no agreement over what should appear on the list of abstract
things and what on the list of the concrete. Some philosophers
think that properties *are* in space and time (see chapter 3) and that
possibilities *are* concrete things after all (see chapter 5). Moreover,
my characterization of the divide being one of whether or not
such things are in space and time or not is also pretty rough. Not
everyone agrees with that (for instance, as already noted, some
people place immaterial things in the concrete category even though
they aren't in space, and others use the word 'abstract' to apply
to entities that are in time but that are not in space), and often
the terms are defined differently as suits the purpose of the individual philosopher. But this rough idea will suffice for our purposes
here.

Terminological Alerts!

'Abstract' and 'concrete' are good examples of where philosophers vary over defining terms. Throughout this book, boxes like these will make clear where there are problems in the literature with how terminology is defined. Not every philosopher uses the same term in the same way, and these boxes make clear when this happens. It is crucial, especially when doing your own independent reading around the subject, that you are clear on exactly what the individual author of a piece of work intends by using certain pieces of terminology, lest serious confusion set in.

Don't get too hung up on asking what the 'correct' definition is. Words like 'abstract' and 'concrete' are terms of art, and one can freely make up a term of art and define it to mean whatever one wants – there's no 'right' or 'wrong' about it! The differences don't arise because someone is right and someone is wrong, but because metaphysicians haven't all sat down and agreed what, precisely, the terms mean. Whether this is a good or bad thing – it's probably not a great thing – it's just a fact of life that, when you study ontology, you have to be keenly aware that different people might mean subtly different things by their terms, and that these subtle differences can often make for not-so-subtle consequences in any given argument.

Nonsense versus sense

Questions about concrete things will be far more familiar than questions about abstract things. If I asked you whether or not there was a hippopotamus in the next room, or whether there was a region of space a trillion light years away from earth, such questions are not radically different from questions you would've thought about before. Certainly there's no reason to, say, think that such questions were either gibberish and meaningless, or trivial and not difficult to answer. The question about whether there's a rather large water-dwelling mammal in the room next to me makes perfect *sense*; you can easily understand what that question *means*. Nor is it trivial to answer. You have to do *something* to find out whether it's true or not, such as open the door and look, or just sit quietly and see if you can hear the sound of a confused two-ton hippo trashing an office. Similarly for the question about the region of space. Physicists do wonder whether or not there are regions of space that far away, and have spent time trying to determine the answer (which still remains unanswered). So, again, it is neither meaningless nor trivial. Likewise for all questions about concreta.

When it comes to abstracta, though, it is less clear that we can say the same thing. Some people think that corresponding questions about the existence of abstract things are somehow defective and so can't be the subject of an intellectually informed debate. Let's have in mind some specific examples:

- Does the number 7 exist?
- Does the property *red* exist?
- Does the possibility that I could be the president of Bolivia exist?

You might think that these questions are just gibberish. It's not an uncommon response – just wander up to the next non-philosopher you meet and try and get them to tell you whether or not the number 7 exists and you might be met with a few odd glances or a lot of 'What do you mean?'s. Such people might think the very question is meaningless. After all, not every string of words is meaningful. Whilst 'Is there a panda pole-dancing over there?' is an odd question, it's meaningful. You know what it means for a panda to pole-dance (even though it's unlikely to be the case that there is such a thing going on). Whereas the string of words 'Panda over dancing there pole?' is just meaningless gibberish. We might think of the above questions in the same light, such that they don't even meet a standard whereby they mean anything in the first place. Questions like, e.g., 'Do numbers exist?' end up being as garbled as asking 'Do numbers municipal?'

Alternatively, you might think that these questions make sense, but believe they are trivial to answer. For instance, we might think that it's just obvious that there *aren't* any such things. 'Material objects exist!' you might say, 'But *numbers*? You can't kick the number 7. You'll never find it hanging in a gallery. We'll never detect it through even the most powerful telescope. So how could it exist?' All one needs is a closely held belief that one should only believe in things you can see (or otherwise empirically detect) and numbers get ruled out straightaway.

Finally, some people swing the opposite way. They believe that the questions are trivial but that it's obvious that *every* such thing exists. For such people it's just *obvious* that the number 7 exists. If it didn't exist, what would three and four add up to? Similarly for the other categories. Properties obviously exist as, because we are both human, there is something that you and I both have in common. And if there's something we have in common, then of course that property exists. After all, what does 'There is a . . .' mean other than 'There exists a . . .'? If *there is* a property that we have in common, then *there exists* a property that we have in common. This triviality response is not an uncommon response either – just ask a mathematician whether there are any numbers and (unless she's particularly philosophically minded) I'm sure she'll happily ream off lots of them for you.

These are all gut reactions some people have when faced with ontological questions (although not simultaneously for, of course, they contradict one another). You might have these gut reactions, or you might not, but they're certainly legitimate – that is, there's *something* to each of them. The rest of this chapter goes through these gut reactions. Each reaction threatens ontology or, at the least, practising ontology as a live discipline. So we must dispense with them if we're to think that ontology is a legitimate, serious subject. In summary, the problematic positions are:

Position One: Ontological questions about abstracta are meaningful, but very easy to answer such that entities like numbers etc. trivially exist.

Position Two: Ontological questions about abstracta are meaningful, but very easy to answer such that entities like numbers etc. trivially don't exist.

Position Three: Ontological questions about abstracta are meaningless.

If all of these positions are false, then ontological questions about abstracta must be meaningful, and must be difficult to answer. And if they're difficult to answer then, you might think, that goes some way to justifying ontology as a discipline. Not the whole way, mind you, for it's meaningful to ask what the shoe size of various dead celebrities is, and that's an intelligible question that's very difficult to answer too, but you don't see the field of Mortgloriapesamplitology being studied in any universities. So it takes more than being meaningful and tricky for a discipline to be worthy of study. But if we dispatch those positions, we'd have made good headway to thinking that ontology was a serious discipline. Moreover, even if the demonstration fails, this still leaves open that ontological questions about concrete objects are meaningful (and difficult to answer), so ontology might not be sunk even if one of the above options did transpire to be the case (and, conversely, demonstrating that ontological questions about abstracta are meaningful and non-trivial doesn't necessarily mean that the same can be said about ontological questions about concreta – see chapter 8 for an example.)

However, it'll be enough to concentrate just on the abstracta for now. So in an effort to show why ontological questions (at least about abstracta) are open questions, we must dispense with the three positions above.

Permissivists

Start with position one; call it **permissivism**. To see the motivation for it, consider the following statements:

- There is a prime number between 5 and 11.
- The Eiffel Tower and the Empire State Building have something in common.
- There is only one way to legitimately win an election, and that is to get the most votes.

These are all true statements. There is a prime number between 5 and 11, namely the number 7; both the Eiffel Tower and the Empire State Building *do* have something in common for they are both tall; and presumably the only legitimate way to win an election is to garner the most votes. Permissivists think this settles the matter – we're done with ontology right here. It might sound a bit odd to say 'There exists something that is a prime number between 5 and 11', rather than simply saying 'There is a prime number between 5 and 11', but that just makes the statement odd to the ear. It doesn't make it *false* by any stretch! If this is right, then numbers do exist, for, as it is true that there is a prime number between 5 and 11, it's true that there exists at least one number (the number 7!). Similarly, properties clearly exist for at least one property, the property of *tallness*, exists for buildings to have in common. And possibilities exist for a possibility is a 'way' and there exists at least one way as there are some 'ways' to legitimately win elections. You can see what the Permissivist is doing: where, in natural English, we have a statement of the form 'There is an X' or 'There are Ys' which we should normally assent to, and which is felicitous to utter, the Permissivist just reads straight off from such sentences that X exists or that Ys exist. Ontology, then, is easy. (And it's just as easy to see what things don't exist, e.g., are there any negative numbers that are also positive? No!)

Permissivists have a problem though, as this line of reasoning leads them into contradiction. This can be demonstrated by using **the paradox of non-self-instantiation** (sometimes called 'the paradox of non-self-exemplification'.) It's a bit fiddly, but if we go through it slowly, you'll easily see how it works. The first stage is to demonstrate that permissivism entails that there is a property of *being non-self-instantiating*.

Stage 1: The property of being non-self-instantiating exists

Take a sentence like:

There is something that I and Barack Obama have in common.

That's true, for we're both men. The permissivist claims this demonstrates beyond a shadow of a doubt that there exists something – the property *being a man* – that both myself and Barack Obama have in common. Further, anyone who believes that properties exist will say that we bear certain special relations to some properties but not others. So the property *being a man* and *being shorter than fifty metres in height* are properties I have, whereas *being a goat* and *being taller than fifty metres in height* are properties I don't have. So whilst these properties may exist, I bear some close connection to the first two that I don't to the latter two. Call this relation **instantiation,** e.g., I instantiate the property *being a man* whereas I don't instantiate the property *being a goat*. So far, so good.

But if these properties exist, those properties themselves will have properties. For instance, the property *being a man* is instantiated by six billion people. So it has the property *being instantiated by six billion people*. Or try this:

There is something that *being a man* and *being a goat* have in common.

That statement is also true, for *being a man* and *being a goat* are both properties. So they have that in common, and the permissivist will say that there exists a property that corresponds to that: namely, *being a property*. So it's true that:

There exists a property that is *being a property*, which is instantiated by all properties.

If that's true, then *being a property*, as it is itself a property, instantiates itself. But that's fine – there's nothing wrong with that. It just turns out that some properties instantiate themselves (which, in turn, means that those properties have something in common, which in turn entails that there exists a property of *being self-instantiating*). Again, so far, so good.

Now turn back to the properties *being a man* and *being a goat*. Are they themselves men or goats? What an odd question! But the answer is surely no. I can go for a drink with John (who is a man and instantiates *being a man*) and I can go for a drink with Jack (who is a man and instantiates *being a man*) but I can't go for a drink with *being a man*. I can't sit around the pub and have a chat and a beer with a property. That'd just be nonsense! It's an abstract thing, not itself a person. So we mustn't mistake the property *being a man* for itself being a man. Ditto for *being a goat*. There could be but one goat in the world (call it Billy). Billy would instantiate *being a goat* – but clearly *being a goat* isn't itself a goat as then there'd be two goats: Billy and *being a goat*. But there *can* be just one goat, so clearly *being a goat* is not itself a goat. But if *being a man* is not a man, it does not instantiate itself. And if *being a goat* is not a goat, it doesn't instantiate itself either. But that means that the following is true:

There is something that the properties *being a goat* and *being a man* have in common.

where that 'something' is their not instantiating themselves. The permissivist must say that the above sentence leads us to say that the 'something' exists (after all, it's a true statement that starts with 'There is . . .' so we should believe that the bit following 'There is . . .' exists). That 'something' that exists is the property *being non-self-instantiating*, and it is that which the properties have in common. Before continuing, look carefully at the moves being made here. It seems that if we accept permissivism (and that for any 'There is an X' statement that we should assent to in English, it entails that X exists) we must accept that the property *being non-self-instantiating* exists. Stage one is complete. The second stage of the argument demonstrates that no such property can exist, for if it did it would entail a contradiction.

Stage 2: There cannot be any such property!

This is where it all goes horribly wrong: there cannot exist a property which is *being non-self-instantiating*. To prove this, take the trivial truth that for any property and any thing, that thing either instantiates that property or it doesn't (an instance of 'the law of excluded middle'). So either:

First disjunct: *Being non-self-instantiating* instantiates itself

or

Second disjunct: It is not the case that *being non-self-instantiating* instantiates itself.

(A 'disjunct' is the thing that flanks the 'or' in logic, e.g., in P v Q, P and Q are the disjuncts.)

Take the first disjunct. Anything that instantiates *being a goat* has to be a goat; anything that instantiates *being a man* has to be a man; in the same vein, anything that instantiates *being non-self-instantiating* cannot instantiate itself. So if the first disjunct was the case, and it instantiated itself, then it cannot instantiate itself. But that's a contradiction! So the first disjunct cannot be the case.

That just leaves the second disjunct. It also proves to be problematic. Anything that doesn't instantiate itself must instantiate *being non-self-instantiating*. So if the second disjunct was true, and *being non-self-instantiating* did not instantiate itself, then it must instantiate *being non-self-instantiating* – which is itself! So if it didn't instantiate itself, then it *would* instantiate itself. But that's a contradiction as well.

So if either disjunct were true (and if *being non-self-instantiating* exists, then one of them must be) we have a serious problem. The only way to avoid contradiction is to deny that *being non-self-instantiating* exists in the first place. But, as Stage 1 demonstrated, if permissivism is true, then *being non-self-instantiating* does exist. Conclusion: to avoid contradiction, permissivism must be false (and, indeed, any theory that entails the existence of such a property must be avoided).

Before we move on to other alternatives, you should note that whilst this line of reasoning may work, it may well not. As with many parts of this book, I don't mean to lay down the final word on the matter, and that is just as true for permissivism. There are still permissivists out there, as well as some who think that things like *being non-self-instantiating* can exist, contrary to the above line of reasoning (for instance some people, 'dialetheists', think this sort of reasoning just demonstrates that *sometimes* a contradiction *can* be true). But, for now, we shall rest content with there being at least a prima facie case against permissivism. We should, therefore, doubt that ontological questions can be trivially answered.

Terminology Alert! Nominalism and Realism

As I've already noted, ontologists are terrible when it comes to terminology. 'Nominalism' and 'realism' make good examples. The word 'nominalism' gets used in many different ways. Here I use it to refer to those theories that don't maintain the existence of abstract objects. This is far from being the only acceptable use of the term.

Example 1: some people use the terms exclusively to refer to a position whereby one thinks properties exist and, more specifically, are things called 'universals'. 'Nominalism' is the position that there are no universals (although not the position that properties do not exist – just as long as they aren't universals, you're a nominalist).

Example 2: nominalism has been used to refer to the position that there are no sets (see chapter 3). This is sometimes called Harvard nominalism.

Example 3: realism is sometimes just taken to be the view that how the world is is independent of what humans think about it.

None of *those* uses are the same as that in this book. So, when reading literature in metaphysics and ontology, do be aware that other metaphysicians might be using slightly different terms. Just as long as we are explicit about what we mean, as I am here, there should be no grounds for confusion. If, on the other hand, you aren't careful in this manner, then you are liable to end up very confused as you engage in further reading around the topic!

Nominalism

The remaining positions that threaten ontology are that it's trivial that abstracta don't exist (position two), or that it's just gibberish to say these things in the first place (position three).*When we don't believe that a certain category of entities exist, we say that we are **anti-realists** about that category (whereas, if we do believe that entities in that category exist, we are **realists** about that category.)* Either option leads us to being anti-realists about all abstract objects – a position called **nominalism**.

If you take position two, and think that ontological questions about whether numbers, properties and so on exist are such that trivially those things don't exist, then you think that anti-realism about abstract objects is trivially true. So you're a nominalist, and think nominalism is trivially true. Those who think that ontological questions are open questions – that is, serious questions that are difficult to answer – are also often nominalists. They just don't think it's *trivial* whether things like properties or numbers exist, and instead agonize over whether to be a realist or anti-realist about them, before settling on them not existing (hence, they become nominalists). One might imagine, though, that the nominalist who thinks nominalism is trivially true and the nominalist who thinks nominalism is a serious, debatable question aren't that far apart. I would suggest that those who think nominalism is trivially true do so for very similar reasons to those who think nominalism is non-trivially true. The only difference is that the former tend to think that the reasons for nominalism being true are so overwhelmingly compelling that they are irresistible; they simply cannot even imagine how one would set about denying them. But then there's no fundamental difference between the two, it's just that the nominalist who thinks nominalism is trivially true is more assured that their nominalist convictions are sound. To get a grip on why we might think this, have a look at the traditional motivations for being a nominalist about abstracta.

Motivation 1: Naturalism

If things like numbers, properties, possibilities and so on exist, where are they? For anything, it's trivial that it's either *in* space and time or it's *not* in space and time (again, another instance of the law of excluded middle). But, so the thought goes, it is just plain bizarre for numbers to be in space and time. It's not as if you'll find the number 7 somewhere in a coal mine in Slough, or the square root of 2 lost somewhere behind the sofa, or the property *being a man* somewhere on Pluto. Those kinds of assertions are just plain crazy (so the thought goes; we'll see positions to the contrary in chapter 3). But this means that these things are *not* in space and time, and not anywhere in the universe. **Naturalism** is the thesis that everything is located somewhere in space and time, and that the contents of reality are contained somewhere in the physical realm. Given naturalism, there are no disembodied spirits, no Gods or angels and, most importantly for our purposes, no abstracta outside space and time. So those who endorse naturalism (which is, so supporters believe, one of the lessons of contemporary science) will not endorse the existence of unlocated abstracta.

Motivation 2: Causal issues

Connected to this are causal issues. If abstracta are outside space and time, then (so the nominalist intuition goes) they can't have any *causal* influence on us or the world around us. After all, if they're outside space and time, it just seems outlandish to think they have causal powers. The standard view of contemporary science is that everything that has causal powers is within space and time, and within the purview of the study of physics and the natural sciences. Even those who disagree, such as those who believe in supernatural entities like God, who can miraculously affect the universe through divine power, are not at all likely to think that abstract objects have such abilities. God might be able to miraculously cause things to happen from beyond the confines of the universe, but it's a big leap from that to thinking that the number 47 does exactly the same – God can magic into life a burning bush, but the number 47 has never done anything!

This is problematic for realists about abstracta, because some find the **Eleatic principle** to be convincing. That principle states that anything that exists must have causal powers, and that it's somehow redundant to believe in things that don't *do* anything. After all, it'd be very strange for physicists to postulate the existence of particles that didn't have any effect on anything. If they don't *do* anything, why believe in them? The Eleatic principle, then, appears to rule out abstract objects.

Motivation 3: Epistemological issues

Following from this: if they don't have causal powers how do we even *know* about them. I know that the chair I sit on exists because it has a causal influence on me (it causes photons to bounce into my eyes, causing me to see a chair); I know that New York exists because, even though I've never been there, there is a chain of events that connect us (for instance, I've seen photographs of New York; people talk about New York; New York features prominently in *Friends*, etc., each being a fact that can trace at least some of its causes back to New York existing). Even things from the past (such as Chingiz Khan, the dinosaurs, the Big Bang, etc.) all have some causal chain between them and me. More generally, it seems that anything that I know exists must have some causal connection to me. To say otherwise sounds a bit weird. Imagine I say that I know there are aliens which exist a billion light years away from us, so far away that I couldn't possibly know about them (for I would have had to, impossibly, travel faster than the speed of light). So not only don't I have any evidence, but it seems *impossible* for me to have any evidence. It seems that this fact alone rules out my being justified in believing that there are such aliens, hence this fact alone rules out my knowing that they exist. So the worry is that, even if abstracta existed, there'd be no way to know. And if there's no way to know about them, you shouldn't go around asserting that you believe in them. For instance, if you meet someone who agreed they had no way of knowing that they were ill but believed it anyway, you'd think them an irrational hypochondriac. Similarly we should doubt people who believe in entities that they could not possibly know about. So believing in abstracta seems to bring with it serious epistemological issues.

Motivation 4: No explanation

We might fear that abstracta, in being outside space and time, won't appear in our best physical theories. Abstracta, in having no causal powers, will never cause anything to happen. Causation and explanation are tightly knit, so you might think that if they don't have causal powers they'll never feature in any explanation of what goes on in the world. Further, if abstracta can never be known about, then they can never feature in any justified explanation of the world.

In other words, it seems abstracta will never explain anything – if you have any phenomenon that needs explanation, rest assured that you will never mention abstracta in that explanation.

But it seems obvious that we shouldn't believe in anything that plays *no* explanatory role whatsoever. Imagine some physicists come up with a theory that explained everything in the universe. As they crack open the champagne, break out the cigars and ready themselves for fame (admittedly, probably not that much fame as physics isn't as sexy as stories about celebrity smut), a single physicist pipes up and says he has a *competing* theory. Worrying that they've been gazumped or outdone, they ask him to explain it. 'Aha!' he says 'It's *exactly* like your theory except it includes extra entities that I call uselessions.' When asked what the uselessions do, and why they should be included in the theory, the physicist just shrugs his shoulders: 'They don't *do* anything, they're just there. You can't see them, you can't find them, you can't detect them, and they don't affect anything. They just hover around doing nothing at all.'

What a ridiculous theory it would be, and how unbelievable. The uselessions have *no* explanatory power. Uselessions are useless! And if they have *no* explanatory power, then you shouldn't believe in them. Similarly, some nominalists worry that the same applies to abstracta, and that they have no explanatory role, so they shouldn't be believed in. (In chapter 4, we shall see arguments to the contrary.)

Back to trivial nominalism

So there are four reasons for one to be a nominalist about abstracta. Certainly, those nominalists who think ontology is a serious discipline, and that it's not obvious that realism is true, have these sorts of motivations. So it's not a stretch of the imagination to think that when someone tells me that they're a nominalist about abstracta, such that it's *trivial* that there are no abstracta, that they have similar motivations. It's just that the latter think it even more obvious that these reasons are the case, or more obvious that such reasons rule out abstracta. But this means that every reason to think these motivations are defeasible is also a reason not to think nominalism is trivially true. And there are such reasons, as we shall see later in the book.

Moreover, as we shall see in the next few chapters, anti-realism about abstracta (whether one thinks it is trivially true or otherwise) raises some very awkward questions. After all, it appears at first glance that we talk about abstract entities all of the time, so if you're a nominalist (whether you're motivated towards nominalism because you think it's trivially true or otherwise), you must still explain away that putative reference. For instance, we say things like 'There is a prime number between 5 and 11' and that seems true enough. But how can it be true if there are no prime numbers? A thorough investigation of how to solve this problem will have to be postponed until later chapters, but it's enough to say that, even if you think nominalism is trivially true, you still have to explain exactly what's going on there. Compare: Imagine you meet a Creationist who says that Creationism is obviously true. When you try and convince them that Creationism is false, because of the fossil record and so on, it'd be deeply unsatisfying if they dismissed your concerns by merely saying that, as their position was *obviously* true, they didn't need to say *anything* about the fossil record. The same applies to the nominalist – even if their position is trivially true, they must still provide explanations of why we appear to truly talk as if there are abstract objects. Indeed, in the same way that the fossil record seems to demonstrate that Creationism cannot be trivially true, we might think that the very presence of such a problem for nominalism demonstrates, in one fell swoop, that nominalism cannot be a trivial thesis either.

Is it all gibberish?

So ontological questions aren't trivially true, nor does it look like ontology is threatened if they're trivially false. The final option was that neither is the case as all of this talk is sheer gibberish. The same factors come into play again. If you think it's *gibberish* to assert that numbers or such exist, then you're also a nominalist in so far as nominalists believe that *all* that exists are concrete things like material objects. Your motivation for nominalism would be somewhat different, for now you would be a nominalist because you cannot even *understand* realism about abstracta. But again, exactly what has just been said about the nominalist above will apply here as well. Nominalism is a bona fide position in ontology, so you are still signing up to a traditional ontological position, and even if you think that assertions about abstract entities existing are nonsense, you are still going to be pressed into having to answer objections to nominalism. Compare with a Creationist who thought evolution was simply meaningless – even then they *still* have to answer the awkward questions about the dinosaur fossils. The same applies here. The nominalist who thinks realism is gibberish is still going to have to pay careful attention to, and form cogent replies to, those objections to their position.

So the remaining two options that seem to threaten ontology as a practice don't seem to be that troublesome. It isn't that they threaten *ontology*, it's just that they threaten *realism* about abstract objects. And threatening realism, whatever your motivation for that, is a mainstream position in ontology. Should you endorse it, you aren't avoiding ontology at all, and will instead find yourself in the company of many contemporary metaphysicians. With that in mind, let's assume that ontology *is* a serious discipline worthy of study, and press on with the project of answering ontological questions. In the next chapter, we will start to introduce some methodology for how we set about answering these questions.

Chapter summary

In this chapter, we have:

- introduced what ontology is.
- shown the problems with thinking ontological questions are easily answered such that just about everything you truly talk about with a 'There is' or 'There are' sentence trivially exists.
- explained what nominalism is, and examined some problems with being a nominalist. So it can't be trivial that ontological questions are easily answered.

Further reading

Those interested in a general introduction to issues with abstract entities should read Chris Swoyer's article (2008). As for attacks on ontology, we will see more of them in later chapters. For permissivism, you might want to look to Amie Thomasson (2010a) and Thomas Hofweber (2005), as well as a theory called 'Neo-Fregeanism' which is very similar to permissivism (a good, although challenging, article on it is by Matti Eklund (2006)).

2

Methodology

Metaontology

Once we've settled on ontological questions being open and difficult questions, we have to figure out how we're meant to answer them. That is, we need to establish a methodology for determining which ontological theory is correct. This chapter lays out some of the more standard methodological principles that metaphysicians rely upon. However, such matters are a mesh of thorny issues. Whilst ontology is one of the oldest areas of study, it has not, as yet, been lucky enough to develop a widely agreed upon methodology. It is a far cry from, say, the scientific disciplines with their hypothetical-deductive method, and their rigorous application of statistics and numbers to yield solid, clearly justified results. The sciences are a mature discipline – whilst their methodology might not be perfect (for proof, pick up a book on the philosophy of science!), their conclusions are built on far more stable foundations than those you'll find in ontology. Normally, there are no predictions to verify or falsify ontological theories (although see chapter 6), no computer program we can run a set of data through to tell us whether abstracta exist or not, no particle accelerator so big or so powerful that it could determine whether or not there were numbers or events. Nor is it entirely clear, at present, exactly what takes the place of such empirical verifications when it comes to a topic like ontology. Essentially, the methodology just isn't clear. As we'll see, different ontologists try and answer these questions in radically different ways, starting off with different preconceptions (and, sometimes, very obscure or apparently groundless preconceptions). And of these different methods and theories concerning how to settle vexing ontological questions, no theory or method has, as yet, come out on top.

So ontology is an old discipline, but an immature one – a misanthrope of the intellectual areas that never quite left home to make it on its own in the world. But don't be deceived into thinking this is a *bad* thing – at least, not in the sense of putting you off studying ontology. That'd be crazy: every discipline needs to mature, and every discipline needs to work hard to both acquire and justify its methodology. Just look at the sciences and the Scientific Revolution. It would have been a damn shame if the scientists of the Enlightenment had given up and gone home because they hadn't entirely sorted out the methodological details of their discipline, rather than powering through to bring about the massive advances in knowledge that they did. Similarly, you'd think that they found it *exciting* to be engaged with the discipline at such a stage, and that participating in the crafting of the overall methodology wasn't a hardship, but an intellectual joy.

The study of how ontology is to proceed, what its methodology should be, and whether ontology is even a worthwhile project, is called **metaontology** (or, sometimes, metametaphysics, which should be etymologically obliged to be about the methodology of metaphysics in general, not just ontology, but at present almost always refers just to the methodology of ontology). So ontology is the study of what things exist, and metaontology is the study of ontology and how ontology is to proceed. And it is indeed an exciting, febrile area of debate which this book will also examine alongside the standard ontological issues. Each chapter of this book will introduce a new metaontological theory (including more metaontological positions like those from the first chapter that deflate ontological inquiry and make ontological questions look relatively trivial to answer). By examining these methodological questions alongside seeing how ontology is practised, you'll have a chance yourself to see how the methodology has evolved, which should give you a better chance of being able to evaluate whether such methodologies are flawed or not.

At this stage, I am sure that you are left with a sense that ontologists are hugely divided over not just the questions that they are trying to answer but also over how they are even to answer them. That sense is the correct one – ontology and metaontology are both practising a roaring trade at the moment, fuelled by some pretty wide-ranging, and often deeply divisive, disagreements. As you approach this subject, and read this book, you will be struck by the divisions, you will be struck by the lack of globally accepted theories and you will be struck by how much of the literature has been produced in the relatively recent present. These disagreements are not (or, at least, I hope are not) a sign of confusion, dissension or that the discipline is somehow defective, but a sign that it is in the process of maturing. You are fortunate to have a chance to study it at such a stage. If this book instils you with enough enthusiasm to carry on keeping up with ontology once you have graduated, you will get the chance to watch the field grow and develop. In studying ontology, then, people should be jealous of you, for only rarely does one get to be there at the moment a discipline begins to flower. Like the scientists during the Enlightenment, you should revel in these questions: about what exists; about the methodology to decide such things; about whether it is worth practising at all. Certainly I do.

Theory choice

Nonetheless, even amongst the dissension, there are some principles used to choose amongst competing theories which are fairly widely accepted. The rest of this chapter lays out these standard pieces of methodology and – as a worked example – shows how we might apply what we have learnt, both in this chapter and the last, to the ontology of holes.

Start with the notion of **theory choice**. We engage in theory choice all of the time. Sometimes we engage with it in fairly simple cases. Imagine you intend to watch a film this evening. One friend tells you that they read in the local newspaper that the film is excellent. The other friend tells you that they downloaded it off the internet and thought it was awful. So you have two theories that say competing things about the film: one that says that such-and-such a film critic's reviews are to be respected (and so you should see the film) and another that says that your friend's own opinions about illegally downloaded films are to be respected (and so you shouldn't). When weighing up those theories, different factors might come into play. You might, for instance, recall that your second friend has been right every time before, so you have evidence that the latter theory is right. Or you might suspect that your second friend has an ulterior motive, and doesn't want you to go to the cinema so he can seduce you instead. You would then have an alternative explanation for your friend's opinions about the film that doesn't involve the film being bad, and this could lead you to favour the first theory. In any case, you can weigh up the theories and decide which is better and decide whether you should see the film.

Theory choice can also be more serious. Detectives investigating murders have to weigh up competing theories all of the time, e.g., did the butler do it? Did the victim fake a suicide? What explanation is there of Dr Lucky's fingerprints being on the murder weapon? (Or what have you.) And, of course, you find theory choice in things like science. We can compare a geocentric view of the solar system (whereby the sun revolves around the earth) with a heliocentric view of the solar system informed by the science of Galileo and Einstein (whereby the earth revolves around the sun). The geocentric theory conflicts with the vast majority of our observations, whereas the heliocentric view predicts most of what we observe (but not everything for even the best, current, physical theory doesn't predict every observation we make). Hence, it's rational to choose the heliocentric theory.

The same thing happens in metaphysics. The generally agreed upon view is that we should carry out what is called a **cost–benefit analysis** of the theories on offer. That is, for each theory we figure out the benefits of that theory and then figure out those things that are detrimental about it. Then we compare how it performs in light of this with each of its competitors and hopefully we will be able to weigh up which theory is better overall. This analysis is particularly apt for ontology, as in most cases where we need a theory to account for a certain phenomenon or solve a certain problem, no theory manages to do so perfectly – there are always some costs or downsides of believing it. So all we are left with being able to do is determine which theory has the best balance of costs and benefits overall.

The divisions in ontology over methodology also stretch to making clear which things count as costs and which as benefits. The rest of this chapter examines some of the theoretical virtues that might factor into one's cost–benefit analysis. Along the way, we'll look at how these virtues feed into an ontological topic – the existence or non-existence of holes – using that as an example to highlight how these virtues are meant to work.

Virtue 1: Coherence with intuitions

One of the virtues that a philosophical theory is often said to possess is that it bears out our intuitions. Where we intuitively think that there are chairs, or that time passes, or that it is morally obligatory to save drowning children, or that there are no true contradictions, or that solipsism is false, etc., it's a good thing when a theory entails that this is true. Conversely, when something is intuitively false, it's a bad thing if it is entailed by the theory. So a theory that entails that there are no chairs, that nothing changes, that it doesn't matter whether you save drowning children or have an ice cream and watch them flounder, that there are contradictory truths or that only you exist, and so on, would, in each case, be a theory with costs. (Those things that we intuitively think are true are often called **folk intuitions,** as they are meant to be the kind of intuition that the everyday kind of person – a member of the 'folk' – believes intuitively.)

Notice that I don't say that a theory which coheres with our intuitions is true, nor do I say that a theory which challenges them is false. I am saying that coherence with our intuitions is one of various costs and benefits in play. So be clear: to consider coherence a virtue is not to believe that all of what we intuitively believe is true and unrevisable on philosophical grounds. Such a position would be exceedingly dubious, both because what we think is intuitively true varies over time (and, indeed, from culture to culture), so we'd be remarkably lucky if our intuitions turned out to be exactly the right set of intuitions to have, and because there might be times when you *have* to give up on a folk intuition, for instance, when we have a paradox (an example of which is, say, the paradox of the statue and the lump in chapter 9). So don't be fooled into thinking that ontology is just apologetics for our gut feelings. Certainly, though, there's something to the idea that coherence with intuition is a good thing – after all, if two theories varied *only* with regard as to what intuitions they bore out, then it'd seem natural to go for the one that bore out the most intuitions.

Turn now to the ontology of holes, which we will use to help explain how these virtues work. By 'holes', I mean those things that appear in jeans when they become frayed, or you find running through toilet rolls, or the holes in a bucket that let water escape. We might be a realist about holes, believing that they existed, or an anti-realist about holes, believing that we should eliminate holes from our ontology.

With realism, we might worry that we offend all sorts of intuitions. Here are some (connected) examples. The first intuition that realism about holes might offend is that holes are absences, and absences aren't things. To get an idea of exactly what this involves, switch to using a metaphor that ontologists are fond of: God creating the universe (remember, it's only a metaphor, so don't worry if you're agnostic or an atheist). Imagine that God is making the universe. When God makes jeans with a hole in the knee, or pieces of Swiss cheese, or what have you, it seems that all he has to do is arrange atoms in a certain way. If God wants to make a pair of jeans with a hole in them, he just makes less of the jeans. If God wants to make Swiss cheese, he just makes slightly less of the cheese, leaving holes in it. What God doesn't have to do is make the jeans *and then add in some holes*. Similarly, for the cheese: a hole is an absence, it's a lack of an entity, not an additional thing that has to be added to the universe. Therefore, intuitively (we might think) holes do not exist. Or, to put it another way: when we point at a hole in something and say 'There's nothing there' that seems to be true (at least, it would if we ignored the air where the hole is, which we can by imagining that we're pointing at the hole whilst in a perfect vacuum). Again, it seems that intuitively holes do not exist.

We get other similar oddities. If we were realists about holes, then it appears that when we make a hole in something, we get a weird result concerning how many things exist. Imagine God makes a perfectly solid sheet of material out of a million atoms, with no holes in it whatsoever (this is physically impossible, as atoms cannot touch one another, but it will do for example purposes). If God then annihilates an atom, you'd think that there were fewer things in existence for he has, after all, destroyed an object. But if the realist is right, then a hole pops into existence to take that atom's place. We still have a million things! And this sounds strange indeed, for how can annihilating an atom, and doing nothing else at all, leave us with exactly the same number of things? So realism is somewhat strange, and we might fear that it doesn't cohere with our intuitions. With that in mind, turn to some of the other virtues to get a taste for some of the problems that anti-realism about holes might suffer from (although you might have ideas of your own as to why anti-realism about holes actually *challenges* our intuitive beliefs! I leave that to you to think about yourself).

Virtue 2: Explanatory power

It is not simply an inexplicable fact about the world that when we put potassium in water it explodes. Nor is it inexplicable that the sun appears to rise every morning and to move across the horizon. Nor is it inexplicable why simply printing more money to distribute to the poor doesn't make them any better off. Nor are we left in the dark as to why the Great Train Robbery (when, in 1963, £2.6 million was stolen from a train) happened. In each case, we can provide an explanation for these things. The laws of chemistry explain the explosive reaction of potassium in water; the laws of gravity and our knowledge of the relative location and movement of stellar bodies explains why it appears that the sun moves across the sky; basic principles of economics explain why you can't inflate your way out of poverty; and we have psychological explanations for why the Great Train Robbers stole a lot of money (namely, that they were both immoral and greedy).

However, theories generally take some truths as inexplicable – what we can call **brute truths**. Our physical theories might explain the truth that potassium explodes in water but will take some facts as brute – say the fundamental laws of physics (of which, physicists hope that there will be only a few). Having as few as possible is a benefit, and having more brute truths is a cost. If I have a theory of physics that has five fundamental laws and yours has three laws that also explain all of my five, it seems that your theory has more explanatory power for, in having less brute truths, it is simpler. Similarly, we often find that theories leave some things unexplained – few theories are wholly explanatory. I might have a physical theory that explains some of the things that go on but leaves some things unexplained. This is pretty much how actual science is. We can explain a lot of things, but some problems remain unsolved, for example, we cannot explain why the Pioneer 10 and Pioneer 11 spacecraft mysteriously slowed down when they reached the edge of our solar system. A theory that does explain those things is more powerful, and hence better (and, indeed, there have been many theories to explain the mysterious slowdown, although none have received universal endorsement). And, as always, we can weigh these things against one another, for there might be times that we have to choose between a theory that is powerful and a theory with brute truths (for instance, take physics and add in, as a brute truth, that man-made satellites slow down when they reach the edge of the solar system – it becomes a more powerful theory as it explains more things, which is a benefit, but now contains an intolerably ad hoc law of physics, which is a cost).

✳ When it comes to ontological theories, exactly the same thinking applies. We want theories that have as few brute truths as possible, whilst still explaining as much as possible✳(we'll also see, in the next chapter, that some metaphysicians think that there is a brand of explanation specific to metaphysics). So when we have to explain, say, water coming out of a bucket, we don't want to assert the ad hoc brute truth that the bucket is the kind of thing which lets water out, but the more sensible explanation that the water comes out of the bucket because it has a hole in it. This is something that the realist can easily do, for their ontology contains holes. The anti-realist, on the other hand, cannot say this and must say something else. Exactly what they must say is tricky, and to explain why, we'll need to introduce the notion of paraphrasing.

Paraphrasing

In sentences like:

> There are pandas
> There are electrons
> Barack Obama exists
> There are leprechauns

it looks like the things talked about have to exist in order for the sentence to be true. For the sentences to be true, there have to be pandas, electrons, Barack Obama or leprechauns (although in chapter 8 we'll see arguments to the contrary). We say that the sentences are **ontologically committed** to those things. But in similar sentences, apparently referring to things we want to be anti-realists about, we run into problems. Take a perfectly natural, seemingly true, sentence of English:

> There are holes in the bucket.

In the same way that 'There are electrons' commits us to electrons, this appears to commit us to holes. Clearly, then, the anti-realist has a problem as sentences like 'There are holes in the bucket' seem to be true of at least some buckets. The anti-realist must revise the naive understanding of ontological commitment. Whilst it may *look* like 'There are holes in the bucket' commits us to holes, the ontological commitments of a sentence aren't always what its surface grammar indicates. This can easily be seen to be the case by using other examples, for which we are certain that the ontological commitments of a sentence differ from the commitments that the sentence appears to have according to its surface grammar.

Example 1 Imagine you speak to an economist about the British economy. Whilst chatting, he says 'The average man has 2.4 children and lives in a London borough'. Economists utter these sorts of sentences all the time, and they sound true enough to the casual listener. But what are the ontological commitments of the sentence? If we thought the ontological commitments of a sentence were to be read off from what the sentence literally asserts, then it seems that there exists some guy – the average man – who owns a house somewhere in London. But that's not true! If I go to London, I won't find 'The Average Man' listed on the census. There is no house in any part of London where I can knock on the door and find him living there. And the idea that some bloke in London lives in a house with two children and the gruesome remains of a child, amassing a full 40 per cent of a whole child, is a chilling image indeed. Or another way of thinking about it: imagine that a non-native English speaker thought the economist's sentence was just like 'The prime minister lives in 10 Downing Street and has three children.' That sentence *is* committed to the existence of some people (the prime minister and his three children) who live in Downing Street. But whilst the economist's sentence is a bit like that – that is, the *surface grammar* is very similar – the ontological commitments of the sentence are radically different and don't seem to have anything to do with such things.

Example 2 Imagine you are in the garden and someone asks why you are sitting in the shade. 'Ah,' you reply. 'The sun has moved behind the elms and now I'm in the shade.' A perfectly fine answer, and one which you might well think was true. But science has shown us that it is *us* who are moving, *not* the sun. The earth's rotation on its axis, and its orbit around the sun, is such that the elms are now interposed between you and the sun – *that's* the fact of the matter. 'The sun has moved behind the elms' seems, strictly and literally, to commit us to a Ptolemaic model of the solar system, with the earth at the centre and the sun moving across the heavens, rather than the (accurate) heliocentric model that we know of today. The surface commitments, then, differ from what we normally think of as the actual commitments.

Example 3 'There is something that the property *being a goat* and *being a man* have in common.' Sound familiar? Back in chapter 1, we saw that a contradiction arose by thinking that the ontological commitments of this sentence should be read off its surface grammar. Whilst we should assent to that statement, we should not say that there exists some property that these things have in common lest we end up believing in the problematic property that led us into contradiction.

Those example sentences are all fine sentences, and yet there exist no average men, the sun does not move across the heavens and no property of *being non-self-instantiating* exists. So it seems common-place for the apparent commitments of a sentence – those commitments it would have if we interpreted it literally and crudely – to be different from its actual ontological commitments.

What we do in these circumstances is say that the sentence's ontological commitments are given by another sentence. We'll call that a **paraphrase** of the original sentence. For instance:

'The average man has 2.4 children'

might be paraphrased as:

'The number of children divided by the number of men equals 2.4.'

And we might think that, when economists talk about the average man, it's that second sentence which they really have in mind. Whilst

'The sun has moved behind the elms'

has as its paraphrase:

'The earth has rotated such that the elms are now between where we are and the sun.'

And

'There is something that the property *being a goat* and *being a man* have in common'

has as its paraphrase:

'Both *being a goat* and *being a man* fail to instantiate themselves.'

The first paraphrase only talks about numbers, and is about demography, rather than talking about oddly named men who live in houses with the grisly remains of their children. The second only asserts heliocentric-friendly facts, not facts contrary to science. The third asserts only that two properties fail to do something, not that a third property – the logically impossible *being non-self-instantiating* – exists. And, in each case, the idea is that we're only ontologically committed to those things that the paraphrase literally asserts: assert that average men exist, and ontologically commit only to numbers; assert that the sun has gone behind the elms, and commit only to the earth rotating; assert sentences about properties being similar, without committing to the impossible properties and so on.

So broadly speaking, the tactic to avoid unwanted ontological commitments is to say of problematic sentences (like 'There are holes in the bucket') that the paraphrase is some, quite different, sentence. This insight is crucial to the anti-realist enterprise. (And paraphrases can be just as useful to realists. For instance, realists about properties will still want to say that *being non-self-instantiating* doesn't exist, and therefore give a paraphrase of sentences apparently committing to it.)

How does paraphrasing work?

Exactly how paraphrases are meant to help is something I won't go into (not least because it is a tricky problem that has, alas, received little attention). As it is, when faced with sentences that, if true, would be problematic for ontology (e.g., 'There is a prime number between 5 and 11' or 'The average man has 2.4 children'), the strategy is to come up with a different sentence that doesn't prove problematic. But it's not clear how that is meant to help! What, we might ask, is it about this process which solves the problem? For much of this book, we will overlook this problem, but this box briefly goes through the options of what a paraphrase is meant to be doing.

We might think the paraphrase is what we should have said. So the original sentence is false and misleading (e.g., by asserting the existence of average men) and the paraphrase is what a more astute speaker, keyed into the ontological principles at play, would have said in its stead. Ontology, then, would be the discipline of creating the most ontologically accurate language.

Or we might think the paraphrase is what we actually mean. So you might have thought that a problematic sentence meant that there existed such-and-such a problematic entity (like a number, or an average man) but it turns out that it means something entirely different. It means whatever the paraphrase says. So the original sentence is true; it just means something different to what we thought.

Or we might think that the sentence is false, but not false in the same way that 'Leprechauns secretly rule the world' is false. It's false, but it's a nice heuristic for navigating the world. We might say the sentence is 'nearly as good as true'.

There are other alternatives, such as thinking that the original sentence is false but fictionally true (see chapter 4 for an example of this), that the paraphrase just needs to say what the 'truthmakers' of the sentence are (see chapter 7), or that the original sentence is true but the paraphrase is a sentence in an alternate language that explains the original sentence being true (see chapter 10). Although in some of these cases people will tend not to call it 'paraphrasing', everyone is looking for some alternative sentence that better captures the ontological commitments of the original sentence. For now, though, we'll overlook these issues and, for the most part, talk as if paraphrasing unproblematically works to relieve us of unwanted ontological commitments. I'll also pretend, for exposition purposes, that the original sentence is true, rather than being false or 'nearly as good as true', etc.

So with hole talk, the anti-realist will need to introduce paraphrases to do the required work. For instance, in the case of:

The water is escaping the bucket because there is a hole in the bucket

they might say:

The water is escaping the bucket because the bucket is ✓ perforated.

You might be wondering exactly how that helps – after all, what is the difference between a bucket being perforated and there being a hole in the bucket?

The Quinean theory of ontological commitment

To answer that, we must turn to the first theory of ontological commitment that we will examine in this book: *the **Quinean theory of ontological commitment**.*

That theory, stemming from the work of Willard van Orman Quine (widely known as the philosopher who helped resurrect ontology as a serious discipline back in the 1960s) is to translate sentences into first-order logic, and then determine the ontological commitments of the sentences on the back of what those translations quantify over. That is, for any given sentence we get the paraphrase of that sentence and translate it into first-order logic. (This is somewhat of a caricature, as Quine both believed in 'ontological relativism' – that there was no, single, objectively correct ontological theory – nor was he overly interested in translating sentences outside of scientific disciplines. But the caricature will suffice.)

As an example, take a simple sentence like: 'There is a man standing over there'. A first-order translation into logic would be:

$\exists x$ (x is a man & x is standing over there)

The ontological commitments of the sentence are, says Quine, what we are quantifying over in the translation – or, more specifically, the value of the **bound variable** (which is what leads to Quine's famous slogan: 'To be is to be the value of a bound variable'). For the logically uninitiated, let's break down what that means. The variable in the above translation is 'x'. It's a *bound* variable because it gets introduced alongside a quantifier, such as the existential quantifier '$\exists$'. (In classical logic, all variables are bound as they all have to be introduced by means of a quantifier, so you don't need to worry about that bit too much. Finally, if the sentence is true, then something is the **value** of the variable in this case, the man who is 'standing over there' would be the value of x. So, if we were Quineans, as the ontological commitments of that sentence are the value of that variable, we would say that we are ontologically committed to the man standing over there.

Let's have a few more example sentences along with a putative translation for each:

* 'All footballs are round' can be translated into '$\forall x$ (x is a ball $\rightarrow$ x is round)', which only quantifies over balls. So that sentence is only ontologically committed to balls.

* 'Some birds can swim' translates as '$\exists x$ (x is bird & x can swim)' which quantifies only over birds. The sentence, then, is ontologically committed to birds.

'Barack Obama is the president of the USA' translates as $\exists x$ (x = Barack Obama & x is president of the USA)' (actually, it doesn't translate to this – see the box – but this translation will do). So that sentence is, if Quinean theories of ontological commitment are right, committed only to the existence of some person, i.e., Barack Obama.

Names, Definite Descriptions and Paraphrasing

The perceptive amongst you, who remember your basic logic, will have noticed that the translation for 'Barack Obama is the president of the USA' is wrong. What I have just given is actually a translation of 'There is something which is Barack Obama and that thing is the president of the USA.' The problem is that as 'Barack Obama is the president of the USA' mentions a specific person, rather than talking more generally about there being some thing that is president, the logical translation should merely introduce a name (represented in logic, as I hope you'll recall, by, e.g., 'a') and translate it as 'a is the president of the USA'. But now there aren't any bound variables (for there aren't any quantifiers!) so how are we meant to use the Quinean method to figure out the commitments of the sentence? This is a nuance that Quine eliminates by using

Bertrand Russell's theory of **definite descriptions** whereby we can turn names into descriptions. So 'Barack Obama' gets treated as a description along the lines of 'The only man who served as the Illinois senator from 2005 until 2008 and who was born in Honolulu and who lots of odd people claimed wasn't born in Honolulu and . . .' so on and so forth. So 'Barack Obama is the president of the USA' becomes:

> $\exists x$ ((x served as the Illinois senator from 2005 to 2008 & x was born in Honolulu & x was such that lots of people claimed he wasn't born in Honolulu . . .) & x is the president of the USA & $\forall y$ (y served as the Illinois senator from 2005 to 2008 & y was born in Honolulu & . . . $\rightarrow x = y$))

It's a bit wordy, but we've removed the name and we now have our bound variable. However, rather than using definite descriptions throughout this book (which is lengthy and over-complicated for our purposes), I'll instead account for names by pretending, falsely, that we should translate them as I have done in the main text (that is, by introducing a variable and then identifying the variable with the named individual).

Given the Quinean theory of ontological commitment in place, it becomes obvious why there are differences between those two sentences about holes. The first sentence gets the following treatment:

'There is a <u>hole</u> in the bucket' translates as: $\exists x \exists y$ (x is a bucket & y is a hole & y is part of x)

whilst the second sentence is treated as follows:

'The bucket is <u>perforated</u>' translates as: $\exists x$ (x is a bucket & x is perforated)

The former <u>quantifies over holes</u>— and is committed to holes, and thus hole realism. <u>The latter has no such quantification.</u> It merely quantifies over buckets and says of them that they are perforated. It tells us only what a bucket is like, not that holes exist. With that in mind, we can see that, at least with these simple sentences, the anti-realist can translate them quite well. However, they have a harder time with other sentences. For instance, take the following:

'The piece of paper has a single hole in it'

versus

'The piece of paper has two holes in it.'

What the anti-realist cannot do is offer the same paraphrase of those two sentences. The paraphrase is meant to capture the conditions under which these sentences are true, but as the sentences describe different states of affairs, the conditions under which the first is true is different from the conditions that the second is true (for instance, if you're putting a piece of paper in a paper binder with two metal prongs then you want the second to be true but not the first, as if the first is true there aren't enough holes in the paper for the prongs to go through). So we cannot simply say that the paraphrase for both is that they are perforated. What we could do is introduce more predicates to do the work. We could say that there are predicates of things being 'singularly perforated', as well as being 'doubly perforated'. We could then say:

'The piece of paper has a single hole in it' translates as $\exists x$ (x is a piece of paper & x is singularly perforated)

'The piece of paper has two holes in it' translates as $\exists x$ (x is a piece of paper & x is doubly perforated)

In each case, we don't quantify over holes and only quantify over pieces of paper, but still manage to give unique paraphrases for each sentence allegedly about holes. So we can account for, we can *explain*, why water comes out of a bucket with a hole in it. The nominalist can say this happens because the bucket is singularly perforated, and so their theory might well have as much explanatory power as a realist's.

Of course, a piece of paper might have any number of holes in it so we'll need to talk about pieces of paper being triply perforated, quadruply perforated, quintuply perforated and so on for an infinite number of predicates. And people often think this is a bad thing. To see why, turn to the next theoretical virtue.

Virtue 3: Ideological parsimony

Let's be clear that there is no problem with a theory featuring an infinite number of predicates. The problem is that we should not have an infinite number of *undefined* predicates – what are called the **primitives**. To illustrate: some predicates can be defined in terms of another. If we were trying to teach someone how to understand familial relations, we only need three predicates to do this:

'__ is a child of __' (as in, Harold is the child of Jill).
'__ is male' (as in, 'Harold is male').
'__ is female' (as in, 'Jill is female').

With that in mind, we can define the other predicates. To say that someone is someone else's father is easy! We just say

x is the father of $y = _{df} x$ is male and y is a child of x.

(The little '$= _{df}$' just indicates that the left-hand side is to be defined in terms of the right-hand side.) We could do the same for being a brother:

x is the brother of $y = _{df} x$ is male & y is the child of z & x is the child of z.

We can extend this to all other relations (for being a mother, being a sister, being a grandfather, being a grandmother, being a niece, nephew or cousin, etc.). So we take three predicates as primitive and then define – or **analyse** – the other predicates in terms of the primitives, and it is those predicates that we are meant to have as few of as possible. We want our stock of primitives to be as low as possible because to have more of them is to add complexity to a theory (and we should always strive to get the simplest theory as possible). We add complexity to the theory by adding primitives because we add to the amount that you need to understand the theory. Imagine you met an alien who was spawned asexually by some xeno-biological polyp on a far-off planet, and who doesn't understand familial relations at all. Call him Kevin. To explain the primitives to Kevin, we would show him lots of examples of those things (say by parading one's family in front of him, or showing him books, pictures and films demonstrating the procreative acts) in the hope that he got the gist of what a male was, what a female was and what a child was. Imagine we succeeded in doing so and were then trying to explain what brothers, fathers, mothers and sisters and so on were. How odd it would be, having taught Kevin the three primitives, to *not* explain those terms simply by using the primitives we had already taught him. For instance, with '__ is the brother of __', we would tell him just that brothers are males who are children of the same people. It would be bizarre and laborious to treat that relation like a primitive again and spend ages showing him examples of brothers – far better to use the definition in terms Kevin already knows. Similarly, then, where we can reduce the number of primitives in our theory, we should jump at the chance.

But when it comes to primitives, the anti-realist about holes is in a bad position compared to the realist. There are an infinite number of perforation predicates, but the realist need not take them as primitive. They can say:

- x is singularly perforated $=_{df}$ there is a single y, which is a hole, and which is a part of x.

- x is doubly perforated $=_{df}$ there are two things, y and z, which are both holes and are both part of x.

    etc.

So they get to define those predicates in terms of what a hole is and one thing being a part of another. A realist can get by with two primitives (indeed, some realists who engage in an ontological reduction – see below for what that involves – can even define what a hole is, leaving them with one primitive). The anti-realist, on the other hand, can't accept this natural analysis of perforation for to say something is perforated would then be to say there is (i.e., there exists!) a hole that's a part of it – we'd be back to committing to holes. So each predicate must be an unanalysable primitive and, as there is an infinite number of such predicates, there will be an infinite number of primitives! So when it comes to ideological parsimony, anti-realism is in a poor position. Indeed, it might be independently absurd for us to think that there is an infinite number of primitives in play. Again, compare to Kevin. When we taught him the primitives, we pointed to examples to make him understand what we meant. For each primitive that Kevin learnt, we would have had to have shown him a number of examples to make him understand what each primitive meant (so a number of men to show him what a man was, a number of women to show him what a woman was, etc.). So for us to have learnt an infinite number of primitives would need us to have seen an infinite number of examples.*That is, to learn what it is for something to be singularly perforated, we'd need to see lots of examples of singularly perforated things. To learn what something was to be doubly perforated, we'd need to see lots of examples of doubly perforated things and so on for all of the primitives. But we've never done *that* – we know what the entire range of 'perforated' predicates means without having gone through the eternally laborious task of seeing examples of every different variation of perforated object. So, one might argue, it just seems to be demonstrably false that these predicates are primitives.

Nor are these the only problems with the primitives, for it's not clear that we can paraphrase all hole talk merely with perforation primitives. Take the following sentence, courtesy of Peter Geach:

'The hole in the tooth was smaller than the dentist's finest probe.'

We cannot paraphrase that in terms merely of perforation. Perhaps we could offer the paraphrase that:

If the tooth were not perforated, then there would exist an extra object which would be part of the tooth, even though it isn't actually part of the tooth (i.e., the bit of the tooth that is missing), and this object would be smaller in width than the tip of the dentist's finest probe.

Whilst it doesn't quantify over any holes, it's not exactly elegant! Moreover, try paraphrasing an alternative sentence:

'There are as many holes in the Swiss cheese as there are in that piece of paper.'

When we quantify over holes (by being realists about holes) this is easy to account for – there are some things (the holes in the cheese) and some other things (the holes in the paper) and there are as many of the former as there are of the latter. The anti-realist has no such luck. They'd be okay if they just had to say that the cheese and the paper had one hole in them (for the paraphrase of that is that they are both singularly perforated) or two holes in them (where it is that they are both doubly perforated) and so on but as the sentence doesn't say exactly how many holes are in either the cheese or the paper, we will need to say something like:

$\exists x \exists y$ (x is a piece of paper & y is a piece of cheese & ([x is singularly perforated & y is singularly perforated] v [x is doubly perforated & y is doubly perforated] v [x is triply perforated v y is triply perforated] v . . .))

Whilst we avoid quantifying over holes, the paraphrase is now infinitely long as it just goes on and on, listing all the ways that the cheese and the paper could both be. This is even less elegant! Even simple sentences now require infinitely long paraphrases. Moreover, consider:

'There were as many bullet holes in the corpse as there were dirty cops on the force.'

You might have thought that the paraphrase for this sentence would be very similar to the one about the paper and cheese. But it can't be! As the police force isn't 'perforated' (that just makes no sense), we cannot say any such thing. Indeed, I'll leave you to figure out a possible paraphrase.

So we've seen a lot of reasons why anti-realism about holes might not be as workable as we'd have hoped (at least, if we assume a Quinean theory of ontological commitment). We might, then, want to reconsider the realist options. Before doing so, we can turn to the final theoretical virtue we'll look at.

Virtue 4: Ontological parsimony

Ontological reduction

A standard aim in ontology is to have as few things as possible in one's ontology (to stop it being 'bloated'). Indeed, it's a common theme in many disciplines that you should make do with less rather than more. Take two examples.

Example 1 An archaeologist discovers that a tool, say an axe, was made on a remote mountain top. Being a simple tool, only one person would be needed to make it. In light of this fact, and in light of the remoteness of the location, the archaeologist concludes that it is likely that only one person made it and was up on the mountainside at that time. Similarly, if it were a more complex device that he surmised needed at least three people to make, it wouldn't be an unreasonable conclusion that exactly three people helped make it. Why suppose *more* were present? Notice, the claim isn't that *it's impossible* for more people to have been involved. But, given the evidence at hand, if the archaeologist were forced to pick a number of people involved, he'd do well to pick the lowest possible (after all, if not that number, what number?)

Example 2 If two physical theories were equal in all other respects, but one said that one particle was involved in a subatomic reaction, and the other theory said a billion were, and there was simply no evidence to tell between them, it seems intuitive that we should conclude only one particle is involved. (Indeed, this is *exactly* what takes place with certain reactions involving neutrinos – in some reactions, the science allows us to describe it as a case of numerous particles being produced, but physicists always assume it's just the one particle: the neutrino.)

Notice that in both examples we're trying to keep the number of entities needed to as few as possible. This is called **quantitative ontological parsimony**. But there is also another dimension to ontological parsimony. We might want to keep the number of *kinds* of entity as low as possible. This is called **qualitative ontological parsimony**. There are good examples of this as well.

Example 1 You've probably already encountered one example during your philosophical studies: substance dualism. Substance dualists, like Descartes, think that there are two kinds of entity. One is the physical, material matter (that makes up tables, chairs, mountains, etc.); the other is some immaterial substance (which is what things like people and angels are identical to). Because an explanation in merely material terms is sufficient for what goes on in the world (that is, physicalism seems to do the trick when it comes to explaining our mental lives), we should naturally favour the theory with just one kind of substance, i.e., discard substance dualism in favour of some physicalist theory about the mind.

Example 2 Back to physics. In physics, scientists tend to postulate
the smallest number of kinds of particles in their theory. They don't
want a new kind of entity to account for every new phenomenon
they observe – far better to draft in the existing kinds of entities,
working in complex ways, to account for the phenomena that
they see.

Similarly, then, in ontology there's a desire to keep the number of
kinds of entity as low as possible (indeed, it is commonplace for
ontologists to think that qualitative ontological parsimony is more
important than quantitative ontological parsimony).

This virtue looks to be one that realism does not meet. If the
realist believes in all of the material objects in the world and then
adds, on top, that there is this extra category of entity – holes – that
exist in addition, then they are being neither quantitatively nor
qualitatively parsimonious. They are not quantitatively parsimonious, for where the anti-realist thinks there is but one thing where a
pair of jeans are, the realist must now think there are two things,
i.e., the jeans plus the hole that they have in them. Nor are they
being qualitatively parsimonious, for they now believe that there
are not just the material objects (one kind of entity) but also holes
(a second kind of entity).

There are options open to the realist to militate against this cost.
One can make a theory more parsimonious by eliminating certain
entities, as the anti-realist about holes does, but one can also have
a parsimonious theory by utilizing entities that already unconten-
tiously exist. For instance, substance dualists say that people are
immaterial souls. We could achieve parsimony by making the
radical move of saying that people don't exist (that is, that we
should be anti-realists about people!). Such a move isn't one that
we should feel forced into making. The natural move is to say that
people exist (so we're still realists about them) but identify them
with things we already believe in – namely brains, or central nervous
systems, or bodies or any of the other physical things that physical-
ists tend to think that people are. Therefore, we can get a theory
more parsimonious than substance dualism without being an anti-
realist about people. Call this process, of identifying a class of entities you want to be a realist about with some entities you already
believe in, **ontological reduction**. Not everyone uses this term in
exactly the same way, and some people think that one (kind of)
entity can be reduced to another (kind of) entity without identifying
one with the other (we shall see an example on p. 204 in the final

chapter). But, for now, we'll just treat ontological reduction as a case of identifying one (kind of) entity with another (kind of) entity.

Holes as hole linings

Return to holes. In an effort to regain parsimony, the realist about holes might decide to engage in an ontological reduction. So, rather than thinking that holes are extra entities in a category of their own (when an entity is in a category of its own, and not reducible to another category, we say it is *sui generis*), we instead identify holes with other entities in our ontology. For instance, take an object with a hole in it – a table, say. It's uncontentious that the table exists, and that the parts of the table exist (although see chapter 8). The top of the table exists, the legs of the table exist, etc., and there also exists the part of the table that we can call the **hole lining**. The hole lining is that part of the table which we would ordinarily think the hole sits just inside: it is the edge of the table that borders where the hole would be. As the hole lining is just a physical part of the table – a chunk of wood not dissimilar to, say, the table leg – it is as uncontentious to say that hole linings exist as it is to say that tables exist. In a famous article by David and Stephanie Lewis, two fictional interlocutors, Argle and Bargle (as in 'argle bargle', a Scottish slang term for 'argument') discuss the ontology of holes. Argle decides to identify holes with hole linings: holes exist, but aren't entities in a category of their own, instead being entities that we already believe in. This theory (sometimes called the **Ludovician theory**) is ontologically parsimonious – it includes holes, but includes them without adding in an extra *sui generis* category. (Indeed, you might want to readdress whether or not the Ludovician theory does, in fact, rally against the intuitions that a realism about holes is thought to be transgressing. For instance, you might want to consider whether the Ludovician theory entails that the number of things in existence remains constant even when you make a hole in something.)

But no theory goes without problems. When we carry out a reduction, what we want to ensure is that the properties of the thing being reduced end up being what they should be. Argle and Bargle discuss a few issues concerning this. For instance, if holes are hole linings, then they're made of what the object they are holes in is itself made of. The hole lining in a wooden table is made of wood, the hole lining in a block of cheese is made of cheese, the hole lining in a pair of jeans is made of denim and so on but it seems odd to think that holes are made of wood, cheese or denim. Holes, you would've thought, aren't made of *anything*. Or if you spin a toilet roll, then the hole lining is spinning, therefore the hole is spinning. But (so worries Bargle in the Lewis article) it doesn't seem right to say that the hole spins. Casati and Varzi, who criticize Argle's theory, add in the following problem. Intuitively, we can make holes bigger (just imagine digging one – the more you dig, the bigger it gets). So take a hole with a funny shape (as shown in the left-hand side of Figure 2.1). Imagine that you dig out more of the object to leave you with a bigger hole (as given in the right-hand side of Figure 2.1).

It seems that the hole has been enlarged. But the lining of the hole, the edge that runs around the hole, has got smaller. Imagine you trace with your finger the hole on the left side, and then do the same on the right. It will take you longer for the hole on the left, so the hole lining on the left is bigger than the one on the right. But if Argle is correct, then the hole lining just is the hole, so the size of the hole is the size of the hole lining. So if the hole lining gets smaller when we change the shape of the hole lining from what it is on the left to what it is on the right, then the hole gets smaller. But how can the hole get smaller when intuitively it's got bigger! In each case, we could try and think of some way to wriggle out of these unwanted consequences (I leave it to you as an exercise to attempt). The realist could also decide to bite some bullets and just accept these counter-intuitive consequences. So we might say (as

Figure 2.1 Size of hole linings

The hole on the right is bigger than that on the left, but the hole lining has got smaller

Argle in fact says) that holes are made of wood (or cheese, or denim, etc.), even though intuitively they are not (or intuitively they can spin, or the size of the hole isn't what you intuitively thought it was, etc.). This incurs a cost (namely, it offends the virtue of cohering with our intuitions) but it still manages to be parsimonious. Exactly whether the parsimony is worth the cost, of course, is just the kind of question that we must answer when we come to weigh the theories up against one another with regard to their costs and benefits.

Holes as regions of space

Let's instead consider an alternative realist reduction. We might believe in regions of space. So in addition to all of the material objects that exist, we might think that there exists space itself, in which objects are located. As we shall see in chapter 6, some people are fond of believing in such regions of space. We could, if we believed that space itself existed, believe that holes were reduced to regions of space – namely, the empty region surrounded by the hole lining.

To help get a grip on it, consider Figure 2.2. On the left, imagine that there are no objects at all. There is, nevertheless, an area of space: the big area, R, and the smaller area that's a part of it, r. When we have a perforated object, as depicted on the right of the diagram,

Figure 2.2 Holes as regions of space

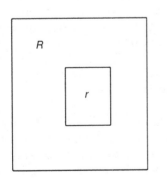

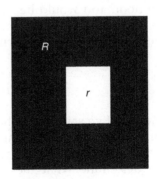

Two regions of (empty) space, R and r

Those regions when an object with a hole in it is placed in R

the object occupies an area of space (in this case R), leaving some area empty because it has a hole in it (in this case r). If we identify holes with regions of space, then the hole is just that region of space (in this case, r).

Now we solve some of the above problems. The hole is made of nothing – it's not made of cheese, or wood, or denim (perhaps it's made of 'spacetime' or whatever goes to make up space, but we might not think this is a problem). When we scoop out more of a hole, the hole lining might get smaller, but the size of the region that is a hole gets bigger – so it solves that problem too. Finally, when the object spins, the region of space stays where it is, so we solve that as well.

Unfortunately, this last move causes problems of its own. Regions of space don't move. That is, where you are now remains where it is when you go. You can go different places, but the places themselves stay where they are. But if holes are regions of space, then, as spatial regions cannot move, the holes cannot move either! This, again, contradicts our intuitions. For instance, imagine I go to your house and, with malice aforethought, burn a hole in your favourite jeans. I then run off back to my own home. Annoyed, you bring the jeans to my house and show me them: 'Look at this hole you've put in my jeans!' you say. 'What are you going to do about it?' But the hole I made in your jeans is a region of space that's still back where your house is. Over at my house, there's *another* region of space where the jeans now are, and that region of space is now the hole I'm looking at. But it's not the same as the region/hole back in your house. If I was stubborn, and so ontologically minded, I would say 'Hole? What hole? I didn't burn *that* hole. I've never seen *that* hole in my life. I don't know what you're talking about.' And then shut the door. You would be rightly annoyed, and fear, therefore, that this theory gets it thoroughly wrong. So this theory, too, has problems with cohering with our intuitions.

Weighing up the theories

Thus far I've said that, when trying to determine which theory is correct, we need to determine what the costs and benefits are of the competing theories and then weigh them up against one another. We determine what the costs and benefits are by considering, amongst other virtues, how well they cohere with our intuitions, how well they explain things and how parsimonious they are with respect to their ideologies and ontologies. Let's consider how this works with holes. We've discussed four theories – an anti-realist theory that tries to provide paraphrases for avoiding a commitment to holes; a realist theory where holes are *sui generis*; a realist theory where holes are reduced to hole linings; and a realist theory where holes are regions of space. Let's chart some of their costs and benefits:

Theory	Theoretical Virtue			
	Coherence with intuition	Explanatory power	Ideological parsimony	Ontological parsimony
Anti-realism	*Benefit*: Doesn't endorse the existence of absences.	*Benefit*: Explains everything (just as long as we get the correct paraphrases).	*Cost*: To get the correct paraphrases, we need lots of primitives, and the paraphrases are all radically dissimilar from one another.	*Benefit*: Doesn't include holes, making it qualitatively and quantitatively more parsimonious than holes as *sui generis* entities.
Sui generis realism	*Cost*: Endorses the existence of things we would've otherwise thought didn't exist.	*Benefit*: No reason to think it doesn't explain things.	*Benefit*: Only needs to take the predicate '__ is a hole' as primitive. (Or is this a cost?)	*Cost*: Includes the existence of a new category of entities.
Ludovician theory	*Cost*: Holes get smaller when they intuitively get bigger. *Cost*: Holes are now made of wood, cheese, denim, etc. *Cost*: Holes can now spin.	*Benefit*: No reason to think it doesn't explain things. (Or does it? I leave you to think about that.)	*Benefit*: No extra ideology (it can even analyse what a hole is in terms of hole lining).	*Benefit*: Doesn't add any extra ontology, making it as parsimonious as the anti-realist theory.
Holes as regions of space	*Cost*: Holes can no longer move.	*Benefit*: No reason to think it doesn't explain things. (Or does it? I leave you to think about that.)	*Benefit*: No extra ideology (as we can analyse what a hole is in terms of being a region of space surrounded by a hole lining).	*Cost or benefit?*: If you believe in space, it's parsimonious (if you don't, then it adds a new category of entity that you otherwise might not need).

There are a few things to note with this table. First, it's still not obvious – even having done this – which theory is correct. What we cannot do is simply tot up the costs and benefits as if they are equal. It's not clear which is more important: are we to attempt to secure our intuitions no matter what, even if this means a bloated ontology or ideology and lots of brute facts? Or are we to try and get a parsimonious ideology/ontology even at the cost of a few of our intuitions about holes, such as whether they can move, or whether they're made of cheese, etc.? It's not clear exactly which option we should go for and you'll find that in many cases we end up with a quandary over what to pick. Different metaphysicians weigh the virtues differently (usually thinking that no virtue is so important that it should be obtained no matter what) and this is something you should be aware of. And if you're looking to find a cast-iron statement of which virtue is better than which other, then the answer has not as yet been settled. Perhaps, as you go through this book, you'll get a better grip on what's at stake, and will form a (hopefully justifiable!) opinion on the matter. Secondly, for each theory there might be a lot more to say in its defence. Perhaps we can explain how to be an anti-realist without needing an infinite number of primitives, or perhaps there are more serious worries with the Ludovician theory that we've missed and so on. One important issue is that I have only discussed the Quinean theory of ontological commitment. There are competitors, which we will introduce throughout this book and in light of which you might, having learnt about them, want to come back and deploy them in the case of holes. We will, however, see more of the Quinean theory of ontological commitment, and how it guides anti-realist paraphrases, in the next two chapters.

Chapter summary

In this chapter, we have:

- introduced the notion of theory choice and the cost benefit analysis.
- introduced some virtues that we can measure a theory by (namely coherence with intuition, explanatory power, ideological parsimony and ontological parsimony).
- introduced one (metaontological) theory for determining what things a theory commits to: the Quinean theory of ontological commitment.

- deployed all of this with regard to the ontology of holes to examine realist and anti-realist theories about whether holes exist and, if they do exist, whether they can be identified with ('reduced to') some other entity.

Further reading

Quine's theory of ontological commitment gets the most standard statement in his 1948 article. The best contemporary statement of that theory – including a strong argument for why we should endorse it – is by Peter van Inwagen (1998). You can find introductions to issues in ontological commitment in Cynthia Macdonald (2005), Stephen Laurence and Cynthia Macdonald (1998) and Bill Aune (1985). More complicated discussion and criticisms of Quine's view include those by Joseph Melia (1995) and Agustín Rayo (2007). Discussions of specific theoretical virtues include those by Daniel Nolan (1997), Elliott Sober (1981) and Michael Huemer (2009).

The most famous article on the ontology of holes is by David and Stephanie Lewis (1970). Roberto Casati and Achille Varzi (1994) have a book dedicated to these issues (with a response by the Lewis's (1996), and a response to that article then appears in Jackson and Priest (2004)). Frank Jackson (1977a) has a discussion of paraphrasing hole talk, whilst Kristie Miller (2007) and Wake, Spencer and Fowler (2007) discuss other theories of holes. Casati has also written a shorter introduction (2009).

3

Properties

Terminology Alert! Universals

Throughout this chapter, I talk about whether 'properties' exist, but in the literature people often talk instead about 'universals'. It's not entirely clear what a universal is meant to be. Here are some examples of how people use the term:

* A universal is any property that can be 'repeated'. That is, which can be instantiated by lots of things.
* A universal is just that thing which can be found in lots of places (it is 'wholly present' (see p. 59) in lots of places).
* Universals are the entities referred to by general terms such as 'horse' or 'blue'.
* A universal is any entity that is both a property and cannot be reduced to an entity from another category.

As there is a lot of division concerning usage, this book opts to not use the term 'universal'. Instead, I talk simply about 'properties'. As always, when you settle down to your further research, you should bear in mind the variation over how the term is used.

A standard question in ontology is whether or not properties exist. That is, given that,

* electrons are charged
* the Taj Mahal is white

- I am about 150,000,000 kilometres from the sun
- Brad Pitt is in love with Angelina Jolie

does it follow that there also exist the properties and relations picked out by those facts, i.e., do *charge, white, being 150,000,000 km away from* or *being in love* exist? This chapter examines the realist and anti-realist theories about this matter, during which we shall see more of the Quinean theory of ontological commitment, as well introducing an alternative method for figuring out a theory's ontological commitments.

Properties and Quinean ontological commitment

Chapter 1 has already introduced some reasons to not believe in properties, e.g., if properties existed, they would be abstract objects so not in space and time, and we'd have no knowledge of them and so on (although, as we shall see at the end of this chapter, not every realist believes there are such difficulties). So let's assume, for now, that such motivations drive us towards anti-realism, and see how that enterprise works out. Certainly, given the Quinean theory of ontological commitment, the simple sentences above do not commit us to realism. To say that electrons are charged is just to say:

$\forall x$ (x is an electron $\rightarrow x$ is charged)

We don't quantify over some property in that case (nor do any of the other sentences – I leave it as an exercise for you to see why). But not all sentences are like this. There are problematic sentences where we do appear to quantify over properties. Start by looking at one that *doesn't* entail such quantification:

'The car on the left and the car on the right are both blue'

which is translated into first-order logic as:

$\exists x \exists y$ (x is the car on the left & y is the car on the right & x is blue & y is blue)

We only quantify over cars, and again there's no quantification over properties. But with the very similar statement:

'The car on the left and the car on the right are the same colour'

such an anti-realist translation proves to be much more difficult. As both cars could be the same colour without both being blue, the earlier translation won't work (for if both cars were pink the sentence would be true, but that paraphrase into first-order logic would be false). We could try a disjunctive paraphrase, e.g., that the cars must be both blue *or* both be yellow *or* both be green and so on. That's translated as:

$\exists\, x\, \exists\, y$ (x is the car on the left & y is the car on the right & ([x is blue & y is blue] v [x is yellow & y is yellow] v [x is green & y is green] v . . .))

where the ellipses are followed by a disjunct for x and y being every colour that there is. That would be a long translation. In fact, because there are different shades of each colour, even that translation wouldn't be complicated enough, for an azure car won't be the same colour as a car that is Alice blue, even though they will both be blue. So the pairs of disjuncts should actually be specific shades, e.g., [x is azure and y is azure] v [x is Alice blue & y is Alice blue] etc. There are about a thousand shades that the human eye can easily differentiate, so the translation will be a thousand pairs of disjuncts long. In fact, if we meant that the cars were *exactly* the same colour – precise in every possible way, even when indistinguishable to human faculties – then even that translation won't be precise enough. We'll need, instead, to have a pair of disjuncts for *every* single one of the infinite shades that there can be. The paraphrase, then, would be *infinitely* long!

Compare that anti-realist paraphrase, with its infinite disjuncts, to this, far shorter, realist paraphrase:

$\exists\, x\, \exists\, y\, \exists\, z$ (x is the car on the left & y is the car on the right & z is a colour & x instantiates z & y instantiates z)

where, you may recall from chapter 1, a thing instantiates a property if it 'is' it or 'has' it, so the cars would instantiate *red* if they were both red, or instantiate *blue* if they were both blue, or instantiate *owned by Barack Obama* if they were owned by Barack Obama. That paraphrase, then, just says that two cars are the same colour if there's a colour that they both instantiate – if there's a colour they both *are*. This second translation is far simpler and far shorter. But as it quantifies over colours (for the value of the bound variable 'z' is a colour, which is a type of property), we would have to be realists. So if that second translation were the correct one, then we would be quantifying over properties (in this case, a colour property) which, according to Quine's theory of ontological commitment, would mean that properties existed.

So the same quandary from the last chapter arises here as well. We have to choose between the anti-realist's paraphrase, which introduces an infinite number of colour primitives and uses complicated paraphrases that are infinitely long, and a simple, realist, paraphrase using only one primitive (namely the primitive relation '__ instantiates __', as in 'The electron instantiates *charge*') that comes lumbered with costs concerning ontological parsimony (as well as any costs you attach to including abstract objects in your ontology!).

Further, there might be many sentences which the anti-realist will be hard pressed to translate at all. For instance:

- Blue is my favourite colour.
- Red resembles orange more than it does blue.
- Electrons have something in common.
- There are as yet undiscovered physical properties.
- There are three fundamental properties of quantum physics.

In those cases, the translations become a lot harder as their surface grammar explicitly appears to quantify over properties:

- $\exists x \, (x = blue \; \& \; x$ is my favourite colour $)$.
- $\exists x \, \exists y \, \exists z \, (x = red \; \& \; y = orange \; \& \; z = blue \; \& \; x$ resembles y to degree $n \; \& \; x$ resembles z to degree $m \; \& \; n > m)$.
- $\exists x \, \exists y \, \exists z \, (x$ is an electron $\& \; y$ is an electron $\& \; x$ instantiates $z \; \& \; y$ instantiates $z)$.
- $\exists x \, (x$ is a property $\& \; x$ has not been discovered as of this time $)$.
- $\exists x \, \exists y \, \exists z \, (x$ is a fundamental property of physics $\& \; y$ is a fundamental property of physics $\& \; z$ is a fundamental property of physics $\& \; x \neq y \neq z)$

The anti-realist can keep banging out their competing paraphrases, but it can get quite difficult to find the correct one. For instance, 'Blue is my favourite colour' might be paraphrased by the anti-realist as:

$\forall\, x\, (\, x \text{ is blue} \rightarrow \text{I will like } x\,)$

We've removed the quantification over properties – now we are only quantifying over things that are blue (like blue balls, blue cars, etc., all things that the nominalist will be happy with) but that doesn't seem to be a good paraphrase at all. Blue might be my favourite colour without me liking all blue things. For instance, I might absolutely hate a given politician, and painting them blue (whilst comical) won't make me like them any the more. At this stage, the anti-realist has three options, either (i) try and come up with a better paraphrase; (ii) deny the Quinean theory of ontological commitment; or (iii) bite the bullet and deny that the sentence is true. I leave (i) for you to attempt (and in the Further Reading section below, I suggest some readings to look at concerning such paraphrases). But, remember, it is not just that sentence which needs to be paraphrased, but all of the problematic sentences. Even if you can offer paraphrases of 'Blue is my favourite colour' it'll be far harder to find adequate paraphrases of 'There are three fundamental properties of quantum physics.' Have fun trying though! Option (ii) I also leave to you. Feel free to read some of the other theories of ontological commitment, given in later chapters, and then come back to bring them to bear on the question of whether or not properties exist. Finally, then, we might just deny that these things are true at all. Now the anti-realist is left with a theory that doesn't cohere with our intuitions. Can it really be the case that blue isn't my favourite colour? I thought it was! I like wearing blue clothing and blue rooms and all of the other things associated with blue being my favourite colour. Or could it really be the case that there aren't any undiscovered physical properties? And, not only this, but we figured out this fact from metaphysics alone, by sitting in our armchairs and thinking very hard? Doubtlessly few physicists would take us seriously when we start saying such things. So whilst this is an option open to us, it's unlikely to be the one we pick.

So if we deploy the Quinean theory of ontological commitment, we find that the anti-realist has problems with ideological parsimony and getting the correct paraphrases (whilst the realist has problems with ontological parsimony and running roughshod over the intuitions that clash with believing in abstract objects). As we've already seen how this works with regard to holes, I shall press on and instead turn to an alternative way of determining what does or does not exist.

The problem of universals

Whilst we'll return to the Quinean theory of ontological commitment at many more junctures in this book, for now let's set it aside and consider another way of trying to determine whether or not properties exist. That way is the **problem of universals**. With a history worming its way from classical metaphysics (where it was called the 'One Over Many' argument), through medieval metaphysics (when it got the name I am using here) and into contemporary times, the problem has quite the pedigree. Unfortunately, having such a long history means that there is also a lot of division over exactly what the problem is meant to be (indeed, it might be more apt to consider it as a grouping of lots of very similar problems).

We'll examine two versions of the problem (although there are more). The first version says that given a sentence of the form '*a* is F', we must find some sort of explanation for *why* '*a* is F'. Realists argue that the explanation involves properties existing. Before going further, note that there are many different types of explanation, and the one sought here is of a specific kind. For instance, one explanation of the Taj Mahal being white is that, when Ustad Ahmad Lahauri (the architect of the Taj Mahal) designed it, he instructed it to be white. That's a *causal* explanation. And that's not the kind of explanation deployed when we explain, say, the transparency of windows by reference to their molecular structure, or explain my being human in terms of my having certain DNA. It doesn't sound correct to say that the structure *causes* the transparency of the window, or that my DNA *causes* me to be human, for when we say that one thing causes another we normally think that the cause happens *earlier* than the effect. As the window's transparency (and my being human) is simultaneous with having a particular molecular structure (or having certain DNA), it doesn't sound right to say that one causes the other. Nevertheless, we still have a type of explanation; it's just a second brand of explanation – a form of *non-causal* explanation.

Neither type of explanation is what the realist has in mind when they think that we must explain the truth of the proposition that the Taj Mahal is white. Those who believe in the problem of universals believe there is a further type of explanation: **metaphysical explanation**. They believe that there are specifically ontological facts which must ground, and *metaphysically* explain, an object being F. The realist explanation, of course, is that *a* is F because *a* instantiates *Fness* – that the facts about instantiation *explain* the facts about what properties it has. So the Taj Mahal's being white is (metaphysically) explained by it instantiating the property *white* (and an electron's being charged is explained by it instantiating the property *charge*, etc.). As anti-realists do not believe in properties, they are denied that explanation and, unless they can provide an alternative, the realist theory has more explanatory power (which is a theoretical virtue) and so we should accept it and believe in properties.

Alternative versions of the problem

Not everyone thinks that the idea of metaphysical explanation makes any sense. To some, it is an esoteric notion of no merit whatsoever, and exactly the kind of thing that gives philosophers a bad reputation. Such people won't be fazed by this realist argument for properties existing, as they won't think any special explanation in terms of properties is required. But, for now, we shall assume that there is a legitimate demand for metaphysical explanation and press on with examining exactly how the anti-realist might otherwise respond to the problem of universals.

Given the present version of the problem of universals, the realist is already going to face some problems as it seems impossible, in general, to give a realist explanation of predication. We've seen examples of this already in chapter 1. In the (true) sentence '*Being a human* is non-self-instantiating', we have a predicate ('__ is non-self-instantiating') that we are predicating of something else (*being a human*). But if we are, in general, required to provide metaphysical explanations of true sentences, what explanation can we give here? As discussed in chapter 1, the explanation *can't* be that there's a property, *being non-self-instantiating*, which the property *being a human* instantiates, since the existence of such a property entails a contradiction. So the realist must think that at least some true sentences go without any explanation in terms of instantiating a given property. And if one sentence goes without such an explanation, why think the others cannot be likewise? But there are alternative versions of the problem of universals. We might instead say that the problem is not that we have to explain predication, but that we have to explain resemblance.

Not every set of objects is such that the objects all resemble one another – for instance, the actor Michael J. Fox does not resemble a 1981 DeLorean car. He is a person made of organic matter, whilst it is an (aesthetically pleasing) mass of metal and other inorganic materials. Whilst we might say that there are things they have in common (say, that they are both not made of cheese or both have appeared in the film *Back to the Future*), this doesn't indicate the presence of **genuine resemblance**. Fox and the DeLorean do not resemble one another in the same way that, say, two negatively charged electrons resemble one another. The resemblance between the electrons is a natural, objective resemblance. The things we might think Michael J. Fox has in common with the car are not natural, genuine resemblances at all.

The existence of properties can explain genuine resemblance, some realists say. At least, if only certain properties exist. We might think that some properties are natural and objective, e.g., *charge*, *having a mass of 0.51 MeV* (which is the mass of an electron), *being white*, etc. Certain other properties, we might think, are not natural or objective, e.g., *not being made of cheese* or *appearing in the 1985 film 'Back to the Future'*, etc. If we thought that only the former properties existed and not the latter, we could explain why two things genuinely resemble one another in terms of their sharing properties. The genuine resemblance of the electrons is explained by them both instantiating *charge* and *having a mass of 0.51 MeV*. Michael J. Fox and the DeLorean car don't resemble one another, and this is explained by there being no properties that they both instantiate (for, whilst they are both not made of cheese, we've just stipulated that no such property corresponds to that). Indeed, we can compare the degrees of resemblance by comparing *how many* properties two things instantiate. So a tall, ginger-haired man might, in some respects, resemble a tall, blonde woman, but will more closely resemble a short, ginger-haired man just because the two of them instantiate more properties than the man does with the woman.

So there are different versions of the problem of universals, varying over what feature of reality stands in need of a metaphysical explanation. But we won't consider the alternative versions too extensively, and the crude caricature of the problem as being about explaining predication will suffice here. What is crucial for my purposes is the introduction of the notion of metaphysical explanation: both versions of the Problem rely upon it, and it's that which is most important to the matter at hand.

Alternative anti-realist theories

We've looked at two reasons that the anti-realist might have for thinking that the realist's demand for a metaphysical explanation is unreasonable (either that metaphysical explanation is just non-sensical or that the realist cannot, in fact, provide a suitable explanation for all sentences). But not every anti-realist about properties thinks that the demand is unreasonable – some agree that the problem of universals is a challenge that an anti-realist enterprise must meet and so suggest alternative, anti-realist, theories to meet it. The rest of this section considers two such attempts.

The first is **trope theory**. 'Trope' is the term of art that ontologists use for specific instantiations of properties. For instance, if I have a black jacket and a black pen, they're both black but they have their own particular 'blacknesses' – the jacket's instance of black is distinct from that of the pen. Or you might look at the sky and revel in how blue it is: in that case you are specifically focusing on the blueness of the sky – not the property *blue* in general but just the sky's particular instantiation of it. Or you might notice how tall someone is, at which point you're noticing not the property *tall* in general, but that man's specific tallness. Or you might be cut by a particularly ornate knife whilst chopping vegetables. In that case, what caused you to bleed would be the sharpness of the knife – not the property *sharpness* in general (nor the ornateness of the knife) but that sharpness which is specific to the knife. Each of these things – the blacknesses of the jacket and the pen, the blueness of the sky, the man's specific tallness and the knife's sharpness and so on – are tropes.

Trope theorists often try and respond to the problem of universals by invoking tropes. Rather than the Taj Mahal being white because it instantiates the property *white*, it's white because it has a particular white trope; an electron is charged because it has its own, specific, trope corresponding to its own particular charge; Obama is a Democrat in virtue of having his 'Democrat' trope and so on. Of course, they have to introduce a category of entities – tropes – to account for this, but trope theorists prefer tropes to properties for several reasons. First, tropes are located in time and space. They are not in platonic heaven and avoid problems that affect abstracta. Indeed, tropes are sometimes called 'concrete properties' (although, just to be utterly confusing, they are sometimes called 'abstract particulars' – another confirmation that terminology in contemporary ontology is an absolute mess). Second, as we shall see below, some philosophers think properties can also be in space and time, but would then be strangely located by being exactly located where their every instance is (as explained in the next section). As tropes are particular to the individual, they are located only at one place, i.e., where the instance is. So they are more normal in that sense. Third, tropes might serve other purposes that properties cannot. For instance, we might think tropes figure in a theory of causation (just think of the example of the knife's sharpness *causing* someone to bleed – tropes, it seems, are causally active). Or we might want to ontologically reduce material objects down to properties (what is called **bundle theory**). Objects would become 'bundles' of properties, constructed from them analogous to how objects are constructed from their atoms. But, with an ontology of just properties, that's hard to pull off. Just as you cannot make two objects out of the same atoms at the same time (although see chapter 9), the analogue would be that you couldn't have two objects which were bundles of the same properties. But that's just to say that you can't have two objects with exactly the same properties. The principle that captures that thesis, the **identity of indiscernibles**, is a most unpopular thesis for it seems relatively easy to imagine counter-examples, e.g., we can imagine a universe containing nothing other than two exactly identical iron balls – they would be two objects with precisely the same properties. But if we shift to tropes (and to objects being reduced to bundles of tropes), then we don't have this problem. As tropes are particular to the individual that has them, we can have two objects with exactly the same properties but they'll have their own *instantiations* of those properties. Hence, they'll be two bundles with totally different parts. One object will be a bundle of its tropes, but a totally different collection of tropes will make up the bundle that is the other (qualitatively identical) bundle. Hence, trope theory makes room for bundle theory to be true and allows us to ontologically reduce objects to tropes. So whilst, like realism about properties, trope theory introduces another category, it might offer extra benefits.

Another anti-realist option that involves adding in no extra categories of entities is **resemblance nominalism** (where here the word 'nominalism' is being used to specifically mean an anti-realism about properties rather than, as I used it in chapter 1, an anti-realism about abstract objects in general). The resemblance nominalist says that an explanation of '*a* is F' can be given in terms of facts about objects resembling other objects. So the Taj Mahal is

white because it resembles other white things; an electron is negatively charged because it resembles all of the other negatively
charged objects in the world; Obama is a Democrat because he
resembles all of the other Democrats out there; and so on. Such
anti-realists take resemblance as a primitive – adding to their ideology – in the hope of providing a metaphysical explanation. (This is
problematic if you had in mind the interpretation of the problem of
universals where we are meant to explain genuine resemblance in
the first place, as it looks as if the explanation will now be circular.
Of course, the resemblance nominalist might simply have in mind
an alternative interpretation, or otherwise think they can escape the
charge of circularity.)

What are properties like?

So far, we have only discussed anti-realist projects versus realist
proposals, both for holes and now for properties. Whilst the realism/
anti-realism divide is a large part of the ontological project, this is
not the be all and end all. Ontology is not only concerned with
whether or not certain things exist, but what they are like if they do
exist. To see how that proceeds, let's assume (out of charity) that
properties should be included in our ontology. Given this, we can
ask questions about what they are like. For instance, we can ask
whether or not they are in spacetime: thus far I've assumed that, if
properties exist, they're abstract, but – as we shall see – that's not
the only viewpoint on offer. Or we can ask *which* properties there
are: just because you believe that there are some properties doesn't
mean you have to believe in any old property. It is consistent to
believe in some properties (like those used in fundamental science)
and not others (like the property of *being a rock star* or properties
that nothing has, like *being a gold sphere twenty miles wide*).

Immanent versus platonic realism

Start with the location of properties. We might think that properties
are abstract entities, outside space and time. This position is often
called transcendental realism or **platonic realism** (not to be confused with Plato's very own theory on this matter – his theory of
Forms – which, whilst historically interesting, we won't talk about
here). Of course, the problems for abstracta in general (covered in

chapter 1) plague such platonic theories, and I tacitly assumed such problems were part of the motivation for anti-realism about properties.

But we needn't think that properties are outside space and time. The position that properties are in space and time is called **immanent realism** (or sometimes Aristotelianism – although, as with Plato, the specifics of Aristotle's own theory will be ignored). The first hurdle for immanent realism is that, if properties are located, *where* are they located? There is a natural answer: they are where their instances are. So the property *being a man* is where every man is; the property *negative charge* is where every electron is; the property *blue* is where every blue object is, and so on. Indeed, immanent realists often go further and say that properties, unlike regular material objects, are **wholly located** where each instance is. To get a sense of what that means, I must first explain what 'wholly located' means. The idea is that you are wholly located at a person-shaped region of space (and a table is wholly located at the table-shaped region of space that it occupies, a cube is wholly located at the cube-shaped region of space that it occupies, etc.). Whereas we normally think objects are wholly located at just one place, the immanent realists tend to think that properties can be wholly located at *lots* of places. *All* of the property is where the instance is, for example the entire of *being a human* is located where every human is, the entire of *negative charge* is located where every electron is, and so on. If this is slightly mind boggling, try and compare it to the (somewhat fantastical) situation of someone time-travelling backwards and standing next to themselves. One person would then be wholly located at two different places through the weirdness of time travel. Immanent realists think that properties do that sort of thing all of the time.

Terminology Alert! Location Relations

There has been a rising interest in the logic and metaphysics of location, with a particularly important essay being Josh Parson's 'Theories of Location'. Unfortunately, this has resulted in a lot of division concerning how to use the terminology. First, the English language suffers quite severely from ambiguity when it comes to saying that an object 'is' somewhere or is 'located' somewhere. Take the following examples:

John is in New York.
Jill is located where her hand is.
Jack is at the human-shaped region of space over there.

The first example is of New York being a place where, somewhere within it, you can find John. Following Josh Parsons,
we might disambiguate this type of location by saying that
John is **weakly located** at New York. In the second example,
we mean that Jill entirely takes up the area where her hand is
– no part of that area is empty of Jill – even though Jill can still
be found elsewhere (for instance, whilst she is where her hand
is, she is also to be found where her head is). We might say Jill
pervades where her hand is (or, alternatively, she is partially
located where her hand is). The final example, of Jack being
at a single human-shaped region of space, is the type of location discussed in the main text – Jack is wholly located there.
(Parsons uses the term **exactly located**, although he argues
that properties cannot be as the immanent realist imagines,
and can't be exactly located at many places.)

So that's one way that we might locate properties in space and
time. Another way, favoured by David Armstrong, is somewhat
weirder. Armstrong is one of the lead proponents of immanent
realism but thinks that properties are in space and time, even though
there is no specific location at which they are at. He believes in entities called **states of affairs** (which we'll return to in chapter 7). They
are neither objects nor properties, but that thing which corresponds
to an individual instantiating a particular property. So a state of
affairs might be 'Bill Gates having invented *Windows*', 'The Empire
State Building is 381 metres tall' or 'The electron in the cloud
chamber is negatively charged.'

Armstrong believes that each state of affairs is composed out of
a property and an individual (such as an object). So the state of
affairs of Bill Gates having invented *Windows* is made up of two
things – an object (i.e., Bill Gates) and a property (i.e., the property
of *having invented Windows*). Similarly for the other states of affairs.
The Empire State Building plus the property *being 381 metres tall*
make up another state of affairs, whilst an electron and the property
negative charge compose a third. These states of affairs together make
up the entirety of reality, says Armstrong (hence the title of his most

famous work, *A World of States of Affairs*, 1997). In that sense, then, properties are in spacetime, as they are 'in' the states of affairs – they are constituents of them – and the states of affairs make up the whole of space and time. This, says Armstrong, is what it means for properties to be immanently located.

So we have two proposals for how we can locate properties in space and time (and thereby avoid problems such as those to do with naturalism, or with epistemological worries concerning how to know about unlocated things). But there are problems with locating properties, one of which is covered in the next subsection.

What properties are there?

Turn to the other question about what properties are like: which properties exist? We can break that question down into two further questions: (i) can there be properties with no instances? (ii) does every predicate correspond to a property?

Properties with no instances – **uninstantiated properties** – would be things like:

- *being a perfect circle* (for whilst there are things which are roughly circular, there are no perfect circles).
- *being exactly 10 metres tall* (for we can imagine that nothing is *exactly* 10 metres tall – certainly, for some given height, nothing is exactly that height).
- *being biniloctium* (biniloctium is the name given to the element that would have the atomic number 208. It is so absurdly unstable that it has never, as far as we know, occurred in nature and is not only impossible, as of yet, to create in the laboratory, it is likely to remain so for a very, very long time, and – quite probably – for ever).

The platonist, who thinks properties are unlocated, abstract things, can make room in their ontology for uninstantiated properties. The immanent realist, on the other hand, has no such luxury. If all properties are wholly located where their instances are, then, as uninstantiated properties have no instances, they cannot be located anywhere (similarly, if we thought properties were located in space and time in Armstrong's sense, then, as they're not instantiated, there won't be any states of affairs involving them, ergo, they can't be part of the collection of all states of affairs, and so won't be part of space and time). Thus, as all properties are to be located, given immanent realism, there cannot be properties like *being a perfect circle* or *being biniloctium*. This might not faze the immanent realist too much, and they might even see this as a pleasant result of their theory. They might be quite happy with the idea that the only properties that exist are those that are instantiated. After all, the above examples are just the tip of the iceberg. We can quickly move to far more fanciful examples of uninstantiated properties, such as the property that a unicorn, witch or Jedi would have. Whilst one might not baulk at including *being a perfect circle* in an ontology, *being a unicorn, being a witch* or *being a Jedi* might give more pause for thought. It is odd to imagine that such properties exist. Aren't Jedi just the creation of George Lucas's imagination? And how strange it would be for reality to have kindly included a property from a fictional galaxy far, far away, even though there never has been, or will be, a Force-wielding Jedi. There are also worries about ontological parsimony. There are an infinite number of such uninstantiated properties, so including them will bloat our ontology, which is especially worrying since (as they are not instantiated) they do not seem to do any work in exchange for this theoretical cost.

Similarly, we might think that just because an object falls under a certain predicate (e.g., '__ is human') doesn't necessarily mean that it instantiates a corresponding property (e.g., *being a human*). Certainly not *every* predicate corresponds to a property: we already have seen that the predicate '__ is not self-instantiating' cannot correspond to the property *being non-self-instantiating*, so some predicates do not correspond to an existing property and it's an open question as to which predicates qualify for that privilege. For instance, take the following predicates:

'__ is negatively charged.'	'__ is a human.'
'__ is in pain.'	'__ is a song by *Arcade Fire*.'
'__ is German.'	'__ is upset because they were dumped by their significant other.'
'__ is a rusty sword.'	'__ is not a rabbit.'

Which of those predicates correspond to a property? The first three, to varying degrees, correspond to what we think might be 'objective' cuts in reality. Some of the other predicates were things we made up – we made up songs, and some people made up *Arcade*

Fire, and some people (albeit a lot of people) made up what it is to be German, etc. The worry is very similar to one from above about *being a Jedi* – it'd somehow be strange if reality was obliging enough to ensure that properties like *being a German* or *being a song by Arcade Fire* existed. The temptation, then, is to think that those predicates don't correspond to properties.

We might also worry that the last two predicates don't correspond to properties because they're somehow derivative of other properties. If you have the property *being rusty,* for instance, and the property *being a sword,* do we really need the property *being a rusty sword*? Isn't it enough that an object instantiates the first two in order for it to be the case that the predicate '__ is a rusty sword' correctly applies to it? Adding in the extra property just seems extravagant. Likewise, isn't it enough to not be a rabbit that you just fail to instantiate the property *being a rabbit*? Do we really need to add in an extra property, *being something that is not a rabbit,* in order to account for this? If we allow in properties like these, we run roughshod over one motivation for believing in properties: accounting for genuine resemblance. If we are meant to be accounting for how things genuinely resemble one another, then we need to exclude such 'negative properties' from our ontology, else Michael J. Fox and a 1981 DeLorean car will both resemble one another for, whilst he is a thinking person made of organic matter, and the DeLorean is a mass of aesthetically pleasing metal and other such inorganic substances, both he and the car are not a rabbit. So if there were a property *being something that is not a rabbit,* they would both instantiate it and thus both genuinely resemble one another to some degree. And, as there is an infinite number of other things they are not, they would both instantiate an infinite number of the same properties. So they would resemble one another to an infinite degree – which is as close a resemblance as you can get. That's not right at all, for no actor and car genuinely resemble each other at all, never mind as closely as can possibly be. So if we are motivated to believe in properties to account for genuine resemblance, we'd better make sure such derivative properties do not exist.

One position that has gained some traction concerning this question is **scientific realism**. This is the thesis (again, closely associated with David Armstrong) that only the predicates that appear in fundamental physics correspond to a property. So '__ is negatively charged' corresponds to the property *negative charge,* but none of the other predicates we are considering correspond to any property, as humans, Germans, songs, being upset about break-ups and so on are not the kinds of thing that quantum physicists talk about.

But before you get too excited about excluding certain properties from your ontology, look at some of the problems posed by thinking that there aren't any uninstantiated properties (or that some predicates don't correspond to properties). There is a danger that we end up undermining the original motivation for realism about properties in the first place. First, return to the realist arguments based upon the Quinean theory of ontological commitment. There were sentences, such as 'There are three, as yet undiscovered, fundamental properties', which prove too difficult for the anti-realist to paraphrase and so we should, says the realist, endorse the existence of properties. If you thought that the only properties which existed were properties that featured in science, then that particular sentence wouldn't be problematic. Out there, somewhere, there would be some things that instantiated the fundamental physical properties we don't know about, so there is no problem with their existing. But other sentences will prove more problematic. Take:

Blue is a colour.

That sentence seems to be true, but, as tiny subatomic particles aren't blue (or green, or red, or any colour), it is unlikely that *blue* will feature in our fundamental physical theory. So if we think that only properties that appear in fundamental scientific theories exist, *blue* won't be one of them. But that means that the realist paraphrase of that sentence (i.e., $\exists x\,(\,x = \text{blue}\;\&\;x \text{ is a colour}\,)$) won't work any more and we must come up with an alternative paraphrase that doesn't quantify over colours. But that was exactly what the anti-realist was trying to do, and exactly what the realist thought couldn't be done. So the realist now faces serious problems. One option is to gloss scientific realism. Armstrong, for instance, adds that not only do the predicates that feature in fundamental scientific theories correspond to properties, but some properties are 'built up' out of those fundamental properties. These properties, what he calls **structural universals**, would be things like *being methane*, which would be constructed out of, say, *being a carbon atom* and *being a hydrogen atom* (which would, in turn, be structural universals themselves). Indeed, Armstrong thinks you can construct a host of properties in this manner, and we might be able to construct things like *blue*. I leave it to you to examine whether this does or does not work.

There are similar problems if you think that uninstantiated properties do not exist. Imagine that you thought colours would exist if only they were instantiated. *Red*, *orange* and *blue* are all instantiated, and so exist. Presumably, you also think the following is true:

Red resembles orange more than it does blue.

If you're a realist, this sentence is true because the property *red* resembles *orange* more than it does *blue*. But some people tend to think this sentence can be true even if nothing turned out to be red, orange or blue. If, say, the Big Bang had been more of a splutter, and it had petered out without creating anything of interest, then there would have been no coloured objects. But, you might think, that does nothing to affect the truth of that sentence. After all, even in our universe where there are such coloured objects, those objects have nothing to do with the truth of that sentence – no matter how many red, orange or blue objects we make, or what we do to them, we'll never be able to make that sentence false. The sentence is true regardless of how those objects are – so why think the sentence turns out to be false just because the number of objects reaches zero? Or imagine that someone hallucinates a colour that has never been instantiated (say, a particular shade of blue). That might, then, become their favourite colour. But then, if there is no such property, how can the sentence 'That particular shade of blue is my favourite colour' turn out to be true, given the standard realist paraphrase? So problems with uninstantiated properties arise as well.

So there are issues, not just with whether there are or aren't properties but, if there are properties, with which properties there are, and what those properties are like.

Chapter summary

In this chapter, we have:

- examined anti-realist strategies for properties and how they gel, or fail to gel, with the Quinean theory of ontological commitment.
- introduced a second way of determining whether or not we should be committed to certain entities: namely, whether they feature in metaphysical explanations of the facts.

- introduced a specific example of this, the problem of universals, and examined some anti-realist responses to it.
- looked at what properties there would be, and whether properties would be located, were realism about properties to be true.

Further reading

An excellent introduction to the ontology of properties is by Alex Oliver (1996). Alternatives include those by David Armstrong (1989a), Fraser MacBride (2009), Michael Loux and Dean Zimmerman (2003) and James Porter Moreland (2001). A selection of essays on properties can be found in D. H. Mellor and Alex Oliver (1997).

The anti-realist case for properties is famously made in Quine (1948), and another proponent includes James van Cleve (1994). You can find a discussion of paraphrases of property talk and how they work, or fail to work, in Frank Jackson (1977b) and Loux (1998). Trope nominalism is discussed by Keith Campbell (1990). An introduction to resemblance nominalism can be found by both David Armstrong (1989a) and E. Jonathan Lowe (2002), with a book-length treatment by Gonzalo Rodriguez-Pereyra (2002). If you are interested in properties and their locations, you should read Fraser MacBride (1998) and Josh Parsons (2007). Properties are also the focus of other alternatives to ontological commitment not discussed above, e.g., those trying to bring theistic beliefs to bear on the problem include Brian Leftow (2006) and Michael Bergmann and Jeffrey Brower (2006).

4

Numbers

In (apparently true) sentences like:

There is a prime number between 5 and 11
There is an infinite number of real numbers
$2 + 3 = 5$

we appear to be talking about numbers. In the first sentence, we apparently assert that there is – that there *exists* – a number that is both prime and which is greater than 5 and less than 11. Interpreted similarly, the second sentence demands an infinite number of real numbers to be out there. And the third sentence is apparently true because two numbers (the number 2 and the number 3) stand in the '__ and __ adds up to __' relation to some other number (the number 5). But, as with properties and holes, there are anti-realist theories which strive to relieve us of these commitments (and, again, because numbers are likely to be abstract, the motivations for such anti-realism will largely be the nominalist motivations from chapter 1).

Psychologism

Some people try and deflate ontological questions – that is, they try and show why the questions are easy to answer or are misguided. We've seen one deflationary theory already (permissivism, back in chapter 1) and will see a more sophisticated theory in chapter 8. Another deflationary effort, often heard in philosophy classes, is that numbers (and, for that matter, properties and other abstracta) exist only in the sense that they are ideas in our head (or are mental states, or some other similar phrase). This **psychologistic** theory is rarely heard of in the literature as it works out very poorly indeed. In natural language, there is a clear distinction drawn between something existing and *the idea of* that thing. Some examples: (i) it seems natural to say that Pegasus does not exist, but eminently natural to say that the idea of Pegasus exists; (ii) if you were hungry, a pizza would be excellent to have; an idea of a pizza would not; (iii) if you're on a plane when someone falls sick and the captain calls for a doctor, you'll find them unimpressed when you tell them that you have just what they need – a picture of a doctor in your head. Just as clearly, the idea of a number is not a number (similarly for other ontological entities).

You might instead say that numbers (etc.) *depend* upon our ideas about them, that is, without our thinking about them, they would not exist. (In the philosophy of mathematics, the position that mathematical entities are created by us is a type of **constructivist** theory, where constructivism in general is the idea that mathematical truth depends upon human activity.) This may or may not be true, but it does little to deflate ontological questions. For numbers to depend upon us, it is clear that they therefore exist, but it's not clear how this fact about dependence helps solve any of our ontological worries with them existing: how do numbers depending on our minds make their being abstracta less concerning, or tell us if they are – or should be – ontologically reduced to some other entity? If anything, the dependence claim makes realism about abstracta even weirder. If numbers depend upon us, then the universe could get along quite happily without them (as it would've done if we had not evolved). The only role they serve is an anthropocentric one. It seems, then, somewhat gratuitous to think that numbers pop into existence solely to service our needs. Indeed, we might think that it's odd that entities can pop into existence by our just thinking about them – the creation of entities by mere thought alone is surely the province of wizardry. Voldemort might be able to do it, but not us! (However, see chapter 10 for examples of entities, such as works of music and fictional characters, for which this may seem less weird.) So there appears to be little sense to be made of a theory where numbers are ideas – at least, that is, if you want that theory to deflate the problem we are faced with.

This chapter is in reverse order to the last. We shall start by assuming that numbers exist and asking what they might be like (more narrowly, what they might be reduced to) before moving on to whether or not they exist in the first place. We proceed this way because, to discuss the metaphysics of numbers, it's expedient to first know about a new category of entity that you're probably unfamiliar with: the **mathematical set**.

Ontological reductions

Introducing sets

Mathematicians introduce the notion of a 'set'. Sets stand in the **membership** relation to other things, for example, there is a set of all people (which takes, as its members, every person); there is a set of all apples (which takes, as its members, every apple); there is a set of more disparate members that don't resemble one another at all (for instance, the set of you, a forklift truck and six hydrogen atoms from a star thousands of light years away). We represent sets by means of braces like this: { and }. What go between the braces are the members of the set; for example, the set of Barack Obama and George Bush is represented by:

{ Barack Obama, George Bush }

Mathematicians have provided us with various axioms that govern how these sets work, some of which are explained in this subsection. One principle is that two sets are identical if and only if they have the same members (so, e.g., { Barack Obama, George Bush } ≠ { Bill Clinton, George Bush }). Another principle is (crudely) that, given that some things exist, there is a set of those things (no matter how disparate those things are from one another). That's why we get sets like the set of apples, or the set of you, the truck and the hydrogen atoms. In this regard, sets are like collections, for if you have some things, then it always makes sense to talk about the collection of those things. Indeed, mathematicians often compare sets to collections of things, thinking that sets and collections are one and the same. For example, imagine we had some plates. We might talk about the collection of the plates, or 'those plates over there', or – as the metaphysically unconcerned mathematician might put it – the set of plates. So we might, naively, think that talking about sets is innocuous and just another way of talking about collections.

Certainly, we sometimes use the word 'set' to talk about collections of things, but mathematical sets are nothing like collections (and mathematicians should know better than to recommend an analogy between the two). In the same way that we can use the word 'bank' in different ways, and shouldn't then become confused by wondering how people can go fishing or look at otters down the high street, we should not think that the sets which mathematicians talk about are anything like 'sets' as understood in regular English (i.e., as collections), for there are a large number of disparities between sets and collections. Indeed, explaining those disparities will allow me to tell you about more of the axioms that mathematicians think govern sets. Given the first axiom from above, if you have some things, you have a set of those things. This works even when you only have one thing, so you can have a set with a single member, for example, { Barack Obama }. But it barely makes sense to talk about collections with only one thing amongst them (imagine you wanted entertaining and I said I had a collection of DVDs at home – how disappointing it would be to find I had just one!). Moreover, not only can sets take objects as members, they can also take other sets as members, but they don't then have the members of those sets as members (membership is a non-transitive relation – it is not necessarily the case that the members of a member of a set are also its members). This means that, say, a set with two members, the set of men and the set of women, is different from the set of all men and women (which has *billions* of members). For collections, the same does not hold (for, surely, the collection of both the collection of men and the collection of women is just the same thing as the collection of men and women? As just demonstrated, the same cannot be said of the set of all men and women being the same thing as the set of the set of all men and set of all women as it has but two members). Finally, one of the biggest oddities about set theory is that there can be a set with no members – what is called the null set or **empty set** (represented by ∅). As it will turn out, the empty set is fairly important to the ontological reductions we might try and execute with regard to numbers. But the idea that there's a collection with nothing in it seems absurd. A collection with nothing in it is . . . well, nothing. Nevertheless, set theory demands that the empty set exist. Further, as we shall see, set theory will demand that there is an infinite number of sets built up out of this empty set. Sets, then, are nothing like collections.

But if they're not collections, what are they? Realists about sets tend to think of them as abstract entities in a category of their own. They are, then, slightly odd entities. You might even wonder why we would contemplate believing in them. But there is a good reason, for it turns out that sets are the basis for most of contemporary mathematics. That numbers can be modelled in set theory (that is, that we can identify numbers with certain sets, or have sets stand as surrogates for numbers) has been embraced by mathematicians for a long time. So whilst sets might be weird entities (they were so weird that, when they were first introduced, the idea was shunned and the man who came up with set theory, Georg Cantor, got quite depressed about the whole affair), they are embraced because of the power that they afford mathematicians. Indeed, some parts of mathematics (such as things called 'Diophantine equations') cannot be proven without using sets and set theory. To get a glimpse of how we are meant to do mathematics using set theory, think about how we might identify numbers with certain sets.

Identifications of numbers with sets

In rough, the axioms of set theory I've introduced thus far are that: there's an empty set; that two sets are identical if and only if they have the same members; if you have some things, you have a set that has those things as members. Whilst not obvious, these axioms entail an explosion of what things exist. For instance, if there were just two things, e.g., Adam and Eve, then there would be at least three sets. Two would be the sets that have just Adam and Eve as members (what are called their **singletons**):

{ Adam }   { Eve }

and another set which has both of them as members:

{ Adam, Eve }

But remember, if you have some things, you have a set of those things (and sets can take other sets as members). So as we now have

Adam, Eve and those three sets, we have lots of other sets in addition. Examples include the set of all of those things:

{ Adam, Eve, { Adam }, { Eve }, { Adam, Eve } }

as well as other sets, such as Adam and his singleton:

{ Adam, { Adam } }

or Eve and Adam's singleton:

{ Eve, { Adam } }

or . . . well, you get the idea. There are a lot of combinations of those five things, and to each combination there is a set with that combination as members. And then there are sets with every combination of *those* things as members. And, as we now have those things, there must be even more sets with every combination of those things as members. We can keep going for ever, and it quickly turns out that there is an infinite number of things (Adam, Eve and the infinite number of sets constructed out of them) where you previously thought only Adam and Eve existed.

Moreover, you don't even need Adam or Eve to get this going, given that set theory demands that the empty set exists. Even if there was nothing – no Adam, no Eve and no material objects at all – that empty set would still be there. And, given set theory, we can generate an infinite number of sets out of just that empty set. If the empty set exists, its singleton exists (i.e., { ∅ }) and now we have two things, so there are sets with those things as members, namely the set of the empty set and its singleton (i.e., { ∅, { ∅ } }) and the singleton of the empty set's singleton (i.e., { { ∅ } }). So now we have *four* things. And so we go again, and again, and again, until we've generated an infinite number of sets out of the empty set. (And, as you don't end up with an infinite number of collections if you start with no objects whatsoever, this should again make clear that sets are not collections and are best thought of as abstract objects.)

People have embraced reductions which identify numbers with sets constructed out of the necessarily existing empty set. Consider the **Zermelo reduction**. Take the empty set. Identify the number 0 with it. Next, stipulate a rule that says that the **successor** of any number (where, say, 1 is the successor of 0, 2 is the successor of 1, 3 is the successor of 2, etc.) is just its predecessor's singleton. In technical terminology we can say that for any number n, $n = \{\ n-1\ \}$. So we would end up with the following identifications:

$0 = \varnothing$
$1 = \{\ \varnothing\ \}$
$2 = \{\ \{\ \varnothing\ \}\ \}$
$3 = \{\ \{\ \{\ \varnothing\ \}\ \}\ \}$
$4 = \{\ \{\ \{\ \{\ \varnothing\ \}\ \}\ \}\ \}$

and so on. Every natural number gets identified with a set, so we can easily reduce the natural numbers to sets. (This doesn't work for negative numbers or real numbers as the reduction given here is only simplistic; needless to say, there are more complex reductions that do a similar thing for real numbers and the like. Refer to the Further Reading if you want to know more.) Once we've done this, we score on various theoretical virtues. First, numbers are ontologically reduced to sets. No longer do we need two different kinds of entities where numbers are in one category and sets in another. (Although this is less convincing given that sets are weird to begin with – we are only achieving the ontological parsimony at the cost of introducing a whole new category of entities!) Second, we achieve some ideological parsimony as mathematical relations are now reduced to set-theoretical relations. That is, relations like one number being a successor of another are now cashed out in terms of set theory (for one number is a successor of another when it is the singleton of its predecessor). Other mathematical relations and terms can be treated similarly. Third, we get more explanatory power. The axioms of arithmetic – which would otherwise be brute truths – can be explained now in terms of set theory and its axioms. The arithmetical axioms, then, are no longer brute, and only the set-theoretical axioms are brute (indeed, as noted above, some parts of mathematics can only be proven using set theory so it garners explanatory power there as well). These are all a metaphorical thumbs-up to the Zermelo reduction.

Reducing Properties to Sets

It is not just numbers which get reduced to sets. All kinds
of ontological entities receive set-theoretic reductions. For
instance, we can be a realist about properties but think that
they can be ontologically reduced to sets. Take every instance
of some property (so every electron would be an instance of
negative charge, every woman would be an instance of *woman*,
every blue thing would be an instance of *blue*, etc.). We can
identify a property with the sets of its instances (so *negative
charge* is the set of all electrons, *woman* is the set of all women
and *blue* is the set of all blue things). In one fell swoop, we
have reduced all properties to sets, as well as achieving
some ideological parsimony (as now we can say that an
object instantiates a property if and only if it is a member of
that property, e.g., something is blue if and only if it is a
member of the set of all blue things). So sets can achieve theoretical parsimony in more areas than just numbers. Indeed,
they are beloved by many metaphysicians for just this sort of
reason and lots of things other than numbers receive the set-
theoretical reductive treatment. Objects, for instance, sometimes get identified with sets of their properties (a strain of
bundle theory, which we briefly examined in the last chapter).
As we have only discussed properties and numbers thus far,
other reductions are difficult to explain, but here are some in
brief: propositions have been identified with sets of possible
worlds (which we will look at in the next chapter); sets of times
and objects have been identified with temporal parts (which
we look at in chapter 9); regions of spacetime (which we
examine in chapter 6) have been identified with sets of spacetime points and so on and so forth. Some people – who are
called Pythagoreans – even think that *everything* is a set (for
instance Quine, on at least one reading, was allied to just
such a view). Sets, then, might be able to do a lot of work in
ontology.

   Of course, it's never all smooth sailing. For instance, we will
have problems with **coextensive** properties – that is, those
·properties which happen to have the same instances. Take a
case where two properties aren't coextensive, such as *being a
terrorist* and *being an honest person*. Many terrorists won't be
honest, and will be very conniving, although some terrorists

might be very honest and always tell the truth. The first property is identified with the set of all terrorists, the second is identified with the set of all honest people and, as those sets have different members, the properties are distinct. But now imagine that, by chance, all honest people are terrorists and all terrorists are honest. That's not actually the case, but it could've come about – perhaps a group of terrorists take over the world (*à la* James Bond) and wipe everyone out who isn't with them. And perhaps they take a particular dislike to dishonest terrorists as well (after all, who'd trust a dishonest terrorist?) and wipe them out alongside. What you would be left with would be a world where every terrorist was honest, and every honest person was a terrorist. But now the members of the two sets, *being a terrorist* and *being an honest person*, would be exactly the same. And if the memberships are the same, then, given the axioms of set theory, the sets are identical. So *being a terrorist* and *being an honest person* would be the same property! But that's not right. For instance, *being an honest person* is a virtue, but *being a terrorist* is not, so they could never be one and the same thing. So whilst some people want to reduce properties to sets, troubles lie ahead.

Benacerraf's problem

But the Zermelo reduction given above isn't the only reduction. There are others, such as the **von Neumann reduction**. That, too, identifies the number 0 with the empty set. It also stipulates which set is the successor of any given number, just like Zermelo. However, rather than saying that the successor of a number is its singleton, von Neumann says that the successor of a number is the set of all of its predecessors. So we get:

$$0 = \varnothing$$
$$1 = \{ \varnothing \}$$
$$2 = \{ \varnothing, \{ \varnothing \} \}$$
$$3 = \{ \varnothing, \{ \varnothing \}, \{ \varnothing, \{ \varnothing \} \} \}$$
$$4 = \{ \varnothing, \{ \varnothing \}, \{ \varnothing, \{ \varnothing \} \}, \{ \varnothing, \{ \varnothing \}, \{ \varnothing, \{ \varnothing \} \} \} \}$$
etc.

Thus we have a competing reduction of what numbers might be. That reduction is just as good as the one that Zermelo relies upon:

mathematicians can use this reduction just as easily as they do the Zermelo reduction; it ends up being just as ontologically parsimonious (as both the Zermelo and the von Neumann reduction need the same sets, and both reduce numbers to sets); both reductions analyse away the same arithmetical relations in terms of set theory; both can explain all of arithmetic in terms of set theory and so on. With this in mind, Paul Benacerraf takes umbrage at the idea of reducing numbers to sets. So, reasons Benacerraf, if we have a competing reduction that's just as good, then whichever reduction we pick, there is no reason to pick that reduction over its competitor. But they can't both be right! The number 2 cannot both be { Ø, { Ø } } and { { Ø } } for obvious reasons: as two sets can only be identical when they have the same members so, as those two sets do not have the same members, they cannot be identical; if 2 were identical to *both* those sets, then (as identity is transitive) those sets *would* be identical; ergo, 2 cannot be both of them. So it looks as if we have to arbitrarily pick one of the reductions, with no argument to prefer it over any other choice. Such arbitrariness, says Benacerraf, is unsavoury – and with good reason, for in general it is bad to say that you have arrived at your conclusion by arbitrary means. These worries, we might think, threaten this putative reduction.

Indispensability arguments for realism

The Quine–Putnam argument for realism about numbers

We shall leave behind questions of ontological reduction – it's enough to have made clear that if we're interested in the ontology of mathematical entities, then we aren't exclusively concerned with whether or not numbers exist, but also with whether there are things like sets. Turn instead to the question of whether we should be realists about mathematical entities (like numbers or sets) in the first place.

Obviously, we have motivations for realism about mathematical entities similar to those we've seen already for things like properties and holes. For instance, we might point out that we appear to refer to such entities in true sentences (e.g., '7 is my favourite number'). Having examined those motivations in previous chapters, we shall instead press on and look at other motivations we might call upon. One is that mathematical entities are indispensable to theories which we think are true. For instance, Lewis believes that set theory is indispensable to mathematics – that is, mathematicians don't look as if they could do without sets. And who are mere philosophers to tell mathematicians that they are wrong? As Lewis argues in *Parts of Classes*, it would strain credulity to think that, having run through a few basic problems in the ontology of abstract entities, we should conclude that there are no sets and then rush over to the Department of Mathematics to tell them that they're mistaken and should give up on set theory. When we got there, would we tell them about all the other results that philosophy has produced? Lewis lists various examples: that nothing can move (i.e., Zeno's arguments against motion); that a being exists such that no being more powerful could be conceived (i.e., Anselm's argument for God); that everything is in the mind (i.e., that idealism is true); that no one believes anything (i.e., Paul and Patricia Churchland's eliminative materialism is true) and so on. And he has a point: in a battle of philosophical opinion versus mathematical assumption, the philosopher is unlikely to come off well. So says Lewis, this demonstrates that we should accept the existence of sets.

Nor is it just indispensability to mathematics that is important. Quine, along with Hilary Putnam, both believed that mathematical entities were indispensable to science, and this indispensability to science is a motivation to believe realism about mathematical entities. Examine Newton's universal law of gravitation. This law is used to calculate the gravitational force between objects, and that force varies, depending upon the masses of the objects and the distance they are away from one another – it's used in all sorts of areas, notably sending rockets to the moon and satellites hurtling through space. But examine the formula in detail:

$$F = [\, G\, (\, m_a \times m_b \,)\,]\, /\, r^2$$

where m_a and m_b are the masses of two objects, F is the gravitational force between those two objects, and r is the distance between the objects. That leaves G. G is the gravitational constant and is approximately 6.7×10^{-11} (the value varies, though, depending upon what units you are working with. If you are using newtons for F, kilograms for m_a and m_b and metres for r, then this is right, but if you use different units, the constant will be different. For instance, if we were measuring on an interstellar background, we might be dealing with distance in parsecs and mass in the terms of how many of our suns its mass is a multiple of. In that case, the constant is about 4.3

$\times\ 10^{-3}$). So it seems that we must talk about, utilize and rely upon numbers, such as G, when doing calculations in physics. Without numbers like the gravitational constant, we'd be unable to calculate the forces between objects. Quine and Putnam (amongst others) held that this means that numbers are indispensable to science. Assuming that we are some brand of naturalist, who believes that the way to find out about the world is through scientific means, it seems we should, therefore, endorse the existence of numbers.

Or another example (this time more recent, from Alan Baker). There are certain species for which it is best for them not to be around one another, say because they compete for the same resources. They evolve such that it is rare that they are around one another. For instance, some insects live underground as larvae and then, after some years (around 15 years, depending on the species), come forth as adults before dying after a brief period. Two subspecies in North America have evolved such that the periods that they spend underground are 13 and 17 years respectively. This minimizes the occasions upon which they are around one another. If, say, they were underground for 14 years and 18 years, they would emerge alongside one another once every 126 years. But with cycles of 13 and 17 years, it's 221 years. This is because 13 and 17 are prime numbers, so their lowest common multiple is usually going to be larger than when the two values are not prime numbers. Therefore, says Baker, in evolutionary biology – specifically in explanations of the life cycles of insects – that the life cycles are *prime numbers* is an explanation of why their life cycles are what they are. So, once again, numbers (in this case, specifically their being prime) feature in scientific explanations.

The indispensability argument is probably the argument that gets the most coverage in the ontology of numbers. It's not without its problems. One problem is that, whilst some mathematical entities may appear to be indispensable to science, others seem more esoteric and deal with abstract matters that barely relate to anything practical (hush your mouth if you're thinking that it's ironic for a metaphysician to say such a thing). For instance, infinity can come in different sizes. We won't go through the relevant proofs for this, but be assured that, say, whilst there are infinitely many natural numbers (e.g., 1, 2, 3, 4, etc.) and there are infinitely many real numbers (where the real numbers are every natural number plus every decimal representation of a number, e.g., 1.2223 or 6.40, where these decimal representations could themselves have infinitely many digits in them), there are *more* real numbers than there are natural numbers. We say there are **countably** many natural numbers and **continuum** many real numbers. These two sizes of infinity crop up fairly often in science, and we'll need to include them in our ontology (so we have to include not just finite numbers but infinite numbers as well – what are called **transfinite cardinals**). However, there are many sizes of infinity beyond those two – indeed, there are infinitely many! But past a handful of the smaller sizes, they *never* feature in scientific explanation. The larger infinities are virtually invisible when it comes to science. Nonetheless, set theory includes them, and mathematicians think about them. Quine once opined that this sort of stuff isn't indispensable at all – it was just 'mathematical recreation', and he gave no time whatsoever to thinking that those recreational parts of mathematics bore on ontology. So, one problem would be that indispensability only guarantees the existence of certain numbers, not all of them.

Anti-realist strategies

Paraphrasing (again)

Turn to anti-realist strategies. In previous chapters, we've examined paraphrasing strategies for holes and for properties. Turn to one Charles Chihara introduced for numbers. Rather than talk about things being members of sets (which seems to entail a commitment to sets existing), Chihara talks about things satisfying **open sentences** (which seems to entail only that sentences exist). An open sentence is a sentence with an unbound variable. Recall that a bound variable was a variable introduced by a quantifier (e.g., '∃ x (F x)' has x as its bound variable). An unbound variable is one introduced *without* a quantifier. For instance, if we simply wrote 'x is a man' we have an open sentence, as the variable x has been introduced without a quantifier. Note that, by itself, that sentence isn't true or false. How could it be, for you don't know what x is! If you went into a room and just said out loud 'x is a man', and demanded to know whether it was true or false, you'd have a room full of confused people (whereas the corresponding sentence with a bound variable *does* have a truth value, e.g., '∃ x (x is man)' has bound the variable and is also true, as it says that there is something that is a man). Chihara then adds that certain things **satisfy** such open sentences if (and only if) it is the case that, were they to be the value of the unbound variable, then the resulting sentence would be true. So I would satisfy the open sentence 'x is a man', as would Barack Obama, for if we replace the variable with our names (to get the sentences 'Nikk Effingham is a man' and 'Barack Obama is a man' respectively) those sentences are true. Angela Merkel, the Eiffel Tower and a piece of chocolate cake would not satisfy the open sentence as none of them are men, and sentences where their names take the place of the unbound variable (e.g., 'The Eiffel Tower is a man') are false. Chihara thinks that we can replace all talk about sets with this sort of talk. Rather than saying that every man is a member of the set of all men, we can say instead that all men satisfy the open sentence 'x is a man.' Rather than saying that Angela Merkel is in the set of all women, we can say instead that she satisfies the open sentence 'x is a woman.' And so on and so forth – all set-theoretical talk is paraphrased in terms of talking about satisfying open sentences.

This alone won't quite work. Set theory says that there are sets of things no matter what we do. Take some particles from the edge of a far-off galaxy that we've never thought about, and never will. According to set theory, there is a set of those things. Chihara needs an open sentence corresponding to that. But there isn't one. I've stipulated that we'll never think about the galaxy in question, nor say or write down anything about it. Given this, there'll never be a sentence – open or otherwise – that mentions it. So there won't be an open sentence surrogate for the set of those particles. What Chihara does at this stage is alter his account slightly. He says that it is enough that there *could* be an open sentence. And, surely, *that's* a possibility. Even though I am sure that there are some things (such as the particles in a far-off galaxy) that we will never utter an open sentence about, we nevertheless *could* have done. We might have evolved on a planet right next to them, where we could have seen them, and we then talked about them using an open sentence. What could be the case, but isn't, is fairly liberal: we should admit that there could be an open sentence about them. So Chihara goes from paraphrasing a sentence of the form 'x is a member of set s' in terms of satisfying an appropriate open sentence that exists, to saying that the paraphrase is that x *could* satisfy some open sentence. Problem solved.

Not everyone is happy with Chihara's theory (in particular, many people are suspicious of explaining away ontological problems by invoking modal terms about what could be the case. As we'll see in the next chapter, those people are fonder of introducing extra ontology – possible worlds – to explain away the modal terms, rather than vice versa). But it remains a contemporary nominalist alternative.

Mathematical Fictionalism

Back in chapter 1, I said that we'd assume that when we produce a paraphrase of a tricky sentence, we'll say the original sentence is true. So whilst we might paraphrase '7 is a prime number' in terms not mentioning numbers, we'll assume the sentence is nevertheless still *true*. Not everyone believes this, and in the metaphysics of mathematics a common alternative, spearheaded by Hartry Field, is **mathematical fictionalism**. Field says that the original sentences (such as '7 is a prime number') *aren't* true, but are instead *fictionally* true (in the same way that 'Sherlock Holmes is a detective' is fictionally true). Mathematical entities end up being fictions, like Snow White, or Hansel and Gretel. When mathematics gets deployed in science, Field argues that we can produce another theory that doesn't mention mathematical entities (so, in this regard, this other theory is akin to a paraphrase scheme). Given that we could drop the theories that talk about mathematical entities in favour of these purely nominalist theories, we shouldn't think we need to commit to numbers, or sets or the like. Nonetheless we may choose to continue using the theories that utilize the fiction of mathematical entities, as long as we remain cognisant of the fact that this isn't indicative of reality.

Formalism

We might move away from paraphrasing entirely. Chihara bought into the idea that mathematical statements appeared to be true, and that we had to produce paraphrases that avoided quantifying over numbers in order to avoid realism about numbers. Not everyone sees it that way. For instance, **formalists** think that mathematical statements are meaningless – and if they're meaningless, then they're neither true nor false. That might sound bizarre, as if they're claiming that mathematicians are charlatans who speak nothing but gibberish. This is not what formalists mean. What is important, says the formalist, is not that sentences in arithmetic or set theory turn out to be true (or false), what is important is that, say, '2 + 2 = 4' follows from the axioms of arithmetic. We need it to be true that they follow from axioms (or are axioms), not that they're true or false themselves – and you can have the former without the latter. To get a grip on that idea, imagine you were playing Sudoku. In Sudoku, there is a 9×9 grid split into nine boxes of 3×3, with certain boxes already filled in with numbers. The rules of the game are that you must fill that grid with numbers between 1 and 9 such that no number appears twice in any row, column or box. So, for instance, if one row of numbers read:

1 3 4 2 6 7 5 8 9

that would be a legitimate string of numbers in Sudoku. Whereas if it read:

1 1 2 8 3 4 5 6 7

that would be an illegitimate string of numbers (as it features '1' twice and does not feature '9' at all). But neither string of numbers has a truth value. They don't *assert* anything. It makes no sense to say that the top one is true and the bottom one is false. The lesson is simple: things can be true *of* the string of numbers, as determined by the rules of the game, even though the string is not *itself* true or false. Or another example: I exist, but *I'm* not true or false. What sense does it make to say 'Nikk Effingham is true?' None at all! Nonetheless, lots of things are true *of* me.

Similarly, we can say the same of mathematical statements. Except rather than saying that some string of numbers is a legitimate Sudoku line, we say that some arithmetical statement, such as '2 + 2 = 4', is an arithmetical theorem. Or we might say that some statement in set theory, such as two sets being identical if and only if they have the same members, is a set-theoretical axiom. It can be an axiom even though we need not ever think that it is true or false. And when I say that *the statement* is an axiom or theorem, I mean that literally. The standard formalist line is that these things aren't true of anything floating around in platonic heaven. It's not some abstract object that turns out to be a theorem or an axiom, but the statement *on the page*. So whilst '2 + 2 = 4' is not true or false, the statement '2 + 2 = 4 is an arithmetical theorem' is true because what it says is that the ink blots on the line above – the ones making up the numerals, and the plus sign, and the equal sign you see before you – are an arithmetical theorem. This, say the formalists, is enough for mathematicians and scientists to be getting on with. Who cares if these things are true or false when we are really interested in whether they are axioms or theorems? So formalists think of mathematics a bit like a game governed by rules. And with any game, there are rules. If we were formalizing the rules of Sudoku, we'd have to define what a grid was, and define the nine numbers, and then state the rules governing which numbers go where and so on. Formalists think mathematics is just the same, although more complicated. We need to define exactly what it takes for certain ink blots to be axioms, or theorems, or proofs and so on. Exactly how we do this is a complicated enterprise, which I leave you to look into.

Meinongianism

We have detailed a variety of anti-realisms. Chihara takes to heart the Quinean principle of ontological commitment: that to be anti-realists we must provide paraphrases that do not quantify over numbers. That's a big assumption. As has already been made clear in the last chapter, not everyone thinks the Quinean theory of ontological commitment is the be all and end all of ontological commitment. At the end of this chapter, we will discuss a theory, **Meinongianism**, which gives up this Quinean assumption.

Return to the Quinean idea – one shared by the permissivist of chapter 1 – that the locution 'There is . . .' is the same as saying 'There exists a . . .' So if I say, for example, that there is a taxi outside, I am saying that there exists a taxi which is outside; if I say there are lots of things we have in common, I say that there exists a property; if I say that there are numbers, I say that there exist numbers. Alexius Meinong denied that such entailments hold. Certainly, it is *sometimes* the case that when it is true that there are such-and-such things, those things exist but, says Meinong, this is not always the case. Sometimes there are things, and yet those things don't exist. 'There is . . .' and 'There exists a . . .' come apart, says Meinong.

Think of it like this: translate the following sentence into first-order logic:

There is a character in *Lord of the Rings* whose name I rarely remember which becomes:

> $\exists\, x$ (x is a character in *Lord of the Rings* & I rarely remember the name of x).

A Quinean says that the translation commits us to the existence of fictional characters as it is a fictional character which is bound by the existential quantifier; if we want to avoid believing that fictional characters exist, we had better offer a paraphrase. Meinong says this is wrong-headed. The logical translation is fine; it's just that the symbol $\exists$ does not quantify solely over things which exist. We should not be calling $\exists$ the *existential* quantifier at all. Similar translations work in other cases, such as negative existentials. When we say:

> The present King of France does not exist.

Meinong takes this to just mean that there is something, the present King of France, and it is true of him that he does not exist. Or, in logic:

> $\exists\, x$ (x = the present King of France & x does not exist)

(Notice we'd have to make existence into a predicate.) So whereas logicians like Quine use quantifiers, that is, $\exists$, to indicate that something exists, Meinong does not. Instead, a predicate is coined, i.e., '__ exists', that applies to all of the existent things (in the same way that a predicate like '__ is red' applies to all of the red things).

Meinong even says such things of impossible objects. Consider:

> Some things could not possibly exist.

Meinongians would just translate that straight into logic as:

> $\exists\, x$ (x is an impossible object)

And, says the Meinongian, there are lots of such things, are there not? If I asked you to tell me what impossible things there were, you could easily construct a list: round squares, spherical cubes, square pentagons, spherical pyramids, cylinders with twelve sides, one dimensional hypercubes, men who are both standing and sitting at the same time, and so on. And it seems natural, then, to say that there are lots of things which are impossible. Meinong agrees, and says that the natural interpretation is the straightforwardly correct one: there are lots of such things, they do not exist and therefore 'There is . . .' and 'There are . . .' do not necessarily entail that the thing(s) that there is (or there are) also exist.

Technically, what has been described here isn't a theory of ontological commitment – after all, it doesn't say how to figure out what exists, rather it just denies that we should embrace Quine's theory of ontological commitment. Once one is a Meinongian, there still remains the question of how, out of all the things that there are, do we figure which of them exist? Nonetheless, it is clearly relevant to our discussions about metaontology, for if the Quineans are wrong about things we quantify over existing, then this radically changes all of the discussions (about holes, properties and numbers) that we've had up until this point.

For instance, it's easy to see how we could start to deploy Meinongianism with regard to numbers, just as some Meinongians – such as Richard Routley – have already done so. Unlike Meinong, who believed that abstract objects like numbers had some sort of 'being', Routley says that there are only two types of things: the existents and the non-existents. Concrete objects go in the former, whilst abstract objects don't exist in any sense – they are Meinongian non-existents – and so belong to the latter. They nevertheless still have properties. Just as Meinong's round squares don't exist but are round and square, the numbers all stand in relation to one another and have properties, but don't exist either. Problems in the metaphysics of mathematics are now solved. Is there a prime number between 5 and 11? Yes, although it doesn't exist. Are there lots of sets like those which mathematicians talk about? Yes! (It's just that they don't exist.) So we just offer the same translations into logic that the realist offers – and don't bother at all with any of the paraphrases that anti-realists like Chihara offer – but deny that quantifying over numbers indicates anything about whether they exist or not. Our difficulties are dissolved and, better yet, at no cost to ontological parsimony (for whilst there are lots of things, they don't exist, and ontological parsimony – so the Meinongian will press – should depend solely upon what does and does not *exist*).

However, Meinongianism is not a popular theory and has not been for many years. This fact alone isn't a good reason to give up on it, though. Perhaps if there were more philosophers, then a theory having the weight of opinion set against it would be an indicator of it being false. That's how it is in science, where every respectable scientist endorsing evolution and climate change gives us a prima facie good reason to believe in evolution and climate change. But as the number of ontologists in the world is only a fraction of the number of scientists, it would be foolhardy to think that the collective endorsements of the community can count as a convincing argument from authority. In fact, it turns out that there isn't all that much literature on Meinongianism (so reviled has it been, it's been somewhat ignored!). But one of the more influential anti-Meinongian arguments comes from Quine, who lambasts Meinong in his famous article 'On What There Is' (although Meinong goes under the pseudonym 'Wyman' in that paper). One of the main problems Quine raises (some people have suggested the *only* problem, and that his other complaints are just rhetoric) is to do with the **individuation** of non-existent objects. Individuation is to do with how we determine whether one thing is identical to another thing. For non-existent objects, this runs into a huge problem. Following Quine, imagine the fat man who is currently standing in the doorway nearest to you. Of course (presumably) no such fat man is present. For Meinong, though, he's still *there*, he just doesn't *exist*. So, asks Quine, how *many* fat men are in the doorway? And what makes each one distinct from the others? Not only is it an awkward question to answer (do you say one fat man? Fifteen? An infinite number?) but Quine is wedded to a principle that says that there can't be an entity unless there are conditions under which it is identical to another entity: 'No entity without identity' as the slogan goes. It strikes Quine that no such principle is available to Meinong, and so he finds Meinong's fat men so repugnant that he rejects Meinongianism. Because of this (rightly or wrongly), Meinongianism has been sidelined for many years.

Chapter summary

In this chapter, we have:

- introduced what a set is and looked at some very basic principles of set theory.
- examined a realist theory where we ontologically reduce numbers to sets.
- examined the indispensability argument for numbers.
- considered some anti-realist views of numbers consistent with something like the Quinean theory of ontological commitment.

- introduced Meinongianism as an alternative to the Quinean theory and seen how it is to be deployed in the case of numbers.

Further reading

General introductions to the philosophy of mathematics, and the problems we've looked at here, include Michelle Friend (2007) and Stewart Shapiro (2000). A good collection of essays is Hart (1996) and Stephen Laurence and Cynthia Macdonald (1998).

Those interested in the weirdness, or not, of sets should refer to Max Black (1971), David Lewis (1990a) and Penelope Maddy (1990). For Benacerraf's problem with sets, see his 1965 article (ways to respond, by endorsing a theory called 'structuralism', can be found in Shapiro (2000) and Michael Resnik (1997)). Hartry Field's mathematical fictionalism is presented in his 1980 book, and Charles Chihara has two books (1990 and 2007; the latter contains a chapter summarizing much of the former). A good exposition of formalism, including a layout of the rules a formalist may use, is a paper written by Nelson Goodman and Quine (1947). On the realist side, defenders include Penelope Maddy (1990) and John Bigelow (1988).

Whilst Meinong and Routley both defend Meinongianism, a more accessible introduction to the theory is Colin McGinn (2000) or Roderick Chisholm (1973). There is a recent book by Graham Priest (2005) defending the view as well (where you will find a slightly different usage of 'Meinongianism'; again, witness the terminological minefield you are faced with). In response to Meinong, there is Quine (1948) as well as David Lewis (1990b).

For the ontological reduction of numbers, if you're interested in the specifics – indeed, how the strategy given above can be extended to all numbers and not just the natural numbers – you should read Alexander George and Daniel Velleman (2002). You might also want to consult Armstrong's alternative reduction of sets to states of affairs (1997). If you want to know more about reducing properties to sets, see the works of David Lewis (1983 and 1986).

5

Possible Worlds

Talk about possible worlds is ubiquitous in philosophy, and doubt-lessly you will have heard of them before. Whilst this chapter will, briefly, recap some of the basics of such talk, we swiftly move on to more relevant questions: why talk about possible worlds; what, if anything, does this indicate about realism about possible worlds; and is there any way to be an anti-realist about possible worlds?

Modal talk and possible worlds talk

Modal logic

Start with modality. Modal talk is all talk concerning what might have been, what could have been, what must have been etc. For example:

- I could have been a fisherman.
- Hitler could have won World War II.
- Hitler could have won World War II by summoning the Balrog to help the Nazis.
- The speed of light could have been twice as fast as it actually is.
- It's impossible for there to be round squares.
- Necessarily, 2 + 2 = 4.

These are all modal statements, for they concern possibility and necessity. Notice that they also concern different kinds of possibility. That I could have been a fisherman or that Hitler could have won World War II, are examples of things which are **physically possible** (sometimes, almost synonymously, 'nomologically possible'). That is, my being a fisherman and Hitler's winning World War II are both compatible with the laws of nature. But not all of the above propositions are like that. That the speed of light could have been twice what it is is physically impossible – once the laws of nature have fixed the speed of light, it is clearly physically *im*possible for these things to be the case. Similarly, as Balrogs – the demons of Tolkien's *Lord of the Rings* – are physically impossible entities, it is as possible for Hitler to have won World War II with them as it is for him to have won it with an army of leprechauns. But there is some sense in which it's still possible – it's not physically possible, but it is **logically possible**. That is, it could have happened if only the laws of physics weren't what they were. We see other variations in the kinds of possibility with the remaining sentences. That it is impossible for there to be round squares, and that it is necessary that 2 + 2 = 4, are not merely a fluke of the laws of physics. It is logically *impossible* for round squares to exist and logically *necessary* that 2 + 2 = 4. And there's no need to limit the brands of possibility to just those two. If I said that it was impossible for a company to pay its debts, I don't mean that it's against the laws of physics that it could do so. It's a weaker form of possibility. I'm saying that, in light of legally binding laws and the financial state of the company's accounts, it can't repay its debts. Whilst the laws of physics and of logic allow the repayments, the laws of economics do not. So it is an *economic* impossibility, even though it's a physical and logical possibility. So there are lots of different kinds of possibility and exactly which one is important will vary upon context (Churchill and Eisenhower, for instance, probably didn't care about Balrogs, and worried about kinds of possibility far less broad than the merely logically possible).

When it comes to such modal talk, basic first-order logic (that is, the logic you are probably most familiar with) doesn't deal well with it. Imagine translating the following two valid arguments:

Socrates is a philosopher.
∴ Socrates could have been a philosopher.

or:

Socrates is essentially a person.
∴ Socrates is a person.

Both of the arguments are valid, for what is the case clearly could be the case, and whatever is essentially some way must actually be that way. But it all goes horribly wrong when first-order logic tries to capture this validity. Let *a* stand for Socrates. The first argument features two predicates: '__ is a philosopher' (call it F) and '__ could have been a philosopher' (call it G). We get:

F*a*
∴ G*a*

Whilst the second also features two predicates: '__ is essentially a person' (call it H) and '__ is a person' (call it I). We get:

H*a*
∴ I*a*

And, as is clear from just looking at them, those argument forms *aren't* valid. But that's okay. When logical systems fail to perspicuously translate what we want them to translate, we can supplement them with more symbols and rules until they can perspicuously translate what we want them to. For instance, that's why we move from *propositional* logic to *predicate* logic. In propositional logic the following argument:

Socrates is a man.
All men are mortal.
∴ Socrates is mortal.

gets represented as

P
Q
∴ R

which is an invalid argument form. Reasons exactly like this led to the creation of predicate logic, where the argument gets translated as the (valid) argument form:

F*a*
∀*x* (F*x* → G*x*)
∴ G*a*

So to represent modal arguments as valid, we must supplement predicate logic with new symbols (and new rules that tell us when we have valid argument forms which feature those new symbols). Start by introducing a possibility operator, represented as ◇. When placed before a proposition, we end up representing that the proposition is possible, for example, 'Possibly, dragons exist' can be translated as '◇ dragons exist', and 'Possibly Socrates is a man' can be translated into '◇ F*a*'. (And it needn't only be placed before them, e.g., 'There is something that could be a man' can be represented as '∃ *x* (◇ F *x*)'.) Then add a rule governing how this operator works. It's intuitive that whatever is the case is possible, so we stipulate that:

$$\varphi \to \Diamond\varphi$$

(Scared by the φ symbol? Don't be. That just stands for any proposition you like, but rather than using P, Q or R – which stand for a *specific* proposition – we use the Greek letter φ. So 'φ → ◇φ' just means that if any proposition is true, then it's possible that the proposition is true.) So the problematic argument:

Socrates is a philosopher.
∴ Socrates could have been a philosopher

can now be translated as:

F*a*
∴ ◇ F*a*

which is, given this new rule, a valid argument form. So, just as we extended propositional logic into predicate logic by adding new symbols (e.g., ∃ and ∀, and predicates, variables and names) and rules governing how they work, we can extend predicate logic by adding ◇, and a rule governing it, to get **modal logic**. Similarly, we can add in a **necessity operator**: □. Stick that before a proposition and it says that the proposition is necessarily true.

It also has a corresponding rule, as whatever is necessarily the case is the case:

$$\Box\ \varphi \rightarrow \varphi$$

(Actually, the operators are interdefinable as '$\Box\ \varphi =_{df} \sim \Diamond \sim \varphi$' and '$\Diamond\ \varphi =_{df} \sim \Box \sim \varphi$', so you only need to take one operator as a primitive.)

Possible worlds talk

'Hang on!' you might say. 'You haven't mentioned possible worlds!' Indeed, possible worlds crop up because, just as predicate logic has a problem with modal talk, the basic modal logic I laid out above *also* has problems with bits of our modal talk. One example problem sentence, focused on by Joseph Melia, is

There could have been one more thing than there actually is.

It proves impossible to translate this using just the $\Box$ and $\Diamond$ operators. That something can't be translated is tricky to prove, so you'll have to take my word for it (you could try translating it yourself, or look at the relevant literature given in the Further Reading section below, to get a better idea of the problems involved). When we include possible worlds, though, we can easily translate that sentence. If we buy into possible worlds talk, we are meant to talk as if there are lots of possible worlds, where one of the worlds is special: the **actual world**. Every proposition is true or false *relative* to a world. At the actual world, all of the actually true things are true (like the Balrog doesn't exist and Hitler lost World War II) and the actually false things are false (like Hitler winning World War II). At other worlds, the propositions true and false relative to those worlds vary. At some world, for instance, it's true that the Balrog doesn't exist but Hitler did win World War II, at some other world it's true that the Balrog does exist and true also that Hitler won the war using it. Indeed, every consistent combination of true and false propositions hold at some world (and so some combinations, such as it being true that Hitler wins World War II but false that Hitler exists, are impossible and are jointly true at no world).

In possible worlds talk, we say that something is possible if it is true *at some world*. We say that something is necessary if it is true *at every world*. (And something is impossible if it's true at no world.) So we can translate modal logic into possible worlds talk:

'◇ P' becomes ' ∃ x (x is a possible world & P is true at x)'
'□ P' becomes ' ∀ x (x is a possible world → P is true at x)'

So, in possible worlds talk, Hitler could have won World War II just because there's a possible world at which he *did* win World War II. 2 + 2 = 4 is necessarily true because it's true at *every* possible world. It is actually true that Johnny Depp starred in *Pirates of the Caribbean* because that proposition is true at the actual world (whereas, at other worlds, it's false and, say, Steve Buscemi starred in it instead, because it's not *impossible* for Buscemi to have played the leading role, so it's true at some world).

How does this help translate the above sentence which modal logic could not translate? Imagine another world, exactly like the actual world, where everything that exists at the actual world exists at this other world. Plus imagine that one extra entity, which doesn't exist at the actual world, does exist at this other world. At that world, there'll be one more thing than there actually is – so the translation of that sentence should say just that. So we would start by saying that there are two worlds, one of which is actual:

∃ x ∃ y (x and y are worlds & x is the actual world).

Next, add that everything that actually exists also exists at the other world:

∃ x ∃ y (x and y are worlds & x is the actual world & ∀ z (z exists at x → z exists at y)

Then finish by saying that there exists something at this other world which doesn't exist at the actual world:

∃ x ∃ y (x and y are worlds & x is the actual world & ∀ z (z exists at x → z exists at y) & ∃ u (u exists at y & ~ u exists at x))

We're now done: by deploying possible worlds we can translate the sentence saying that there could have been one more thing than there actually is. And you could easily imagine how we could construct arguments with valid forms along those lines. So if you really want to translate arguments with premises and conclusions containing modal terms, it looks like you'll need to deploy possible worlds talk.

Back to ontology

This is, more or less, why people are fond of possible worlds talk. Of course, just because people like talking about possible worlds doesn't mean that every philosopher is a realist about them. After all, even the hardened anti-realist about properties likes *talking* about properties, and even the most hardened anti-realist about numbers still says things like 'The number of planets in the solar system is seven.' The same lessons apply here – some people want to talk about possible worlds, without necessarily committing to their existing (and we'll come to the anti-realists later).

Those who believe in possible worlds are called **modal realists** (although be careful with terminology – some people reserve the phrase 'modal realism' solely for David Lewis's formulation). The first motivation is, of course, that we might endorse a Quinean theory of ontological commitment. If the translations of modal talk into possible worlds talk are the best we can do – that is, they are the sentences in logical notation that will appear in our best theory – then, as they quantify over worlds, we must ontologically commit to worlds if we are to secure modal talk. (Ironically, Quine goes the other way and gives up on modal talk for he despises modal terms.) So, if you buy into that theory of ontological commitment, you might well end up endorsing possible worlds realism for those reasons.

There are also other motivations (just as, say, the problem of universals was another motivation for the existence of properties, and the indispensability argument was another argument for the existence of numbers). David Lewis, one of Quine's students and arguably the most accoladed metaphysician of recent years, hoped that it would secure ideological parsimony. Remember that reducing the number of primitives in one's theory is a mark of success. Lewis thought that possible worlds could do away with the need for modal primitives. We've already seen, broadly speaking, how this would work. Where you would otherwise say something like 'Possibly I might go out this evening', we can remove the modal ideology by translating it into possible worlds talk:

$\exists\, x\, (\, x$ is a world & at x, it is the case that I go out this evening)

So we no longer talk about what could or would be, but only about what things exist (namely, what worlds exist). Modal ideology is therefore dropped by analysing the modal terms away in favour of purely existential statements. Of course, this demands that the realist theory cannot itself contain any modal terms. For instance, there has to be a **principle of plenitude** to entail that there's a world at which Hitler wins World War II, a world at which I'm a fisherman, that at every world $2 + 2 = 4$, etc. An example of such a principle would be:

> For all of the ways that the world could be, there is a world at which that is the case.

But we can't use *that* principle in our theory, for that principle contains modal terms (namely 'could'). So if that principle appeared, we wouldn't be able to analyse away the modal terms using possible worlds talk. If you're looking to remove modal terms from your theory, you will need a principle of plenitude which entails that there are enough possible worlds without mentioning any modal terms. As we shall see, this will prove hard to achieve.

Finally, we might deploy possible worlds (and their contents) to guarantee some ontological parsimony. In the last chapter, we discussed reducing properties to sets. One problem was that, at worlds where distinct properties were instantiated by all and only the same things, the properties wrongly turned out to be identical (recall the example of a world where all of the honest people were terrorists, and every terrorist was honest, so *being a terrorist* and *being an honest person* turned out to be one and the same property). We can now fix this problem by saying that properties aren't just sets of their actual instances. Instead, they are sets of all of their instances, no matter what world they exist at, e.g., *negative charge* won't just be the set of all electrons at our world, but the set of all electrons at any world. If we do this, then *being a terrorist* won't have the same members as *being an honest person*. The former property will have as members terrorists from every world, and the latter will have as members the honest people from every world. As those things differ (as, at some world, there's a dishonest terrorist and an honest person who isn't a terrorist), the memberships differ and the sets end up being distinct. Adding in possible objects, then, offers us a chance to solve some of the problems with ontological reductions of sets and achieve a more parsimonious ontology. (Problems still remain, though, with properties which are necessarily coextensive, such as *having three sides* and *having interior angles that add up to 180°*, which – some people say – are different properties but the sets of their instances are still one and the same. I leave it to you how, if at all, one might set about solving that problem.)

We can also reduce other things. For instance, we might want to be realists about propositions. If we already believe in sets and possible worlds, it looks like we can do that. We can reduce propositions down to sets of worlds at which that proposition is true. So the proposition < Hitler lost World War II > (we represent propositions by means of < and > around what the proposition expresses) is identical to the set of every world at which Hitler lost World War II. The proposition < Kangaroos are marsupials > is identical to the set of every world at which kangaroos are marsupials, and so on. So we get to be realists about propositions without having to introduce a whole new category of entities. Again, sets offer us some important parsimonious power.

Genuine modal realism

Assume that we are moved by the above motivations and settle on being realists about possible worlds (later, we'll look at a metaontological theory intended to relieve us of that commitment). As with numbers (and properties, and holes), we can ask what, exactly, a possible world is meant to be. Start by looking at David Lewis's proposed answer: a possible world is just a single maximally connected spacetime (more technically: x is world $=_{df}$ (i) every part of x is spatiotemporally related to every other part and (ii) if some object is spatiotemporally related to a part of x then that object is a part of x). So a part of our universe isn't a possible world (as it is spatiotemporally related to things that aren't parts of it) whereas the entire universe *is* a possible world. Instantly, **genuine modal realism** (GMR) starts producing results that most people think are a little bit strange. Hitler might have won World War II, so there's a world – an entirely separate universe – where he *does* win World War II. It is logically possible that the speed of light could have been faster, so there is a universe where that takes place. Let your imagination go wild: there are universes with Balrogs in them; universes where the events of your favourite soap opera are played out in exact detail; universes where people very much like us spontaneously stop, put on clown outfits and start singing every song that Lady Gaga has ever written. Whatever *could* happen *does* happen at some universe. You can't *go* to any of these universes, for they are disconnected from us. They're not just a far way off, or hard to reach, but they are totally isolated from us. Nonetheless, says Lewis, they are there, and we are best off thinking that possible worlds should be reduced to such disconnected spacetimes.

This is a pretty weird thing to believe. If you don't think it's a weird thing to believe, I suggest you haven't understood the last paragraph correctly – go back and read it again. So why does Lewis believe this? He puts it best himself: 'Why believe in a plurality of worlds? Because the hypothesis is serviceable, and that is a reason to think that it is true' (1986: 3). That is, this theory – what is sometimes called genuine modal realism – captures all of the benefits from above (so, clearly, Lewis thinks he can ultimately overcome the difficulties levelled against the above motivations for possible worlds realism). So Lewis thinks GMR can: take possible worlds talk at face value; guarantee ontological parsimony by reducing propositions down to sets of spacetimes and properties to sets of the inhabitants of those spacetimes; and analyse away modal terms. The last bears some particular note. As explained above, to analyse modality we need to guarantee that there are enough worlds – one for every way that the world could be – and achieve this without mentioning any modal terms. Here Lewis introduces the **principle of recombination**. Roughly speaking, it says that, for any two things that exist, and for any spatiotemporal separation, there is at least one spacetime where duplicates of those things exist and are separated by that relation. For example, as both Obama and Bush exist, there is a world at which they exist and are separated by 1 metre (and another where they are separated by 2 metres, another by 3 metres, etc.). Or another crude example: as there are wings in our world, and lizards in our world, there is a world where those wings are attached to a lizard. As there are also actually gouts of flame, there are worlds where those gouts of flame are coming from the lizard's mouth, i.e., there is a world – a universe – with a dragon in it. That's the gist of the Principle of Recombination (the details are more sophisticated) but Lewis argues that, if it were true, we could recombine all variety of possibilities (and, as we can imagine recombining almost anything out of the tiny little particles that make us all up, arranged in whatever arrangement you care for, we can 'recombine' even more things). So it guarantees the plenitude of worlds that we need. At first glance, it also does this without using any modal terms – it just says that for any two things, and any separation, there *is* (not there *could* be or any similar modal term) a spacetime at which duplicates of those things exist, separated by that relation. Lewis, then, has a theory that appears to analyse away modal terms (thus guaranteeing ideological parsimony).

The incredulous stare

Whilst GMR may capture the benefits that we want a realism about possible worlds to have, it doesn't mean that it's necessarily the best theory. It might have costs that we have not noted, or there might be other theories which are better still. For the rest of this section we shall look at possible costs (and in the next section we'll move to examining the competing theories). The most common cost that is levied against GMR is that it is radically counter-intuitive – Lewis coins the term 'incredulous stare' for the look he got from people when he first suggested GMR. He did not, however, believe such incredulity was persuasive. Certainly, the mere fact that it's weird isn't a deal-breaker. Lots of theories we think are true are weird. For instance, quantum physics is weird – flick open a book on science and just witness the horde of strange and bizarre things that quantum physics entails. This is especially ironic given that one theory in quantum physics, Everett's many-worlds interpretation, likewise states that there are numerous universes where all sorts of possibilities play out (although Everett would not countenance as many as Lewis, for he wouldn't think, say, that the events of Harry Potter are taking place at some universe. So the two theories must be distinguished). So we can't rule the theory out straight away, although we can claim that, as GMR fails to cohere with our intuitions, it suffers a cost. The intuitions we might have in mind are that, whereas we think there aren't any Balrogs, wizards, unicorns or an infinite plethora of disconnected spacetimes, GMR says that there are.

But Lewis has a further reply at this stage. Lewis says that, intuitively, there aren't actually any Balrogs and aren't actually any disconnected spacetimes. But GMR doesn't deny *that*. This is because, according to GMR, what *actually* exists is different from what exists. 'Actually existing' is, for Lewis, a lot like existing *here*.

If I'm lying in bed one morning and say 'I'm here' this is true because 'here' would refer to my bedroom (or someone else's if it's been a particularly good evening). Similarly, even though you aren't in my bedroom, and the sentence 'You are here' is false when it leaves my lips, when *you* say 'I'm here', *you* utter something true. This isn't weird in the slightest, of course, as 'here' just refers to wherever you are when you say it – it's an **indexical** term, which changes where it refers to depending upon the context in which it is uttered. And with 'here' it's impossible to utter that sentence and for it to be false – you're always 'here' in the sense that, whenever you utter the sentence, you are where you are when you say it (answering machine messages that go 'I'm not here at the moment' notwithstanding).

Lewis thinks 'actually' functions the same, and just refers to whichever spacetime you happen to be in when you utter sentences containing that word. So when I say 'I actually exist' that's true just because I am part of the spacetime I am in when I utter that sentence. Similarly, in the same way that there are no Balrogs here (for there aren't any Balrogs nearby), there aren't actually any Balrogs (for they only exist in spacetimes other than the one I am in). But when Bilbo Baggins utters the sentence 'Balrogs actually exist', then that sentence is true, for they are part of the spacetime *he*'s in when he utters the sentence. This, says Lewis, remedies GMR's conflict with our intuitions – even though disconnected spacetimes and Balrogs (etc.) exist, it is enough that they do not *actually* exist, which is a fact GMR agrees with.

Missing possibilities

Don't get too hung up on that first cost though. Whilst most people find GMR too incredible to be believed, it's not clear that it comes cost free, even if we forgive it the commitment to large quantities of disconnected spacetimes. Start looking at such problems by turning to the claim that GMR doesn't cohere with our modal intuitions to begin with – it seems to entail that things we think are intuitively possible aren't, in fact, possible at all. One possibility people have in mind when they say this is that there could be **island universes**. There would be island universes if there were *actually* other spacetimes disconnected from our own. And it certainly looks as if this could be a possibility. To see why, imagine a normal universe (Figure 5.1a). Now imagine another universe, which is very similar, but there's a tiny bridge between one part of the universe and the other (Figure 5.1b). That seems possible. We can even imagine that there's a universe with only the tiniest of connections between the two parts – they are almost entirely separate, connected by only a wafer-thin stretch (Figure 5.1c). That, too, seems possible (indeed, modern physics has proposed that this might be how our world actually is, with lots of universes budding off from one another). But if all of this seems possible, then why not believe that there can be a world exactly like that in Figure 5.1a, but with that tiny, wafer thin stretch connecting them removed (Figure 5.1d). In that case, anything in one part of the universe is totally disconnected from anything in the other part of the universe. For all we know, we could be in such a situation, where – isolated from us and impossible for us to reach – there is another spacetime. That is, for all we know, there could actually be disconnected spacetimes:

Figure 5.1 A series of universes culminating in an island universe

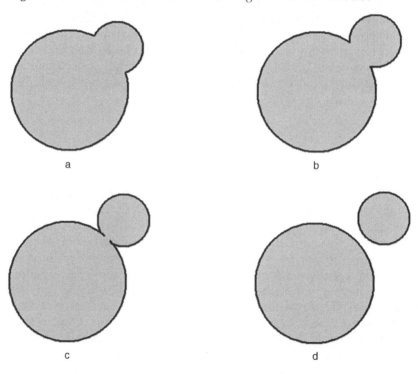

a

b

c

d

Spacetime versus Space

Notice we need disconnected spacetimes, not disconnected spaces. So the universes depicted in Figure 5.1a–5.1c don't represent universes where there's a tiny area of *space* that connects them, but universes where there's only a tiny stretch of *spacetime*. So the island universe in Figure 5.1c might be such that at almost no time whatsoever can you pass between the parts of the universe, except at a specific day in 2020 AD when a tiny doorway opens up and connects the two. On the other hand, the universe in Figure 5.1d is just like the one in Figure 5.1c, but without that door! So when picturing 5.1d, *don't* picture a universe which starts connected, and then evolves over time such that, at some times but not others, things in one part of it cannot reach things in the other part. That wouldn't be an island universe, for it is connected in time, if not always in space.

But GMR, so people have argued, can't handle the possibility of island universes. You might have thought it could – after all, Lewis says there are lots of disconnected spacetimes, and that's just what island universes are, right? Wrong! Following from the last section, Lewis is very clear that, whilst there are lots of disconnected spacetimes, only one of them – the one you are in – actually exists. So there is no world at which there *actually* are disconnected spacetimes and there can be no island universes. Let's go through that slowly. It's a basic principle of possible worlds talk that if something is possible, it is the case at some world. So if island universes were possible, there would be at least one world at which there were two (or more) disconnected areas of spacetime. But GMR rules that out because (given GMR) a world is one big, connected spacetime. So for island universes to be possible, there would have to be one big, connected spacetime which was two disconnected spacetimes. But that's a clear contradiction – you can no more have such a thing than there can be an unbroken stick where one bit is in New York and another bit is in London – for it to be in those places at the same time it must be broken, not *unbroken*. Or here's another way to think about it. In Figure 5.1d, we have two spacetimes disconnected from one another. If you believe GMR, then what you have are two possible worlds, not one. So there'll never be *a* possible world at which there are two (or more) disconnected spacetimes. Given this, then, GMR seems to miss out guaranteeing all of our modal intuitions, which many people count as a cost that outweighs the alleged benefits.

Ethical dilemmas

Nor is this the only proposed cost. Imagine that, in the name of philosophical advancement or perhaps because I turn to a life of the criminal geniuses that I see in James Bond, I construct a machine that automatically captures a random child. Then, when it senses that somewhere in the world a child has been saved from drowning, the machine immediately drives to the ocean and drowns the captured child. So if you saw a child, Anne, drowning in the ocean, you'd also see my machine – poised, ready to dart into the sea and drown a totally different child, Beatrice, were you to rescue Anne. One way or another, a child will drown: either Anne (because of your inaction) or Beatrice (because when you save Anne, my machine drowns Beatrice). What, then, should you do when you see that Anne is drowning? You might think that there's no moral difference either way, whether you save Anne or not, because either way a child dies.

Mark Heller has argued that GMR puts us in that position even without the construction of such a device. When you see a child drowning in the ocean, you might not see Nikk Effingham's Patented Child Drowning-o-matic machine, but you should consider yourself to be in the same situation. This is because every possibility must play out at some possible world. If you see Anne drowning, then (as it's possible that Anne *might* have drowned) if you save Anne you know that there's a disconnected spacetime where a duplicate of you just stands and watches a duplicate of Anne drown. Whereas, if you *don't* save Anne in this world – and just stand and watch her drown – you know that at the other spacetime (as all possibilities must play out) your duplicate dives in and rescues the duplicate of Anne. Either way, then, a child lives and a child dies. One might die in a spacetime you're in, whilst the other dies in a disconnected spacetime but, in the same way that we (should) value the lives of people in Third World countries as highly as our own, no matter where they are, it seems irrelevant where the child is when they die, i.e., irrelevant whether they're in our spacetime or not. The situation is therefore very similar to the one in which we find ourselves with the machine that drowns children. And if you think that it makes no difference what you do in the case of the machine, and if GMR is true (and Heller is correct that there is an analogy here), then it seems that there's no longer a moral obligation to save drowning children. Or, for that matter, to stop people getting hit by cars (for, if you stop a car hitting someone, you know that in another spacetime someone else *does* get hit by a car) or sending money to the Third World to stop children dying of easily preventable diseases (as, for every £10 you send that saves a dying child, in a disconnected spacetime another child is denied the money and dies) and so on. So, if GMR is true, then we should make serious revisions to what we think our ethical obligations are, revisions which rally against our intuitions.

These are just some of the possible costs GMR might incur. We'll set aside the possible costs at this stage and turn to examining competing theories and checking to see if GMR really is the best theory with respect to costs and benefits.

Ersatz modal realism

Start with alternative realisms: can we believe in possible worlds without believing they're concrete spacetimes, disconnected from our own? Certainly, when possible worlds were first introduced, those who talked about them *didn't* think of them as enormous, really existing, concrete spacetimes but thought possible worlds talk was just a heuristic. If anything, possible worlds were abstract entities like numbers and propositions. Such theories have been dubbed 'ersatz' theories of possible worlds.

As a caricature example of such an ersatz theory, imagine that we identified possible worlds with sets of propositions (so our ontology would now be one of objects, propositions and sets). Specifically, we identify them with sets of the propositions which are true at that world. For instance, imagine you have a set corresponding to the world at which I am prime minister of Britain. At that world, the propositions < Nikk Effingham is prime minister > and < David Cameron is not prime minister > are both true, and so those propositions are two of the (many) propositions that are members of that set.

The problem is that this sort of theory, even if it does avoid costs that you may think are associated with GMR, doesn't have any obvious *benefits*. Run through some of the benefits that GMR was meant to guarantee. First, Lewis could take possible worlds talk literally – where possible worlds translations quantified over something, Lewis accepted that the value of that variable exists. But the ersatzist has problems saying this. Take the sentence:

> There could have been at least one more thing than there actually is.

When we translated that into possible worlds talk, we said that all of the things that exist at the actual world exist at some other world *plus* there is an extra thing, which doesn't actually exist, but which does exist at that other world as well. The translation was:

> $\exists x \exists y$ (x and y are worlds & x is the actual world & $\forall z$ (z exists at $x \rightarrow z$ exists at y) & **$\exists u$ (u exists at y & $\sim u$ exists at x)**)

But the bit in bold quantifies over something – not a world, but an object – that doesn't actually exist. These things are called **possibilia**. Possibilia are the possible objects which exist at possible worlds (if possibilia don't actually exist, we say they are 'mere possibilia'). If you accept GMR, this is not a problem – possibilia are just the inhabitants of the other spacetimes. If you accept ersatzism, though, this is not fine. First, there are no 'inhabitants' of worlds for my caricature ersatzist. Their worlds are abstract objects – they are not inhabited by *anything*. They need to instead introduce more entities to play the role of possibilia. But whilst they may have introduced an ontological reduction for worlds, it's not obvious that this will work for possibilia, so they might need to introduce a whole new category of entities to play that role (and, in association, if they can't analyse what it is for a given possibilium to exist at a world, that'll need to be taken as a brute fact – which is also a cost). Second, this move denies us an objection to GMR. Many people think GMR is problematic as it says that some things exist which don't actually exist. These people, called **actualists**, think that if something exists, it must actually exist – this is just, they often say, what 'existence' means. Given possibilia – ersatz or otherwise – there exist some things which don't *actually* exist. So the actualists will think this version of ersatzism is as bad as GMR.

Next, GMR can analyse away modal terms because of Lewis's principle of recombination guaranteeing that there are enough worlds out there. My caricature ersatzism will be harder pressed to do this, as it will need a corresponding principle that says which sets of propositions count as worlds. Certainly, not every set of propositions can count as such. For instance, take the following propositions:

< Hitler won World War II >
< Hitler never existed >

There is a set of those propositions, but that set can't be a *possible* world as then it'd be possible for Hitler to have won World War II without existing. That seems contradictory, and so it'd be possible for there to be true contradictions! As that's impossible, we need to ensure that no world has both of those propositions as members, and that not any old set of propositions gets to be a world. So we must whittle down which sets are worlds and say something like:

x is a world = df *x* is a set of propositions such that all of the propositions in that set are consistent with one another.

We now have a principle that gets us what we want, for if this was true, there'd be a possible world for every way the actual world could have been. But now we won't be able to analyse away modal terms, for the word 'consistent' is itself a modal term: propositions are consistent with one another just in case they *could* all be true together. So whilst our theory can get the correct worlds, it can only do that by utilizing a modal term in the theory itself. Ergo, it cannot analyse away modal terms like GMR can.

Finally, it cannot guarantee ontological parsimony. GMR could ontologically reduce two things: propositions and properties. Propositions became sets of worlds. But it would be ludicrous to think the caricature ersatzist we are considering could do the same. Worlds are now sets of propositions and it'd be viciously circular to think that propositions were also then sets of worlds. So that reduction won't work. For properties, GMR treated them as sets of objects at the other worlds. That is, it treated them as sets of possibilia. Again, as this ersatzism has no obvious room for possibilia, it has no obvious room for this reduction.

So the theory might avoid the supposed madness that is GMR, but only by failing to achieve every benefit that GMR achieved. Nor is it clear what benefit it offers in return! Even if you think it avoids costs (although it does include abstracta reprehensible to nominalist sensibilities!), that it doesn't have any benefits is enough reason to give up on it. This is just a caricature theory, but it gives you an idea of what problems plague ersatz theories of possible worlds – whilst they avoid possible worlds being concrete, it's just not clear that they actually earn anything in return. It's like the government constructing a large building with no doors or rooms. 'But it was cheaper than the alternative design!' a politician might say. Fair enough, but if it doesn't *do* anything, then what was the point?

There are less crude ersatz theories out there. For instance, Stalnaker advances a more sophisticated theory of worlds as sets of propositions. And there are other alternatives:

- Alvin Plantinga believes possible worlds are types of states of affairs.
- Peter Forrest has argued that worlds might be a variety of property (namely, the property that the universe would instantiate were it the way depicted at that world).
- David Armstrong has argued that worlds might be sets of objects and the properties those objects have at those worlds.
- We might try and do away with abstract propositions and imagine that worlds are sets of sentences (although we have to try very hard to ensure that there are enough sentences out there to express the world being every way the world could've been; similarly to Chihara's anti-realist theory of numbers, the apparent lack of enough sentences is a hurdle to overcome).
- You might want to give up on giving a reduction entirely and just treat possible worlds and possibilia as *sui generis*.

You should feel free to explore these realist alternatives, and see how they deal (or fail to deal) with problems like those above. They are not all like the caricature, but you should carefully ask yourself, for each, what costs and benefits there are, and whether they are – at the end of the day – better than Lewis's GMR alternative.

Modal fictionalism

Fictionalism

Let's consider anti-realist theories about possible worlds, whereby we have modal truths without using possible worlds (or, alternatively, that we don't need the modal truths and that it's those truths which are dispensable!). Indeed, many of the metaontological theories presented later in this book (such as, say, truthmaking) can be deployed with modality in an effort to relieve us of unwanted ontological commitments (such as to worlds). But, for now, we'll stick with introducing just one new theory: **fictionalism**. (And, as mentioned in the previous chapter, it is not just with regard to possible worlds that it has been deployed – there are fictionalist accounts for various ontological categories.) The core idea is that we often talk about things that don't exist, and do so without any qualms, so why not think this can work in ontology? The fictionalist has in mind our talk of fictions and fictional entities. We often assert sentences like:

> Gandalf killed the Balrog.
> Buffy slays vampires.
> Gregory House works at Princeton-Plainsboro Teaching Hospital.

Concentrate on that last example. In many cases we should say it's a false statement. For instance, if I was suffering a mysterious illness and my doctor said 'Don't worry, apparently there's a great doctor called House at Princeton-Plainsboro Teaching Hospital. You should go there,' he'd be grossly mistaken (and probably I should doubt whether he was a real doctor) for both House and the hospital are fictional. In that case, the doctor who mistakes the fictional for the real would be asserting something like:

> $\exists x$ (x = Gregory House & x works at Princeton-Plainsboro Teaching Hospital)

whereas, sometimes we seem to utter that sentence and think it's true. For instance, if I was at a quiz and the question was 'In the show *House*, who is the lead character, and where does he work?' then that sentence would appear to be a true answer – certainly I'd be unamused if the quizmaster said I was wrong. But that is because we seem to be asserting something different than the above. I'm not asserting that there is such a person, but instead asserting that *according to the fiction of House* there is such a person. We can represent this by introducing some more logical machinery. Just as we introduced $\Diamond$ and $\Box$ as operators that preceded a proposition to say when it was possibly true or necessarily true, we can introduce a

fictional operator. We won't use a symbol and will instead just say 'According to the fiction of *House*' to get:

According to the fiction of *House*: ∃ x (x = Gregory House & x works at Princeton-Plainsboro Teaching Hospital)

And because the (false) proposition about Gregory House existing and working at a certain hospital is preceded by an operator, there's no need to think the proposition itself is true, in the same way that a false proposition (e.g., < Hitler won World War II >) can be preceded by an operator (e.g., ◇) and the two stuck together can be true (as Hitler could've won World War II). Some operators, then, are **non-factive**, such that what follows the operator needn't be true, even though the overall proposition including the operator is (not all operators are non-factive, e.g., □ is factive, since whatever is necessarily the case is the case).

Modal fictionalism deploys just such a fictional operator by saying that modal sentences are to be paraphrased as (or are true in virtue of) what is true according to Lewis's fiction of GMR. For instance, GMR says that what's possibly true is what is the case at some disconnected spacetime:

Possibly P is true iff ∃ x (x is a disconnected spacetime & P is the case at x)

What modal fictionalism does is say that that something is possible if it's true that, according to GMR's fiction, those things are the case at some disconnected spacetime:

Possibly P is true iff according to the fiction of GMR : ∃ x (x is a disconnected spacetime & P is the case at x)

And *that* sentence can be true without there being any disconnected spacetimes (in the same way that the sentence featuring the operator 'According to the fiction of *House*' can be true without House existing). Repeat this for every other translation: where GMR translates a modal sentence into some proposition about such-and-such being true at a disconnected spacetime, modal fictionalism translates it into some proposition about what is true according to Lewis's fiction of GMR that such-and-such is the case at some disconnected spacetime. Modal fictionalism, then, treats Lewis's possible worlds as *fictional* entities. (Note, also, that it is badly named – it should be 'possible worlds fictionalism' rather than 'modal fictionalism', as modal sentences are still literally true whilst it is only possible worlds that get the fictional treatment.)

Incompleteness

Fictions are generally incomplete. For instance, according to Shakespeare's *Hamlet*, we know that Hamlet is the Prince of Denmark as that's explicitly stated. We can also assume some things too, which are implicit in the play (that he isn't a girl pretending to be a boy, that he has a working heart, that he doesn't walk around painted like a clown, etc.). But some things are left totally undetermined. For instance, it's not true that Hamlet is shoe size 9, nor that he's size 10, or 8 or . . . well, any particular shoe size (although – as it's implicitly true according to the fiction that he has feet – it must be true according to the fiction that he has *a* shoe size, even though he doesn't have a *specific* shoe size). Or take a film or soap opera. Rarely do we ever see characters in films and soap operas going to the toilet, but it's implicit in the fiction that they do. So it's true that they go to the toilet but the sentence 'Jack Bauer went to the toilet six times during the first season of 24' is undetermined.

So fictions are often *incomplete* and certain propositions are, according to the fiction, neither true nor false. (In fact, when I was giving the example above of worlds at which *Lord of the Rings* is true, this was somewhat misleading. For just this reason, there is not *a* world where the events of *Lord of the Rings* play out, but many, each differing over the details of the incomplete propositions that Tolkien left undetermined such as, for example, Gandalf's shoe size.)

This is a problem for modal fictionalism because Lewis's theory of GMR leaves some things undetermined. Unsurprisingly, Lewis's book *On the Plurality of Worlds*, and the other articles he wrote defending GMR, don't cover every last thing. Like most theories, some bits of GMR remain to be worked out. For instance, some subatomic particles have one property and other particles have another property. In some cases, no actual particle has both at our world. But, says Lewis, we shouldn't draw from this that it's logically impossible for them to have both properties (for instance, there's a mass such that no particle actually has that mass, but we don't conclude that it's logically *impossible* for a particle to have that mass). On the other hand, we shouldn't draw from this that they *could* have them together – for all we know, it might be impossible. The specific example Lewis has in mind is that electrons have the property *negative charge*, positrons have the property *positive charge* and nothing in the actual world is both negatively and positively charged. Lewis says that, whilst it's physically impossible, we have no idea whether it's logically impossible for a particle to be both. It'd clearly be impossible if they were the polar opposites of one another, but the opposite of *negative charge* is not *positive charge* but the property of *not* being negatively charged, i.e., *being such that it is not negatively charged*. Lots of things fail to be negatively charged without being positively charged; these two properties are not the opposite of one another. But it might still be logically impossible for a particle to have both properties as properties do not have to be the opposite of one another to make it impossible for them to both be instantiated by the same object at the same time. For example, *being red* and *being blue* cannot both be instantiated by the same thing, for nothing is red all over and blue all over. But one isn't the negative property of the other for the opposite of *being red* is *being such that it isn't red*, which isn't the same as *being blue* (for lots of things aren't red without being blue). So maybe *negative charge* and *positive charge* are like that, and *are* contradictory properties. Lewis says that we've got no idea which it is, so we remain ignorant over some of the modal facts. Of course, given his own theory, the facts are still settled one way or another – either there is, or is not, a disconnected spacetime with a particle that is both negatively and positively charged. So 'It is possible that a particle is both negatively and positively charged' is either true or false according to GMR. We don't *know* which it is, but it's just life that some propositions can't be known. So it's not a problem for Lewis. But when we move to modal fictionalism it does become a problem. The fictionalist says:

> 'It is possible that a particle is both negatively and positively charged' is true if and only if according to GMR: $\exists x$ (x is a disconnected spacetime & at x there exists a particle that is both negatively and positively charged)

But that translation is just like Hamlet's shoe size and Jack Bauer's toilet habits – it's undetermined by Lewis's works (and, therefore, undetermined by the fiction of GMR). But whilst it makes sense to say that propositions about Hamlet's shoe size aren't determined by the fiction, it's harder to believe that modal facts are undetermined. Surely every modal fact is just true or false?

The Brock–Rosen problem

The second problem for modal fictionalism is so named after its progenitors: Stuart Brock and Gideon Rosen. Modal fictionalists want to avoid having to believe in an infinite number of disconnected spacetimes – that is, they want to reap the benefits of GMR whilst endorsing the incredulous stare that:

> It is not actually the case that there is an infinite number of disconnected spacetimes.

This is a tricky sentence for the fictionalist for not only does GMR say that there are an infinite number of disconnected spacetimes, it appears that it's true at every world. In the same way that 'There are lots of countries' is true no matter what country you are in:

> According to GMR, it is true at every world that there are an infinite number of disconnected spacetimes.

is true as well. Here's the rub. The fictionalist says that the following principle determines what's necessary:

> 'P' is necessarily true = $_{df}$ According to GMR, it is true at every world that < P > is true.

But it is true, according to GMR, that at every world there is an infinite number of disconnected spacetimes, so the modal fictionalist should say that it *is* necessarily true. Whatever is necessarily true is true, so it follows that it's actually the case that there is an infinite number of disconnected spacetimes. But this was *exactly* what the modal fictionalist wanted to avoid. So fictionalists have to deal with this problem (although they have, of course, made headway).

Costs/benefits

Finally, we might wonder what work modal fictionalism is really doing. Take ontological parsimony. Although it eliminates possible worlds from our ontology, that obviously means we cannot identify propositions (or properties) with sets of worlds (or possibilia). Further, some people think there are serious ontological and ideological questions to be asked about fictions. Whilst we might be translating talk of possible worlds into talk about fictions, we're still left asking how we deal with the fictional entities that we apparently talk about. Must we add to our ontology fictional entities like Hamlet, Jack Bauer and, now, possible worlds? And, if so, whilst we've excluded possible worlds from our ontology, we've just put fictional entities in their stead. So there are issues with ontological parsimony. Similarly for ideological parsimony. The operator 'According to the fiction of GMR' looks like an odd thing to take as a primitive. Indeed, it appears to be a *modal* primitive, for what does it mean for φ to be true according to a fiction other than for it be interpreted as saying:

Were GMR the case, φ would be the case

or

It is impossible that GMR be true, and φ not be true

or some such? And those translations are modal – so the fictionalist operator appears to be a modal operator anyhow. Thus, modal fictionalism is *not* removing modal terms from our theory and cannot provide – as GMR can allegedly provide – an analysis of modal terms. Of course, this might not worry you too much, for perhaps you never intended to guarantee this benefit (in the same way that some ersatzists don't care that they don't get this benefit). But at this stage we should start wondering, as we did with ersatzism, what benefit modal fictionalism is meant to guarantee? If we are not analysing modal terms, aren't guaranteeing ontological parsimony and can't take possible worlds talk at face value, then what is the point of the theory? Such are the worries that anti-fictionalists have raised.

Chapter summary

In this chapter, we have:

- introduced the reasons why philosophers talk about possible worlds.
- introduced the motivations for, not just talking about worlds, but including them in our ontology.

- examined realist theories for possible worlds (Lewis's Genuine Modal Realism and some ersatz options).
- introduced fictionalism and then explored fictionalism about possible worlds as a specific example of it in action.

Further reading

General introductions to modality include Joseph Melia (2003), E. Jonathan Lowe (2002), John Divers (2002), Louis DeRosset (2009a, 2009b) and Rod Girle (2003). Melia's book explains the difficulties of translating modal sentences without using possible worlds. A good collection of papers can be found in Stephen Laurence and Cynthia Macdonald (1998), Michael Loux (1979, 2001) and Loux and Zimmerman (2003).

There is a lot of literature on Genuine Modal Realism. The famous introduction is Lewis's 1986 book. The problem with GMR missing out worlds is discussed in many places, such as the work of Philip Bricker (2001, 2006), David Efird and Tom Stoneham (2005) and Gonzalo Rodriguez-Pereyra (2004). The problem of morality and GMR is briefly discussed in Lewis (1986) and at great length by Mark Heller (2003). Nor are these the only problems. Others are discussed by Lewis himself (again, 1986), and other objections include those by Divers and Melia (2002) and Richard Sheehy (2006). Modal fictionalism is discussed at length by Gideon Rosen (1990) and also endorsed by Armstrong (1989b). An accessible introduction is by Daniel Nolan (2011).

There is more to modality than just what this chapter covers. For instance, there are other anti-realist programmes concerning possible worlds – see Divers (2004, 2006) – as well as attempts to account for modality without ever mentioning possible worlds; see, e.g., Barbara Vetter (2011) and Michael Jubien (2007).

6

Space

Substantivalism and relationism

So far, this book has looked only at abstract entities, but there are also lots of interesting ontological issues concerning concrete entities. The most obvious concrete entities are material objects and, in chapters 7, 8 and 9, we'll explore the issues surrounding them in detail. However, in this chapter, I concentrate on something else that is commonly thought to be concrete but that isn't in the category of material objects: **regions**. To get a grip on what a region is, imagine that I sell you some land. What have I actually sold you? You might think that it's an object and that, in selling you a plot of land, you are now the owner of the building that is there, and the soil and dirt that it is built upon. But that's not true. Imagine you knock down the building and then scoop out all of the dirt and soil, so you're left with an enormous pit. It's still true that you own *something* for you still own that *place*. You could, for instance, sell that empty pit on to someone else – you would be selling a *region of space*. Here's another example. Bob Hope is dead and buried and is obviously therefore buried somewhere. So the sentence 'There's somewhere where Bob Hope is buried' is true. The straightforward translation of that sentence into logic would be something like:

$\exists x \, \exists y \, (\, x = \text{Bob Hope} \, \& \, y = \text{a region of space under a lot of soil} \, \& \, x \text{ is located at } y \,)$

So there's some reason to think it comes with a commitment to regions; after all, we are quantifying over them.

At least, this is what realists would say. Anti-realists about space say something quite different. From their point of view, regions are an unnecessary addition. Shift to the metaphor of God creating the universe to make things clear. The anti-realist thinks that all God has to do to make the universe is make a bunch of objects, and then arrange them in a certain way. The realist about regions thinks that God has first to make an enormous container – the regions – in order to put the objects in. Only once he has made that container – that is, made the regions – could he start to make the objects. The anti-realist believes that there is no reason to add this extra step. In the same way that the anti-realist about properties thinks objects can be blue without us believing in the property *blue* (and, more generally, that we can talk about something whilst being anti-realist about it), the anti-realist about space thinks things can be separated and located without there being anything which they are located at, and without there being anything that they are separated by, i.e., that there are no regions of space.

To be terminologically awkward, this debate has its own terms of art. Those who are realists about regions are called **substantivalists,** whilst those who are anti-realists about regions are often called **relationists**. What's interesting about the substantivalist/relationist debate is how it differs from previous debates in this book. The debates that substantivalists and relationists standardly have do not revolve around paraphrasing talk about regions of space, or trying to eliminate ideological primitives and so on; those things that figure prominently in debates about holes, properties, numbers and possible worlds don't figure prominently here. Instead, the substantivalists and relationists tend to focus on the *explanatory* role of regions – specifically, their role in scientific theories. So they say: if regions play a role in those theories, then we should include them; if they do not, then we should not. This chapter will therefore give us an insight into another way that people think ontological questions should be solved: rather than thinking about issues with ontological parsimony, or analysing away unwanted primitives (like modal primitives), we instead try to see if scientific theories can cast some light on the problem. (The reason for this, by the way, isn't necessarily that there's something particularly special about the substantivalism/relationism debate but that those philosophers working the most on the ontology of regions haven't been vanilla ontologists, in the vein of David Armstrong, David Lewis and others, but philosophers of science and so they obviously tend to focus on how science relates to these issues.)

Newton's argument for absolute space

Crash course in basic physics

Before we begin, you'll need a quick refresher in some basic physics. Start with **velocity**. The velocity of an object is a bit like the speed of an object. But the difference is that the *direction* that an object is travelling in makes a difference to its velocity. So two things can have the same speed whilst having different velocities, just as long as they are going in different directions. If you and I are both travelling at 3 m/s, but you're going north and I am going south, then, whilst we have the same speed, we don't have the same velocity. Similarly, there are two ways for you to change your velocity. One way is to increase your speed in the same direction you are going. Alternatively, you can change your velocity by changing which direction you are going in.

Velocity is generally thought to be relative to something (although, as we shall see, whether this is correct or not is part of the debate). For instance, imagine you're stationary whilst two other people – Mr Slow and Ms Fast – drive away from you on motorcycles. Say that Mr Slow is moving away from you at 5 m/s, whilst Ms Fast moves away from you at 10 m/s. How fast Ms Fast is going from Mr Slow's point of view is going to be different from how fast she is going from your point of view. From his perspective she is not moving at 10 m/s, but moving away at 5 m/s. Ms Fast's velocity, then, depends upon your point of view: 10 m/s relative to your point of view, and 5 m/s relative to Mr Slow's point of view. In fact, when I said that you were stationary that was somewhat misleading. At best, I should have said that you were stationary *relative to the earth*, for someone else might think you were whizzing along rather than not moving at all. Just imagine someone stood on the surface of the sun. Seconds before they're burnt to a crisp, they would see you hurtling at thousands of kilometres a second through space, because the earth is – from their point of view – orbiting the sun at a speed of thousands of kilometres per second.

But you may have thought that we could ask what the velocity of something was without mentioning what it was relative to. That is, that we could ask what its **absolute velocity** was. You might think that there is a God's eye viewpoint we could take, where the Almighty looks down at Ms Fast and, whilst you, Mr Slow and the person on the sun each think she's going at a different velocity, God sees how fast she's *really* going. The problem with absolute velocity is that, if things have an absolute velocity, then we could never know what it was. To illustrate, imagine that you light a match or smoke a cigarette in the saloon bar of an airport. The smoke from it would trickle up in a (more or less) straight line. Now imagine you light a match or a cigarette on an aeroplane in mid-flight (I recommend neither, by the way, not even for philosophical and scientific experimentation). What does the smoke do now? It doesn't zoom off behind you as the plane flies through the air at high speed. Instead the smoke, again, just trickles upwards in a (more or less) straight line. As long as you're travelling at a constant velocity, the smoke would do nothing different to what it would do if you were in the saloon bar. Indeed, everything else that you do is exactly the same. Whether you're stationary on the ground or zipping through the air at a constant 800 miles per hour, every action you take, and test you perform, will turn out exactly the same. You might think that one thing would be different: if you look out of the window, you would see the landscape moving below you (on the plane) or not moving at all (if it was the window of the bar). But that's exactly the point! Looking out of the window tells you only that you are moving *relative to the earth*. It doesn't tell you what your 'absolute' velocity would be.

Here's another example. Imagine I put you inside an enormous box and sedate you for two hours. When you come to, I ask you to try and decide – without looking out of the window – how fast you are going. I tell you that either I left the box where it was, or I had it chucked down a bottomless pit and we're now plummeting at a constant, terminal velocity. How would you figure out which it was? There's no way! The only way would be to look out, find an object you want to determine your velocity relative to and see how fast you were moving away from that object. And how would that help? Unless you knew what you were looking at was (absolutely) stationary in the first place, you still wouldn't know what your absolute velocity was.

That's the first part of our physics refresher. The second is that this is not the case for acceleration. For both examples, you may have erroneously insisted that you'd be able to tell the difference. You might think that you could tell when you were on a plane as opposed to being in the bar because of the buffeting on the plane, or the surge in your stomach as it took off. Or you might think that, if I dropped you down a bottomless pit, you'd feel your stomach going strange as we do when in fast-moving lifts or on roller coasters. This would be misguided because in *those* cases your velocity isn't *constant*. If you take off in an aeroplane or fall down a lift shaft, you experience forces acting upon you (weightlessness as you fall, or a pressure forcing you back in a plane seat) because your velocity is changing. These forces, what are called **inertial forces**, are a result of changing your velocity – what we more commonly call **acceleration**. Unlike velocity, there *is* absolute acceleration. We can know whether or not we're absolutely accelerating, and can perform experiments (or, indeed, just feel the forces acting on our body) to determine whether we're really accelerating or not. But once you *stop* accelerating (and the plane has levelled out, or the box in the pit has reached terminal velocity), those forces abate.

Newton's bucket

With the refresher complete, we can turn to Isaac Newton's argument for substantivalism. Here's Newton's argument for substantivalism in short: Newton reasoned that if velocity has to be relative to something, and acceleration is a change in velocity, then acceleration has to be relative to something as well. But, says Newton, it's possible for one object to accelerate even though there's no *object* that the acceleration could be relative to. But, as it must be relative to *something*, it must be relative to something that was not an object: it must be relative to space itself; ergo, space must exist.

Here's Newton's argument for substantivalism in full: imagine, says Newton, a universe that consisted of nothing other than a bucket full of water suspended by a piece of rope (you'll need to set aside qualms about there not being enough gravity to keep the water in the bucket or what the rope would be attached to – if these things really bother you, I leave it as an exercise for you to construct an example more in line with your sensibilities). Now imagine that the rope was twisted. As the rope begins to unwind, the bucket will rotate. As the bucket rotates, picture in your mind what happens to the water. It doesn't just remain still, it starts to rotate as well. At some point the water is rotating as fast as the edge of the bucket, and the level of the water will dip slightly, curving in the centre (an effect I'm sure we've all witnessed, and you could easily witness yourself if you got an actual bucket, tied it to the ceiling and did this; if you happen to have a lecturer foolish enough to deface university property, you might try and convince them to demonstrate this for you). So we can split the bucket twisting into three stages:

Stage 1: The rope is twisted but has not been let loose. The bucket and the water are at rest with respect to one another.

Stage 2: The rope has been let loose and the bucket has started to rotate. But the water is still at rest because the bucket hasn't yet started to churn it into motion.

Stage 3: The bucket is rotating, the water is now rotating as fast as the bucket and the water level is now concave.

Look at the first and third stage. Since the water level is concave rather than flat, there's a difference – a testable, empirical difference – between the two situations. The reason it's concave is because the water is accelerating: as the water is going around and around, it changes direction; since velocity is not just speed but speed in a certain direction, as the water changes direction, it changes its velocity; as acceleration is just a change in velocity, the water is therefore accelerating; as the water is accelerating, inertial forces act upon it and it is those forces which cause it to be concave.

If Newton is right that acceleration always has to be relative to something, what can it be relative to in this case? The only objects we have are the bucket, the water and the rope (and we could imagine the rope being annihilated at the instant that it unravels and the bucket has started spinning, so let's ignore the rope). The water can't be accelerating with respect to itself (its acceleration relative to itself is always zero – in the same way that you never end up leaving yourself behind, the water cannot accelerate away from itself!). But nor can it be accelerating with respect to the bucket. As the bucket is going as fast as the water, and its velocity is changing at exactly the same rate as the water, the two are at rest relative to one another. But now we've run out of objects for the acceleration to be relative to. It's at this stage that Newton adds in regions. Take all of the regions and stick them together to get the largest region. This largest region is what Newton calls **absolute space**. Before the rope is twisted, and it is not rotating, the water and the bucket aren't accelerating at all with respect to absolute space. When we get to the third stage, the water may not be accelerating relative to the bucket, but it *is* accelerating relative to absolute space. So, Newton surmised, we need absolute space in order to account for the inertial forces in those cases.

Before moving to possible responses to Newton, notice how – in the case of absolute space – he is using substantially different tactics for settling ontological questions than we've seen before. We are moving away from paraphrasing sentences of natural language, or talking about things like metaphysical explanation, and instead are entering the arena of physics. So we have another possible avenue for discovering what things there are.

Ernst Mach and the fixed stars

Ernst Mach noted that the supposed absolute accelerations resulting from, say, the earth rotating were identical to the accelerations that the earth bore relative to the **fixed stars**. By 'fixed stars', Mach was referring to the stars in the heavens which he thought did not move relative to one another (which, as we now know, aren't, in fact, fixed at all). So where we thought something was accelerating at 5 m/s/s relative to absolute space, it also appeared that it was accelerating at 5 m/s/s relative to the fixed stars in the heavens. Mach supposed, contrary to Newton, that there was no absolute space; instead, the inertial forces were produced because of acceleration relative to the fixed stars. Even though the fixed stars are far away, this isn't entirely unreasonable. There are other forces that are produced when two objects interact, more or less regardless of their distance from one another, e.g., when two electrons pass through a magnetic field, the force produced is barely affected by how far they are from one another, and what's instead relevant is how fast they are moving relative to one another. Mach thought the same might be true of the inertial forces and that they were a result of interacting with the fixed stars, even though these were far away.

So in the bucket experiment, the water would indeed go concave if we imagined that the bucket, rope and water were the only things that existed with the exception of the distant stars. You might reply that we could simply delete the stars from our thought experiment: 'Imagine *just* the bucket and water, and you still get the same result!', you might claim. Mach would not be happy with this line of reasoning. He believed that we should only ask questions about what went on in our universe – and as our universe comes with the heavens as well as the earth, we shouldn't run thought experiments about what would happen if there were no such things. Essentially, Mach thought that, for all we know, a rotating bucket with no fixed stars whatsoever *would* look very different (i.e., not suffer inertial forces and not be concave) from one with fixed stars. It is illegitimate and question-begging, then, to claim that you know what would happen if the stars didn't exist.

Whatever its merits, the Machian argument spurred on another great scientist: Albert Einstein. Einstein developed his theory of **general relativity** (a sequel to his theory of special relativity, which we will examine in some depth in the next chapter). Einstein initially aimed to produce a theory that, like Mach's, accounted for inertial forces by making them the result of not the fixed stars but the distribution of all of the matter in the universe. The downside though, and a blow to Machianism, is that general relativity allowed for all of the matter in the universe to rotate in the same direction. This possibility is a problem. If acceleration is the result of velocity changes relative to matter distributed across the entire universe, rather than relative to absolute space, then that doesn't allow for the matter *itself* to rotate. For it to rotate, it would have to absolutely accelerate, but we are to imagine that absolute acceleration just is the relative acceleration something has to all of the matter in the universe. So for the matter to rotate, it would have to accelerate away from itself – and *nothing* can accelerate away from itself (for by definition you can never leave yourself behind!). Einstein's hopes of rekindling the Machian philosophy of inertial forces were therefore dashed.

Brute accelerations

Whilst Newton makes the acceleration relative to absolute space responsible for inertial forces, and Mach does similar but says that it is acceleration relative to the fixed stars, there is another alternative. Both theories would have to leave something unexplained: why is it acceleration relative to *that* thing that brings about the inertial forces, and *how* does that mechanism take effect? Recall from chapter 2 that inexplicable truths are not inherently bad; it's perfectly acceptable to allow brute truths into one's theory. However, the brute truth in this case might help the relationist's case for anti-realism about regions. The relationist may say that, contrary to the idea that absolute acceleration is to be analysed as acceleration relative to some particular thing (e.g., absolute space or the fixed stars), acceleration has no such analysis and is simply a fundamental property of the universe, irreducible to accelerations relative to other things. So they agree with Newton and Mach that acceleration is absolute but disagree that it can be analysed in terms of acceleration relative to some distinct entity or entities (such as absolute space or the fixed stars). At first glance, this looks inferior to substantivalism, as substantivalists can explain why something has the absolute acceleration that it does. But they only achieve that explanatory power by introducing absolute space, which is a cost to the theory. Moreover, they still leave unexplained why it is acceleration relative to *that* which brings about inertial forces as opposed to acceleration relative to something else. So *both* theories leave at least something unexplained, except substantivalism *also* has an extra entity in its ontology. Further, whilst absolute space is meant to be responsible for inertial forces, you might think that it is otherwise empirically undetectable, so it's a somewhat odd entity to believe in. Compare: every physical theory will have to take some facts as brute, e.g., the most fundamental particles instantiating the most fundamental properties. Call that brute fact X. We could explain X by saying that the fundamental particles weren't actually fundamental and that there was an extra variety of particles: the Uselessions. We could say that the arrangement and organization of the Uselessions explained why the fundamental particles had the properties they do. But if the existence of the Uselessions was otherwise unverifiable, then we might doubt that we've got a genuinely better theory. After all, you could do this for every theory ad infinitum. Once you came up with the Uselessions, I can posit a theory that explains what the Uselessions do in terms of the Pointlessions, and then a better theory that explains what they do in terms of Irrelevantions, etc. So the relationist might claim that Newton would be wrong to think that introducing absolute space brought with it any explanatory power, and that taking absolute acceleration to be brute is a superior option. But is it true that absolute space serves no purpose other than to account for absolute acceleration? The next section investigates what other explanatory role regions might have.

Leibniz's shift argument

Gottfried Leibniz, a seventeenth-century philosopher, was a notable proponent of relationism and his **shift argument** was his main reason for endorsing it. The argument is intended to be a *reductio ad absurdum* of being a realist about regions of space. Start by imagining a universe with two balls in it, Lefty and Righty, plus absolute space. We'll concentrate on just three regions that make up that space. There's the region of space that Lefty is located at (call it r_1),

Figure 6.1 Leibniz's shift argument

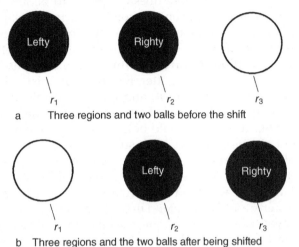

a   Three regions and two balls before the shift

b   Three regions and the two balls after being shifted

the region of space that Righty is located at (call it r_2) – which is one metre to the right of r_1 – and finally an empty region of space one metre to the right of r_2 (call it r_3).

Figure 6.1a shows this set up. The problems arise when we imagine a second universe – one which was made differently, and where everything was shifted one metre to the right. Lefty would be where Righty was, i.e., located at r_2, whereas Righty would fill up what, in the other universe, was the empty space r_3. The place where Lefty was, r_1, would now be devoid of balls (see Figure 6.1b). As the places would be occupied by different things, these universes are two distinct possibilities.

Leibniz had problems with such a possibility, mainly stemming from ancillary metaphysical principles he endorsed. For instance, he endorsed the Principle of Sufficient Reason: that for everything that was the case, there had to be a reason for why it was that way rather than some other way. Examples abound of things for which there are sufficient reasons: if a kettle is boiling water, the sufficient reason for it doing so is that I turned it on rather than leaving it alone; the planets orbit the sun not spontaneously but because of the laws of gravity; if Poirot comes across a body, he presumes there is a reason that person died, rather than thinking it happened for no reason at all, and so on. Given the Principle of Sufficient Reason, substantivalism has a problem, for what reason is there for Lefty being at r_1 (and Righty being at r_2) rather than Lefty being at r_2 (and Righty being at r_3)? As there doesn't appear to be any reason for that, the Principle of Sufficient Reason is breached. Relationism, on the other hand, solves the problem neatly. Given relationism, there is no sense to be made of 'shifting' the objects. If (a metaphorical) God makes a relationist universe with Lefty and Righty one metre apart, that's the end of the matter. For the relationist, all there is to a universe are the objects in it, and the spatial relations between them, so it's impossible to shift Lefty and Righty one metre further to the right because they would both have to be one metre further to the right *of something else*. With substantivalism, the 'something else' would be a part of absolute space, so we can have a difference between the universes. There is no such parallel for relationism. So, given relationism, we don't have two worlds which are different but where Lefty and Righty stand in the same relation to one another and we never have to ask the question about whether the situation depicted in Figure 6.1a holds or whether the situation depicted in Figure 6.1b holds – for the relationist, they are one and the same situation. Leibniz also believed the **identity of indiscernibles**: if two things are indistinguishable – if they have the same properties – then they are one and the same thing. Leibniz thought this, again, favoured relationism. As the two worlds posited by the substantivalist are indiscernible – even God, thought Leibniz, would not be able to tell the difference – then they must be identical. But that would be a contradiction, for substantivalists clearly thought they were distinct. So substantivalism must be false and relationism must be true.

But both principles – the principle of sufficient reason and the identity of indiscernibles – are not well favoured nowadays. That there could be distinct but indiscernible objects seems possible (look back at page 57). That some things have no reason for being seems also to be possible (for instance, there appear to be events which, according to physics, have no cause – certain quantum events and the Big Bang have been mooted as examples). But many still think that, whilst Leibniz's own reasons for thinking indiscernible differences were a problem are not good reasons, it is problematic for there to be such possibilities. For instance, if there was such a difference, it'd be empirically undetectable. In the same way that we might take absolute velocity being undetectable to be a reason to think that there is no such thing as absolute velocity, we can think similarly of these distinct possibilities.

Non-Euclidean geometries

So far, I have said that substantival space has no effects other than inertial forces and (as a corollary) there is no way to distinguish between the two shifted universes that Leibniz imagines. But this is only true if Euclidean geometry, that is, the system of geometric axioms laid down by the ancient Greek Euclid, is true of our world. In particular, it requires the truth of the **parallel postulate**: that for any line and any point not on that line, there's only one line that can be drawn through that point that doesn't cross the original line. That one line is, of course, the line *parallel* to the original line. Draw a line anywhere else, and it'll cross the original one (see Figure 6.2).

For a long time, people thought the parallel postulate was incontrovertibly true. But then people developed **non-Euclidean geometries** where the postulate was false. The postulate only holds when we imagine geometries on a flat surface. If we picture instead drawing lines on a surface that isn't flat, the postulate turns out to be false. Imagine a sphere. If you draw a line on that sphere, and take another point off that line, then there isn't any straight line that fails to cross the original line (there are other lines but there aren't

Figure 6.2 The parallel postulate

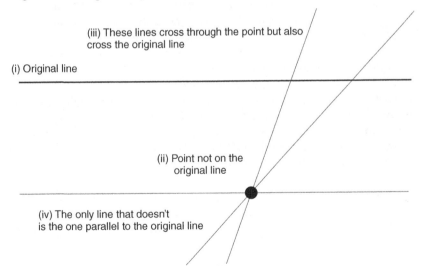

(iii) These lines cross through the point but also cross the original line

(i) Original line

(ii) Point not on the original line

(iv) The only line that doesn't is the one parallel to the original line

any *straight* lines for on a sphere the lines that don't cross the original always count as being curved). Indeed, on such spheres other geometrical principles fail, such as triangles having to have interior angles that add up to 180 degrees. That's true of triangles on a *flat* surface but not of triangles on curved surfaces (try it and see!).

Einstein's theory of general relativity indicated that spacetime might be non-Euclidean – that is, that it might be curved. If it was curved, we'd notice differences because of this. To see how it would make a difference, imagine the following situation. For simplicity, we'll only talk about regions of space and we'll imagine that space is two-dimensional rather than three-dimensional. This is a rather common move when discussing space and spacetime as it's much easier to imagine (and draw!) a two-dimensional region of space than it is to do the same for a four-dimensional region of spacetime. So commonly are such two-dimensional worlds used in examples that they even have a common name: such a world is a **flatland** (named after a book of the same name by Edwin Abbott, about two-dimensional people living in a two-dimensional world). What is made clear by flatland examples holds by analogy for three-dimensional regions of space and four-dimensional spacetimes, so flatland is a useful heuristic device.

Imagine a room in flatland that is 10 metres across. In the centre of the room is a 4 m × 4 m area with a curtain around it. If our flatlanders walked from one side of the room to the other, they'd cross 10 m if they avoided the curtained area (as shown by the bottom line in Figure 6.3a). If they walked *around* the curtain area, they'd have to walk a bit further as they deviated from their straight line, say 14 m (as depicted by the top line). But imagine that when a flatlander goes through the curtained area, she takes an awful long time to come out on the other side and, when she does, she insists that she's been walking the whole time. Refusing to believe her, a fellow flatlander goes in with a long tape measure or metre wheel. The same thing happens and, when he emerges and reaches the other wall, he measures the distance he travelled from one wall to the other, not at 10 m but at 50 m!

If space were curved, we would have an excellent explanation for what has taken place. Imagine that the area curtained off was deformed rather than flat, making a deep dip in the fabric of space itself (see Figure 6.3b). Now picture what would happen to the flatlanders who travelled through the curtain. They'd have to go all the way down one side of space and then come out of the trough on the other side. It would, certainly, take them a lot longer to

Figure 6.3 Non-Euclidean space

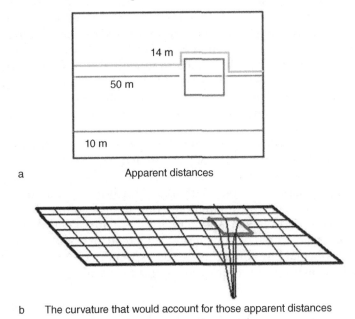

a   Apparent distances

b   The curvature that would account for those apparent distances

traverse from one side of the room to the other if they took this route. In such a world, the shape of space would have an explanatory role: the flatlanders would explain why it took them so long to travel certain places by saying that space existed and was shaped in a certain bizarre way in that region.

Einstein's theory of general relativity seems to indicate that the same is true of our world. So it goes, spacetime can be deformed by the presence of things like mass, and if you deform spacetime correctly, then you end up with similar effects. Whilst Einstein's deformations of spacetime are more complex than the above curtained-off area of flatland, the same idea holds – we might find that spacetime has an effect on us, and thus infer that it exists because of the shape it has in certain places. And, indeed, the predictions of Einstein's theory have been confirmed many times (although, as we shall see soon, there can be competing explanations to Einstein's).

The relationist still has options even at this stage. Whilst spacetime having a certain shape, and being warped, might explain certain phenomena, there are alternative explanations available. Henri Poincaré offered such an argument. Returning to flatland, Poincaré would say that there were certain laws of nature which meant that any object travelling through the zone covered by the curtain ended up shrinking. As it shrank, that would mean distances would *appear* to be larger even though, in fact, they were not. As you came out of the zone, the laws of nature would be such that objects expanded again until they were the same size at the other end. And as *everything* shrank and expanded when it went through the curtains, including light rays, even if you pulled the curtains away, you wouldn't see lots of tiny people; you'd see what appeared to be a huge stretch of space which objects (which appeared normal sized) took longer to traverse. Such a world of strange laws would be indistinguishable from one with a non-Euclidean geometry. So we have two competing explanations: one that is compatible with a relationist's anti-realism about regions but invokes lots of brute laws of nature versus a substantivalist's realism about regions that invokes normal laws but adds warped spacetime into our ontology. Exactly which you find more enticing, I leave up to you.

Ontological reductions

Reductions of regions

To end this chapter, put aside the question of substantivalism versus relationism, and ask what might be the case if substantivalism were true. Just as we can deploy ontological reductions if we are realists about possible worlds (are they sets of propositions? or disconnected spacetimes?), numbers (are they sets?), or holes (are they hole linings? or regions of space?) and so on, we can do the same in the case of substantivalism. We might commit to regions but reduce space to something else. I examine this option in this subsection. Alternatively, we might reduce other things to space (this is examined in the last subsection).

Some people are happy with the existence of regions but want to reduce them to something else. Regions, they say, exist but are not in an ontological category of their own (remember, moves like this are generally thought to relieve the pressure of ontological parsimony). One way is to identify regions with sets (so, once again, mathematical entities make an appearance). Start by introducing the notion of a **Cartesian coordinate system** which can be used to map space (and, yes, by 'Cartesian' we do mean 'introduced by Descartes' – he did more than evil demons and blobs of wax in his time). What coordinates to use depends upon what dimensions we are considering. If we were considering three-dimensional space, we'd use three (one for each axis of the dimension). If we were considering four dimensions – say we were considering a spacetime which has three dimensions of space and one of time – we'd use four numbers. Because it's easier, we'll again just imagine a two-dimensional flatland.

Each point in the flatland would be represented by two numbers – each number representing its position in one of the dimensions. One point is arbitrarily selected to be the 'origin' of the system, represented by 0,0. Places away from that origin are represented by positive or negative numbers giving their distance away from it, and you stipulate what each number represents. So we might stipulate that the unit of our coordinate system is the metre. So if a point was 2 metres in the eastwards direction of the origin, and 3 metres in the northwards direction, that point could be represented by 2,3. If it was 2 metres westwards of it and 4 metres north of it, that'd be represented with –2,4 (see Figure 6.4).

It's not hard to see how we might think a reduction of space to sets might proceed. Each point in flatland corresponds to a coordinate of two numbers. We can identify the point with a set of those numbers. So the point at 2,3 is identified with the set of 2 and 3, and the point at –2,4 is identified with the set of –2 and 4 (actually, normal sets don't recognize order, so the point at 2,3 would end up being identified with the point at 3,2. Fortunately we can introduce a type of set that *does* recognize order – what are called **ordered sets**, represented by using < > instead of { }. So the point at 2,3 would be <2,3> and the point at 3,2 would be <3,2>. Unlike ordinary sets, as the members of the ordered set are in a different order, they end up being distinct).

With the points identified with sets, regions are identified with sets of points that fall within that region. So the shaded region in Figure 6.4 is identified with the set of all of the points in that shaded region (of which, there'd be an infinite number). So every point ends up being an ordered set of numbers (which, as numbers might also be sets, might be an ordered set of other sets), and every region ends up a set of those ordered sets. Regions, then, end up being mathematical objects.

Figure 6.4 Cartesian coordinates

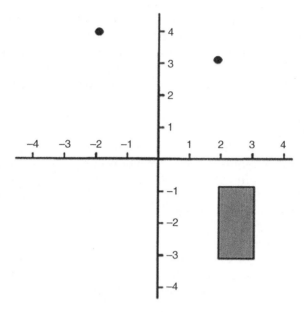

Reductions to regions

We can also go the other way around and reduce other things to regions (of which, we've seen examples already, such as holes in chapter 2). We'll end this chapter by just briefly discussing one further example: **supersubstantivalism**. This is the thesis that material objects – including things like you and me – are identical to regions. This should initially sound strange; after all, you wouldn't have thought that the toast you ate this morning, the bed you slept on or the lover you kissed last night are, in fact, regions of spacetime (Ted Sider makes the point by saying how strange it would be to say that a region of spacetime bounded out the door and barked at the postman). But, whilst it's a bit strange, there are reasons to believe supersubstantivalism. Obviously, it offers the benefits of ontological parsimony. Whereas an ontology of regions and distinct objects has two categories, an ontology where the objects are identified with regions of spacetime has but one category. It also offers ideological and explanatory benefits. Objects are located in certain places, e.g., the Eiffel Tower is exactly located at a particular region in Paris. If you believe in regions and objects as separate categories, then that relation appears to be a primitive – there's no way to analyse an object being at such-and-such a region. But the super-substantivalist, who thinks that objects just *are* the regions they are located at, can analyse away that relation: an object is exactly located at a region if and only if it *is* that region. Similarly, many people have pointed out that there are necessary connections between an object and regions:

- Objects always have the same size and shape as the region they occupy (it's not as if a cube could exactly occupy a spherical region!).
- Every object – every single one – occupies *some* region (none are left 'floating around', untethered from space and time).
- We tend to think that only one object can be located at a region at any given time (although see chapter 9).

We might take these facts as brute facts but we can 'up' the explanatory power of our theory if we accept supersubstantivalism. Now the explanation for the above is obvious:

- As objects just are the regions which they occupy, they must clearly have the same properties as it – including size and shape.
- As every object is a region, and an object is located at a region just in case it is that region, it follows that they *must* be in space and time.
- Clearly, two distinct objects cannot be in the same region as then two distinct things would be identical to the same thing, which is logically impossible.

Further, and in keeping with the metaontological theme of this chapter, people argue that contemporary physics demonstrates that supersubstantivalism is true, claiming that quantum physics or general relativity demand that objects are the regions that they inhabit (issues which are a tad too complex to go into here – see Further Reading for more detail).

Chapter summary

In this chapter, we have:

- introduced realism and anti-realism about regions of space (and spacetime). These are substantivalism and relationism respectively.

- examined Newton's bucket argument that acceleration must be relative to absolute space.
- examined Leibniz's shift argument for substantivalism having no explanatory power.
- examined non-Euclidean geometries where substantival regions have explanatory power.
- looked at ontological reduction and regions, either of regions to something else (mathematical objects) or something else to regions (material objects).

Further reading

One of the definitive introductions to the ontology of space is by Barry Dainton (2010). Other introductions worth looking at include those by Nick Huggett (1999), Tim Maudlin (2009) and E. Jonathan Lowe (2002), with more complex introductions by Graham Nerlich (2003), Lawrence Sklar (1992) and John Earman (1989). Relationists include Gordon Belot (1999) and Clifford Hooker (1971). Maudlin (1993) is a substantivalist, and Nerlich has written on the explanatory role of spacetime (1976, 1994). Another good, albeit complex, paper on the subject is Paul Teller's article (1991). For supersubstantivalism, Jonathan Schaffer (2009b) has written a paper on it, which also offers a comprehensive survey of the extant arguments.

7

Time

Over the next three chapters, we will look at the ontology of material objects. You might think this issue to be cut and dried; after all, isn't it obvious both that material objects exist and *which* material objects exist? What follows shows that an answer to the latter question isn't that straightforward. We start not by looking at whether things like chairs or tables exist (although that's the subject of the next chapter) but at whether or not things like dinosaurs, Chingiz Khan and outposts on Mars exist.

Realism about entities from other times

Intuitively, such things do not exist – or at least, I expect that to be your gut reaction. Isn't it straightforwardly obvious that there are no dinosaurs (for, unless you believe in the Loch Ness Monster, there aren't any to be found), that Chingiz Khan no longer exists and that – having looked at Mars carefully and seen that there are no aliens on it – there are no outposts on Mars. These things *did* exist (dinosaurs once roamed the earth and Chingiz Khan was once the ruler of a mighty empire) and *will* exist (for I shall optimistically assume for the purpose of discussion that we will build outposts on Mars) but, as they don't *currently* exist, then they don't exist at all. This position – that the only material objects which exist are those that presently exist – is called **presentism**. So the presentist is an anti-realist about things from other times (and this might include things other than objects, such as *events* like the Mongolian invasion of Europe or what have you, but we'll stick to just discussing objects).

This is not the only position available. One alternative is **eternalism**: that objects from all of those times exist. So not only do I exist, and you exist, and Barack Obama exists but so do the past things (the dinosaurs, Chingiz Khan, Napoleon, etc.) and the future things (people from future generations, outposts on Mars, the killer virus that wipes out humanity, etc.). Of course, the eternalist doesn't believe these things exist *now*. Sure enough, look wherever you want on our planet and you'll never find any dinosaurs, nor get a chance to meet Chingiz Khan. The eternalist isn't insane – he doesn't believe we can talk to the dead. Instead, the eternalist believes these things exist but are temporally removed from us in the same way that objects can exist even though they are spatially removed from us. Just as many things can exist without being here, and exist even though they are spatially distant from us, the eternalist thinks things can exist even though they're in the past or future and are separated by a gulf of time.

There are other positions besides presentism and eternalism. For instance, there is **growing block theory**: that objects from the past and present exist, but the future entities don't. So dinosaurs exist, as do you and I, but the outposts on Mars are excluded from the party – they don't exist, although one day they will (such as when we get around to building them). Thus, the world is like a block that is growing over time, getting bigger and bigger as more future entities come into existence, and then stay in existence even when they are no longer present. We could also imagine deviant theories such as Futurism (where only the present and future entities exist), or Biblicism (where only entities from the years 4004 BC onwards exists), or 1964ism (where only entities from 1964 exist). But we shall stick just with the standard two options of presentism and eternalism. I shall leave researching growing block theory to the interested reader (and you'll find the deviant theories are barely worth considering, except as foils and stalking horses).

In the ontology of time, the normal dialectic is that presentists assume that their position is intuitively true and leave it up to other people to convince them that they're wrong. I'll follow this format and examine arguments against presentism, with the working assumption that if presentism fails, then eternalism is true. There are two kinds of argument that are used against presentism. The first kind is purely metaphysical, with no empirical content whatsoever (what is sometimes called **armchair philosophy**, as one is trying to figure out what is true or false about the nature of reality without leaving the comfort of an armchair). During a discussion of this, we'll have a chance to see a new metaontological principle in play: truthmaking. The second kind of argument follows on from the thrust of the last chapter: it is empirically informed, showing how contemporary physics causes problems for presentism.

Singular propositions

Start with the purely metaphysical problems. First, introduce **singular propositions**: the propositions that are about some specific, single thing. So the following propositions (I give their logical form to clarify matters) *aren't* singular:

All men are mortal	$\forall x \,(\, x \text{ is a man} \rightarrow x \text{ is mortal} \,)$
There is a black pigeon	$\exists x \,(\, x \text{ is a pigeon} \,\&\, x \text{ is black} \,)$

whereas the following *are* singular:

Nikk Effingham is a lecturer	$F\,a$
Barack Obama is president of the USA	$G\,b$

(where what a, b, F and G stand for should be obvious).

So in the case of the first set of propositions, we're talking about things generally (e.g., *all* men), or some unspecific thing (e.g., *some* black pigeon), whereas the singular propositions are about some specific thing (e.g., myself or Barack Obama). (And, when translated into their logical form, it's easy to see which are singular: those propositions which feature a logical name, like a, b, c, etc., rather than quantifying over variables like x, y, z, etc. are singular propositions.)

Some singular propositions are about objects from the past:

Chingiz Khan once existed.
Napoleon was French.

So, the argument goes, this is a dead giveaway that Chingiz Khan, Napoleon and so forth exist. One reason to believe this would be the Quinean theory of ontological commitment. As noted all the way back in chapter 2, propositions involving names can be converted into sentences that quantify over things by means of 'definite descriptions'. For instance, to translate 'Chingiz Khan once existed' into its logical form, you might think you introduce a name, *a*, for Chingiz Khan and then attach it to the predicate '__ once existed' to get:

  a once existed.

Quine turns that into a definite description by dropping the reference to *a* and instead says that there is one thing that has all of the features that Chingiz Khan has (previously being called Temujin, having built Karakorum, having invaded China, etc.) where that entity exists to get:

$\exists x \, [\, (\, x$ used to be called Temujin & x built Karakorum & x invaded China & . . . & x once existed) & $(\, \forall y \, [\, y$ used to be called Temujin & y built Karakorum & y invaded China . . . $\rightarrow x = y \,] \,) \,]$

As we drop the name and replace it with a quantifier, we thereby quantify over past objects. Given the Quinean theory of ontological commitment, the value of that variable, i.e., Chingiz Khan, must exist. So presentism must be false (and presumably eternalism is true).

An alternative reason for thinking singular propositions are problematic begins by assuming, as some philosophers do, that propositions are complex metaphysical entities that are built up out of constituents. For instance, the constituents of a proposition like < Nikk Effingham is a lecturer > would be myself and, say, the property *being a lecturer*. Similarly, the proposition < Chingiz Khan once existed > is built up out of Chingiz Khan and the property *having once existed*. Now add that, in the same way that if a house exists and has bricks and mortar as parts, then it follows that the bricks and mortar must exist, the constituents of the proposition must exist. In that case, as < Chingiz Khan once existed > is a proposition, it follows that Chingiz Khan must exist (as too must the property *having once existed*).

In response to these problems, the presentist might argue that there are no propositions, or that they don't need to be 'built up' out of constituents like objects and properties (which, given that not everyone believes in properties, is far from absurd). With regard to the problem stemming from Quinean ontological commitment, they might offer up some sort of paraphrase for singular propositions that doesn't require reference to the past and future entities (having already looked at paraphrases for things from other categories, I leave it up to you to find and/or think of some). Alternatively, they might give up on the Quinean theory of ontological commitment. In any case, rather than continuing to debate the application of a metaontological theory we've already discussed, let's turn to a new theory for determining ontological commitment: truthmaking.

Truthmaking

Those who believe in truthmaking believe that for every true proposition there must be something that *makes* that proposition true. Those things that make propositions true are called **truthmakers**. So, for instance, I am the truthmaker for the proposition < Nikk Effingham exists > and Barack Obama is the truthmaker for the proposition < Barack Obama exists >; we are the things that make those propositions true.

It gets more complicated when we talk about propositions which don't just assert the existence of something. For instance, < Barack Obama is the president of the USA > is a true proposition, but truthmaker theorists tend not to think that it's made true by Barack Obama. The reason for this is that Barack Obama doesn't *necessitate* the truth of the proposition – he can exist and yet that proposition can be false (for, of course, he might have lost the presidential election). And truthmaker theorists almost always say that truthmaking is a relation that holds of necessity – that if X is a truthmaker for a proposition then, no matter what, if X exists, that proposition will be true. This principle is called **truthmaker necessitarianism** and (besides being a bit of a tongue-twister) is meant to guarantee that once you have listed what truthmakers there are, nothing else needs to be done to determine what things are true. So the truthmaker theorist imagines that if the metaphorical God of ontology wants to make a universe where certain things are the case, all he has to do is make the truthmakers. Once he's done that, every proposition has its truth value fixed and no more work remains to be done. So Barack Obama cannot, given that principle, be the truthmaker for the proposition about him being president, for God could have made Obama without having made him president. Instead, the truthmaker theorist says, we must commit to other entities to do the work.

The most popular such entities are David Armstrong's states of affairs (recall them from chapter 2). In addition to Barack Obama, Armstrong believes that there are states of affairs about Obama. For instance, there exists a state of affairs of 'Barack Obama being president of the USA'. States of affairs are the truthmakers for true propositions, as it is impossible for there to be a state of affairs of Obama being president without the proposition that he is president being true. Thus, we introduce a new category of entities to do the hard work. (An alternative would be to use tropes, also from chapter 2. If a trope is peculiar to its instance – so the 'presidential trope' that Barack Obama has is non-transferable and could only ever be *his* trope, whilst all of the other presidents have their own presidential tropes – then whenever the trope exists, it must be the case that Obama is president. So tropes could be truthmakers as well.)

Demonstrating that we must commit to states of affairs (or tropes) to account for true propositions is just one example of how truthmaking is deployed in deciding our ontological commitments. But its ramifications for ontology are meant to stretch further than just that. Truthmaking has its roots in debunking the theory of **phenomenalism**: that there are no material objects, and there is only sensory data. Given phenomenalism, there isn't, say, a table in front of me and there only exist the sensations of a table – that's the be all and end all of the explanation. Adding in objects *as well* is just pointless, says the phenomenalist. Similarly, if I look left I will see a picture of my family, to which the phenomenalist says it is just a brute fact that if I look left I will see a picture of my family. Most people do not find phenomenalism plausible, and truthmaker theorists think they have accurately identified why: the phenomenalist has no truthmaker for the fact that when I turn my head left I will see a picture of my family. The regular non-phenomenalist, however, does – the truthmaker would be the state of affairs of there being a picture, of there being me, and of the picture being to the left of me (as well as it being the case that I'm not sitting in the dark, etc.). Obviously, those states of affairs require objects to exist and phenomenalism to be false. So this hopefully gives you some idea of truthmaking theory's original motivations.

Similar worries affect presentism. If I say 'Chingiz Khan once existed', what makes that true? The eternalist says that both the sentence and Chingiz Khan exist, and that the truthmaker is the state of affairs of Chingiz Khan being earlier than the sentence by hundreds of years. The presentist, though, can't say this as Chingiz Khan doesn't exist, so there can't be a state of affairs involving him.

Or here's another way of thinking about it. The truthmaker theorist's metaphor is that God only has to create certain things in order to make everything true. But if God only made the presently existing things, that'd leave the truth of the sentence about Chingiz Khan undetermined. What presently exists could remain the same and yet it be false that Chingiz Khan existed. Maybe some scurrilous scribe in the thirteenth century wrote fabulous tales about a famous Mongolian warlord that, over time, people mistook for truth. We might end up in exactly the same situation now, with exactly the same entities presently existing, and yet that sentence about the past would be false. So it seems that thinking that only the presently existing entities exist riles the very core of the truthmaking enterprise.

Denying truthmaker theory

The presentist has a wide variety of responses to pick from. Obviously, the presentist might not sign up to a theory of truthmaking. Like the Quinean theory of ontological commitment, the jury is still out on whether it's true (oh, and as you're reading this book, welcome to the jury). They might try and argue against truthmaking theory on the grounds that it has problems of its own. The truthmaker theorist tends to believe that *every* true proposition needs a truthmaker, and none get off the hook (a principle called **truthmaker maximalism**). But some propositions prove incredibly problematic to find truthmakers for, e.g., < There are no unicorns >. This proposition is true, but it's not obvious what would be a truthmaker for it. As with holes, in chapter 2, it seems strange to think that an 'absence' exists – a 'lack of unicorns' – to make true that there are no unicorns.

Truthmaker theorists might respond by weakening truthmaker maximalism. Perhaps they'll say that not all propositions need truthmakers – perhaps the 'negative' propositions get off the hook. Only if a proposition asserts that something *is* the case do they need truthmakers; if they say what is *not* the case (e.g., that there *aren't* any unicorns), then they don't need a truthmaker. The truthmaker theorist would, of course, have to get clear on exactly what counts as a positive and negative proposition. However, if they do this, then the presentist can probably remedy their own truthmaker issues. If it is okay for *some* propositions to lack truthmakers, the presentist might want to expand the number of propositions in that position. In the same way that only certain propositions need truthmakers, which doesn't include those about how the world is not, the presentist may say that they don't need truthmakers for how the world was or will be. After all, generally speaking, how the world was or will be is also a way that the world isn't. So if we can restrict truthmaking theory in one area, to avoid problems with negative truths, the presentist may argue that we can restrict it so we don't have any problems with temporal truths. Given this, truthmaker theorists tend to want to leave truthmaker maximalism untouched (and so have to find truthmakers for the 'negative' propositions, the details of which I will leave to the interested reader to research).

Alternative truthmakers

Alternatively, the presentist may embrace the truthmaker's challenge and try to find truthmakers for the past and future truths that don't require the past and future things to exist. For instance, we might say that when Chingiz Khan died, a state of affairs came into being – the state of affairs of him being dead – and that this has hung around ever since. That state of affairs, then, makes true the proposition < Chingiz Khan once existed >. But truthmaker theorists tend to think that these states of affairs are suspicious in some way. Exactly what is suspicious about them will be a good, and difficult to answer, question for the truthmaker theorist – but the gist of the worry is that states of affairs shouldn't 'float free' of the things that they are states *of*. In the same way that metaphysicians think that singular propositions about a particular thing demand that the particular thing exist, Chingiz Khan must exist in order for there to be a state of affairs about him. We might be motivated to believe this because we think that Chingiz Khan is a constituent of the state of affairs – he makes it up in the same way that a table top makes up a table, and therefore requires the table top to exist. (Look back at chapter 2 where we discussed a similar issue with regard to properties existing.)

Further, were we to allow in such states of affairs, we would undo all the good work that truthmaking is meant to achieve. If, when faced with propositions that were apparently true but were tricky to find truthmakers for, we simply allowed that we can introduce any old state of affairs to be its truthmaker, then truthmaking will never be able to play a serious role in deciding between ontological theories. For instance, it would no longer be able to rule out, say, phenomenalism. With regard to the counterfactual proposition:

> < If I looked left, I would have a wall-like phenomenal experience >

the phenomenalist *could* find truthmakers for that proposition if we allowed in such dubious states of affairs like 'Chingiz Khan once existed'. If we can have *that* state of affairs, then why not have a state of affairs of it being such that if Nikk Effingham looked left, Nikk would have a wall-like phenomenal experience? Given the existence of that state of affairs, the counterfactual is necessarily true and therefore the state of affairs looks like it can be a truthmaker for the propositions that phenomenalists were meant to find tricky. So if truthmaking theory is to carry the methodological burden it is intended to shoulder – of eliminating metaphysical theories that somehow cut corners they shouldn't cut (e.g., phenomenalism) – there needs to be some way to restrict what does or does not count as an acceptable state of affairs. And that had better disqualify both states of affairs, such as what sensations I would have if I looked left as well as Chingiz Khan having once existed.

The presentist might say that this is all a bit murky, and until the truthmaker theorist can lay down compelling criteria for what does, or does not, count as an acceptable truthmaker, she or he will ignore any alleged problems with truthmaking. But as we're meant to be imagining a presentist amiable to truthmaking, who is unlikely to be bull-headed on this issue, let's assume that the truthmaker theorist is right to disqualify the existence of such states of affairs. Instead, they must find more sensible truthmakers for the past truths. One possibility might be to invoke **distributional properties** as truthmakers for past and present truths. Imagine I have a Scottish kilt that is tartan. The truthmaker for that is, presumably, the state of affairs of the kilt being tartan. That sounds reasonable enough. But the property *being tartan* tells us how the qualities of an object vary across space; it is a property that tells us about how colour is distributed across the entire kilt. A particular tartan property might, for instance, entail that the kilt is green in one place (say, the lines running down the tartan) and red in another (say the main background of the tartan). If you knew exactly which tartan I was talking about, then you'd know the varying colours of the tartan object in intricate detail.

We could imagine distributional properties being deployed to help the presentist. We'd first have to imagine that there could be distributional properties that didn't just tell us what an object was like across a certain area of space but throughout a certain stretch of time. For instance, imagine a man having the property of *being a toddler and then later an older man*. That property would be a distributional property across his lifetime. In the same way that instantiating *being tartan* tell us that the object is green in one place and red in another (or whatever colours correspond to the tartan in question), *being a toddler and then later an older man* tells us that the person who instantiates that property was, earlier in time, a toddler and is later an older man. That property doesn't tell us exactly how the man is at every moment during his life (in the same way that the property *being tartan* doesn't tell you everything about a kilt, for it entails nothing about, say, the kilt's mass or shape) but we can imagine distributional properties that are more detailed, and that instantiating them entails everything about the object that instantiates them. Indeed, we can imagine the entire universe having a distributional property that is so complex that it entails everything about the universe, and all of its contents, at every moment that it exists. The state of affairs of the universe instantiating that property can do all of the truthmaking work. For instance, the universe could instantiate a distributional property so complex that it entails how the universe was billions of years ago, and that the universe was distributed in such a way that it contained nothing but tiny subatomic particles back then (and so that state of affairs makes true the proposition < It was the case billions of years ago that there was nothing but subatomic particles >), as well as entailing that our time is as it is now (and so the state of affairs can necessitate all of the propositions about how the world is at the moment). Similarly for the future. And unlike Chingiz Khan and the state of affairs of his having once existed, which exists without the Khan himself, the state of affairs of the world instantiating a certain distributional property never exists without either the property or the world (as the world *always* exists). Distributional properties, then, might be able to play the truthmaking role, and the presentist who endorses truthmaking theory has at least one avenue he can pursue if he wants to have a theory consistent with a truthmaker's scruples.

Special relativity

A brief introduction to the special theory of relativity

For the rest of the chapter, let's set aside the purely metaphysical reasons for endorsing presentism and return to trying to settle onto-logical questions using contemporary science. When it comes to the presentism/eternalism debate, the scientific theory that is most rel-evant is Einstein's **special theory of relativity** (STR) which entails that simultaneity is relative to one's inertial frame of reference. Not sure what those words mean? Let me explain.

Start with the fact that things look different depending upon what frame of reference you are in. If you are standing close to the Empire State Building, it will tower over you, whereas if you are far away from it, it looks small. Simply put, as you vary your frame of reference, how things look will likewise vary. An **inertial frame of reference** is a frame of reference specifically concerned with your velocity. Recall from the last chapter that your velocity is always relative to other things. On a train hurtling across the countryside, you will appear stationary relative to the passenger sat opposite you but in quick-moving motion relative to people stood in the fields outside. Crudely, when you are travelling at a different veloc-ity relative to something, you are in a different inertial frame of reference. When you are stationary relative to something, you are in the same inertial frame of reference.

Further, recall from the last chapter that I said you cannot deter-mine what your absolute velocity is and therefore, no matter where you are, you cannot tell whether you are 'truly' moving or whether you are 'truly' stationary. But in the mid-nineteenth-century, a phys-icist called James Clerk Maxwell published a paper on electrody-namics that seemed, at first, to indicate the exact opposite. The specifics won't interest us, only that he proved that the speed of light was ~300,000 kilometres per second (which we'll represent by the normal symbol for such a thing: c). Interestingly, the value of c wasn't measured from a particular inertial frame, it was simply *the* velocity of light. So, it seemed, physicists could now figure out anything's absolute velocity. All we had to do was measure the velocity of light from our inertial frame of reference. If light was, say, going at ~200,000 km/s then, as we know that the true, absolute velocity of light is c, we would know we were travelling at

~100,000 km/s in the direction the light was travelling (and similarly for whatever other speed light was measured at). The universe, it seemed, had given us a clue to figuring out the absolute velocity of things.

So, in 1887, Albert Michelson and Edward Morley conducted an experiment, the **Michelson–Morley experiment**, to find out the relative speed of light in order to calculate the absolute velocity of earth and its inhabitants. They discovered that the speed of light from our inertial frame of reference was . . . *c*. So, by the above logic, the earth was in the rest frame. How remarkably unlikely! Of all the velocities the planet could have been travelling at, the chance of it happening to be the one at absolute rest is ridiculously small. But Michelson and Morley realized it was stranger still. The earth's velocity changes as it goes around the sun (since it's orbiting the sun, it is changing direction and therefore changing velocity). In the same way that my velocity relative to you will change as I accelerate and decelerate, the velocity of light should have changed as the earth orbited the sun. But this never happened! No matter where the experiment was conducted, the speed of light was exactly the same. That seemed totally absurd. To demonstrate the absurdity, imagine the situation where you stand on the pavement watching Ms Fast driving off at 5 m/s and Mr Slow sat stationary in his car. Imagine that as Ms Fast passes Mr Slow, he slams the accelerator down. Further, imagine that Ms Fast keeps moving away from him at 5 m/s. No matter how hard Mr Slow pushes his car, Ms Fast is always advancing away that bit faster. It's easy to see how this could happen: if Ms Fast uses her accelerator just as Mr Slow does and to exactly the same extent, she'll continue to travel at 5 m/s relative to him. Now imagine what it looks like from *your* perspective. You'll see *both* Mr Slow and Ms Fast accelerating, faster and faster, with Ms Fast's velocity getting ever bigger, even as Mr Slow tries to catch up. That is how we naturally think of velocity as working, but light obeys no such laws. Bizarrely, light always travels at a constant velocity *c* from *everyone's* inertial frame of reference. That's like Mr Slow speeding up, Ms Fast *still* going faster than him from his perspective, but from *your* perspective Ms Fast *doesn't* have an increasing velocity and only goes at 5 m/s throughout. That just sounds crazy! How can Mr Slow accelerate and yet from both his perspective and your perspective, Ms Fast never changes her velocity, advancing forwards at 5 m/s from both your viewpoint and Mr Slow's? The Michelson–Morley experiment demonstrated light was just like this.

The solution was to introduce something called **Lorentz contractions**. The idea was that, if you moved faster, then, amongst other things, time appeared to slow down. So imagine now that Ms Fast is travelling at *c*. Mr Slow accelerates to 0.5 *c* (a whopping 150,000 km/s!) and follows her. From your perspective, on the pavement side, Mr Slow will have traversed 150,000 km over the course of one second, whilst Ms Fast would have traversed 300,000 km – and so should have a velocity, relative to Mr Slow, of 150,000 km/s from your frame of reference. But imagine that time slowed down for Mr Slow because he was going so fast, such that it's now running at half the rate. So during what you think is a second, Mr Slow will see Ms Fast travel 150,000 km ahead of him. But as time has slowed down for Mr Slow, according to his watch only half a second has elapsed. So when Mr Slow calculates Ms Fast's velocity relative to him he calculates her velocity as . . . *c* (for she's travelled 150,000 km in 0.5 seconds, so is travelling at 300,000 km/s)! So, if time slowed down the faster you go, it's possible for everyone to think that Ms Fast is travelling at the same velocity relative to them. The idea is that something very similar to this goes on with objects in our universe and accounts for the bizarre phenomenon Michelson and Morley witnessed. The actual story is more complicated than this (as time does not only slow down, but the objects gain mass and change shape as well, and the numbers given here are made up – time does not slow down by half when travelling at 0.5 *c*, and Lorentz contractions only become apparent at *very* high velocities) but this should be enough for you to get an idea of what's going on.

All of this has been observed, so we know that these Lorentz contractions take place. For instance, some particles have a very short half-life – they decay and cease to exist very quickly. But when travelling at high speed, they decay much more slowly, as if time were slowed down from their point of view, in exact accordance with Lorentz's predictions. Obviously, we don't notice it most of the time, but that's because this phenomena only kicks in at very high velocities approaching the speed of light. Such velocities rarely bother any of us (although things like GPS have to take account of this kind of thing, otherwise they would slowly stop working).

Now enter Einstein. The special theory of relativity was meant to explain why these Lorentz contractions took place. All we had to do was make the bold move of accepting that the relation of simultaneity was relative to our inertial frame of reference. For example, this would mean that one event being simultaneous with another (say,

Johnny Depp's birth being simultaneous with the 1963 Icelandic election) isn't true for everyone and varies depending on one's inertial frame (so for Mr Slow they might be simultaneous whilst for Ms Fast they aren't, and one is later than the other). Einstein achieves this by redefining simultaneity. To get a grip on his definition, and how it relativizes simultaneity, imagine that we start a stopwatch when we shine a beam of light at another event, and when the beam returns we stop the stopwatch (and, as the light has bounced back, we also see what event it was shone at). Take the time elapsed on the stopwatch and call it T. The event we are now seeing took place, says Einstein, at $\frac{1}{2}T$. For example, imagine you shine a beam of light at an asteroid blowing up over the earth, and by the time it returns two seconds have elapsed (which means that the asteroid's blowing up is 300,000 kilometres away, so we should be fairly safe from any debris!). Assuming, as Einstein does, that light moves at the same speed in every direction, the light beam took as long to get to the asteroid as it did to get back (which was two seconds). Einstein's definition says that the event took place half that time ago – that is, that it took place one second ago. (So if you started the watch, scratched your head after a second and then a second later saw the asteroid blowing up, the scratching of your head was simultaneous with the asteroid blowing up. See Figure 7.1a.)

From Einstein's definition, it follows that things in different inertial frames (that is, travelling at a velocity different from you) will register different answers as to when something is simultaneous. Imagine you and your friend both shine a light at the asteroid and start a stopwatch, but then your friend leaves in a spaceship at high speed. As your friend moves away from the asteroid, it takes slightly longer for the beam of light to return to him. Let's say it takes three seconds for the light to bounce back to his spaceship. Half of that interval is 1.5 seconds, so it's the event that took place when his stopwatch read 1.5 seconds (say, his sneezing) that is simultaneous with the asteroid blowing up (see Figure 7.1b). Note also that, whilst you think your friend thinks his sneezing is at the same time as the asteroid blowing up, and you think it's at the same time as you scratch your head, you think that his sneezing comes *after* you scratch your head. His moving away from you at high velocity – being in a different inertial frame of reference – means the two of you have to disagree over what things are simultaneous with what other things.

But this means that if something is going at a high velocity relative to you, then you'll think time is slowing down for your friend.

Figure 7.1 Simultaneity according to Einstein

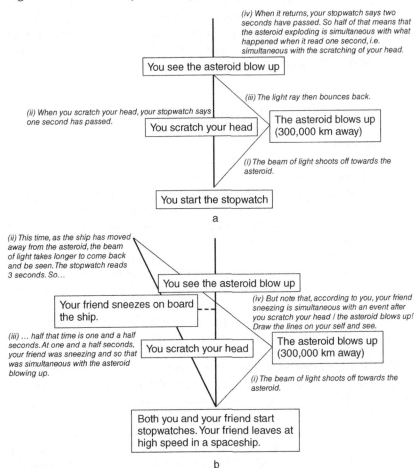

He thinks the asteroid blew up 1.5 seconds after he left in a space-ship – you think it was only one second. If he had left in an even faster spaceship, then he might think hours elapsed between his leaving and the asteroid blowing up. Indeed, as we imagine the spaceship leaving at velocities arbitrarily close to *c*, we can imagine arbitrarily long periods of time elapsing (from the ship's crew's point of view) between its leaving and the asteroid exploding. So Einstein's redefinition of simultaneity entails the weird effects of the

Lorentz contractions – when one thing is moving at a high velocity relative to something else, events appear to go slower relative to the other party. (Again, the contractions are more complex, involving change in shape and mass; Einstein's redefinition can account for these too, but we'll ignore those details in favour of the more salient issue of time dilation.)

STR and presentism

It's not hard to see how this might cause problems for presentism. According to presentism, only presently existing things exist. That seems to be synonymous with saying that all and only the things that are simultaneous with us exist. But if STR is true, then what things are simultaneous with us vary depending upon our inertial frame so what *exists* depends upon what inertial frame we are in (crudely, what exists depends upon how fast we're going). But it seems bizarre to think that what exists depends upon how fast you're going. It runs roughshod over other intuitive beliefs as well. If you exist from my point of view, and something else exists from my point of view, it seems natural to think that the something in question also exists from your point of view (i.e., that the 'exists for' relation is transitive). It seems odd to think that it's true for me that both Ms Fast and Mr Slow exist but, from Mr Slow's point of view, only I exist. Given STR, however, such situations can come about just as long as all three things are in different inertial frames of reference (i.e., travelling at different velocities). Some people think that this spells the end for presentism. Contemporary science, they say, rules out presentist theories (certainly Einstein was an eternalist, going as far as telling people at funerals to bear in mind that their deceased loved ones still exist, just not anywhere temporally local to them). Presentists, though, have fought back and do have some replies open to them.

First, presentists might say that STR is a somewhat speculative theory, and hope for a superior scientific theory to take its place – one that doesn't require the relativity of simultaneity. I don't mean that they simply hope that Einstein was wrong in the way that homeopaths or creationists are wrong – presentists aren't ignorantly flying in the face of established science. Rather, they try and play on existing scientific concerns about the theory in question. For instance, relativity appears to be inconsistent with quantum mechanics. Certain resolutions of this conflict, produced by contemporary physicists, involve giving up on Einstein's theory and reintroducing absolute simultaneity. Whilst not overwhelmingly popular, the presentist may say that we're too quick in thinking that contemporary science has delivered the final word on the matter and shown their theory to be false. As this is clearly more physics than metaphysics, we'll say no more about this option.

Second, some presentists have produced alternative theories of their own which allegedly have as much explanatory power as STR, but in which simultaneity is absolute rather than relative. All of the variations along this line assume that there is a matter of fact as to which events are simultaneous with which other events but admit that, because of things like Lorentz contractions, you'll never know exactly which events they are. This is somewhat like the situation Newton finds himself in with absolute space: there is a matter of fact as to whether you are in motion or not relative to unmoving absolute space, but there is no experiment that can tell you whether this is the case. The presentist may think likewise of our world: there is a matter of fact as to whether one event is simultaneous with another but, because of Lorentz contractions, there's no experiment which we can conduct to tell us what the facts of the matter are. The big problem is that we now posit things that are, in theory, untestable. The facts about simultaneity can never be proved one way or another. But some presentists, such as Michael Tooley, reply that even Einstein had to make untestable assumptions. Look back at his definition of simultaneity. The event is only simultaneous with the event that took place at half the elapsed time on the stopwatch given the *assumption* that light travels at the same speed in every direction. But there's no way to test that assumption, and light might go at varying speeds depending upon what direction it goes in (although it would always *appear* to be going at the same speed). So, as Einstein's theory has untestable assumptions, maybe it's not so bad that the presentist does too.

Third, the presentist might bite the bullet. They can say that what exists *does* depend upon what inertial frame of reference you are in. They then must deny that the resulting theory is too crazy to be believable. They might say that it is STR which is responsible for the weirdness, not presentism. STR itself has lots of weird ramifications; pointing at just another of its weird ramifications, and complaining that it's weird that what exists depends upon your inertial frame of reference, is just flogging a dead horse. Blame Einstein and the physical theory for this counter-intuitive result – don't blame the presentist and his ontological theory!

There are, then, still options for the presentist even in the face of contemporary physics. Whilst it is clear that contemporary science has some bearing on this debate in the ontology of objects, it is not a foregone conclusion that presentism is false and eternalism is true. As always, I leave you to investigate this further on your own.

Chapter summary

In this chapter, we have:

- introduced the different theories about time: presentism, eternalism and (more briefly) the growing block theory.
- introduced another theory of ontological commitment: truthmaking.
- introduced two purely metaphysical motivations for thinking that eternalism is true: issues about singular propositions and truthmakers.
- introduced the special theory of relativity and looked at how it might cause problems for the presentist.

Further reading

Further introductions to these issues include those by E. Jonathan Lowe (2002), Thomas Crisp (2003) and Michael Rea (2003). Ned Markosian (2004) is the definitive starting point concerning singular propositions and time. Gonzalo Rodriguez-Pereyra (2006) and Jonathan Tallant (2011) are both good introductions to truthmaking (indeed, Tallant's book deploys truthmaking in a wide variety of areas other than the ontology of time). David Armstrong's 2004 book is a more complex monograph about truthmaking in general, including motivating eternalism. The specific case of using distributional properties to help out presentism is defended by Ross Cameron in his 2011 article (with distributional properties discussed more generally by Josh Parsons (2004)) and other alternative theories of truthmakers are examined by Simon Keller (2004). Attacks on truthmaking, particularly regarding its use in arguing for eternalism, have been advanced by Trenton Merricks (2007) and Dean Zimmerman (2008).

The material on special relativity is harder, although a good chapter on the issues is by Katherine Hawley (2009). More extensive introductions are those by William Lane Craig (2001) and Lawrence Sklar (1992). The issues are further discussed by Craig Bourne (2006) and Ted Sider (2001), and reconciling special relativity with the growing block theory is discussed by Michael Tooley (1997). And if you're interested in philosophers challenging what physicists say, with particular reference to relativity, you should read Bradley Monton (2011).

8

Mereology

Mereology is the logic of parts and wholes (it stems from *meros*, the Greek for 'part'). It is concerned with any kind of parthood relation, such as the parts of a week (e.g., days); parts of the number series (e.g., the natural numbers); or, more directly of interest to the metaphysician, parts of things like structural universals. However, metaphysicians tend to concentrate on the mereology of material objects, and this chapter follows that focus. Indeed, we'll concentrate mainly on just one mereological relation: **composition**. This chapter introduces you to the basics of mereology and the varying positions concerning the composition of material objects. Near the end of the chapter, we will again introduce metaontological issues, and look at 'Neo-Carnapianism' – a theory which says that all of these questions, in fact much of ontology, is merely a verbal confusion.

A crash course in mereology

First, let's introduce mereology and some of the terminology involved. We'll need a primitive to begin with and shall use **proper parthood**. This notion gels, more or less, with how you use the word 'parthood' in natural English. So your hand, your eye, your lower half, various atoms and so on are all proper parts of you. It's prefaced by the word 'proper' because (for reasons we won't concern ourselves with here) an **improper part** of something is defined as being the thing itself – so you are an improper part of yourself (and the Taj Mahal is an improper part of itself, and the Eiffel Tower is an improper part of itself, etc.), whereas to say something is just a 'part' is, in mereology, to simply say that something is either a proper or an improper part. This distinction between an improper and a proper part will likely strike you as unnecessary – and, indeed, it rarely comes into play – but it's worth being aware of, especially as metaphysicians routinely deploy this terminology in their published papers and you are likely to come across it in your independent research.

We can define different relations in terms of parthood. For instance, we can define what it is for two things to overlap by saying:

x and y overlap = $_{df}$ there is a z which is a part of both x and y.

Better yet, we can define the relation of composition. That is the relation that holds between lots of things and the thing that they compose, e.g., my atoms compose me; bricks and mortar compose a house; an electron and a proton compose a hydrogen atom; parts of an Ikea flatpack compose a bedside table and so on. The definition for composition is:

The xs compose y = $_{df}$ (i) each x is a part of y; (ii) no two of the xs overlap; and (iii) every part of y overlaps at least one of the xs.

Note that it is true of many different pluralities of things that they compose the same thing. So not only am I composed of a bunch of atoms, but I'm also composed of my top half and my bottom half. And I am also composed of my head, limbs and torso. But I am not composed of, say, my head and arms, for there is more to me than merely my head and arms – the things I am composed of must account for *all* of me, not just bits of me. Just to be terminologically gratuitous, metaphysicians have coined special names for the composite objects. Sometimes they are called **mereological sums** or sometimes **mereological fusions**, or simply 'sum' or 'fusion' (just to be *really* annoying, some metaphysicians use the term 'sum' or 'fusion' solely for composite objects that are composed of the xs *and* have those xs as parts essentially – that is, the sums cannot change their parts, or survive the loss of their parts. Be aware of these uses).

The special composition question

Intuitively, some things compose other things; after all, you think that you are composed of atoms and that, say, your bed is composed of bits and pieces from the flatpack used to put it together. But it's also intuitive that some things don't compose anything at all. You and I, for instance, don't compose anything; there is no object that has just you and I as parts. So there is no four-armed, four-legged being with two brains that is in two separate locations at the same time. Maybe if you glued us together, or attached us in some way in the vein of a hideous horror film, we might compose a further object – but as this has not happened, we do not compose anything. Or another example: take all of the toilets in New York and the cast of *Friends*. Those things don't compose anything either. What a weird object that would be! Call these things, these crazy objects that intuitively don't exist, **gerrymandered objects**.

So it seems intuitive that sometimes some things compose a further thing, and sometimes they do not. Peter van Inwagen raised the question of when such composition takes place. This is called the **special composition question** (SCQ for short): What are the necessary and jointly sufficient conditions that any *y*s must satisfy at time *t* in order for it to be the case that there is an object composed of those *y*s at time *t*? Or, more straightforwardly, under what conditions do some things compose some further thing? We will look at three varieties of response to the SCQ. We'll, briefly, examine restricted answers which say that sometimes composition takes place and sometimes it doesn't – that is, an answer which attempts to bear out our intuitions. But it turns out that, whilst I kept saying that such an answer is intuitive, metaphysicians are strongly attracted to denying it and instead say either that composition always takes place (so that things like the weird toilet–*Friends* object exist!) or that it never takes place (and there are no composite objects at all!).

Restricted composition

Start, then, with an answer trying to secure our intuitions. Finding an answer that bears out our intuitions is actually quite tricky. For instance, one candidate is:

> *Contact*: The *y*s compose a further object if and only if they stand in the contacting-relation to one another

where you are in the 'contacting-relation' with something if you're touching it (so if we shake hands, we're touching), or you're touching something that's touching it (so if I shake hands with you, and you shake hands with Barack Obama at the same time, we're all in contact with one another), or you're touching something that's touching something that's touching it (so if Obama then shakes hands with George Bush at the same time, we are, again, all in contact with one another) or . . . well, you get the idea. *Contact*, then, might be a good answer to the SCQ. Certainly, there's something intuitive about the idea that the toilets in New York and the cast of *Friends* don't compose because they are separated from one another and aren't in contact with one another, whereas my body parts, being in contact with one another, do compose. *Contact*, then, seems somewhat intuitive.

But there are problems. First, nothing actually ever touches. If we take physics seriously, everything only ever gets quite *close* to another thing. Second, it seems to miss out certain objects. Don't the stars compose a galaxy? And they're *really* far apart! Third, it seems to include some objects that intuitively don't exist. Just go back to you and I shaking hands. Given *Contact*, a new object pops into existence as soon as we do that. That doesn't sound right! So *Contact* doesn't quite fit the bill. We might modify it slightly. For example, we might say that it's more to do with the forces binding the objects together. If objects are fastened to one another in a certain way – say by superglue or by the laws of gravity – then they compose a further object. Again, the toilets and cast of *Friends* aren't appreciably bound to one another by any force, so fail to compose. And, this time, the stars do compose a galaxy, as they are bound to one another by gravity. And, this time, you and I don't compose a further object just by shaking hands as we're not stuck to one another. But this new answer is itself open to further counter-examples. For instance, if I accidentally had a small blob of glue on my hand when I shook yours, it does seem a little weird that this small blob of glue causes an object to pop into existence! So trying to get an answer that mimics our intuitions will be a tricky task indeed (although more can be said in favour of these stock answers – references can be found in the Further Reading section). Of course, this is not the end of the world. Maybe the task is just harder than we thought, and it'll take some time to get the correct restricted answer (indeed, the answer might be impossible to find – this position is discussed by Karen Bennett). Or perhaps there's *no* informative answer to the SCQ, and which things compose and which don't is just a matter of brute fact, with no rhyme or reason that we can capture by laying out some necessary and sufficient conditions (this is the position of Ned Markosian). However, not only is this a cost with regard to the overall explanatory power of the theory you end up with, there are some arguments which set out to demonstrate that any restricted answer to the SCQ is false. It is to those arguments that we now turn.

Against restricted composition

The argument from cultural prejudice

Some cultures believe in a plethora of deities ruling the cosmos (e.g., Hindu cultures) – others do not. Some cultures have believed that human sacrifice was morally permissible (e.g., the Aztecs) – others did not. Some cultures have believed that the universe began about 15 billion years ago (e.g., contemporary western culture) – some others do not. Either from ignorance, a refusal to accept the truth or by an alternative reading of the known facts, cultures vary over what they generally believe. Cultural beliefs also vary concerning what material objects there are. By this, I don't mean that they vary over whether, say, there are things like dragons (for, sure enough, some cultures have previously thought that there were and now we tend not to). Instead, I am concerned with cultural variation of a different sort. Consider the following examples:

Example 1 Sirloin steak is a particular cut of beef from a cow. Presumably you believe that there are sirloin steaks in the world. But not every culture cuts the beef in the same way. Whilst Anglo-Americans have sirloin cuts, the French do not – the sirloin is not a proper cut of a dead cow. But that cut of meat is an object so (one might argue) the Anglo-Americans believe in an object (sirloin steak) that the French do not. There is cultural variation over what objects exist!

Example 2 We might think that a country is just a special type of material object – a really large object made mainly of dirt and stone and soil. But there is cultural variation over what countries there are. For instance, western society recognizes the existence of Israel and Cyprus. But these claims are politically contentious and some cultures don't recognize the existence of Israel and Cyprus. Conversely, some people recognize the existence of countries western society does not, for instance the country of Transnistria (if you've never heard of it, that's not surprising given that we don't count it as a country!) So there is cultural variation concerning what countries there are and, if countries are just objects, then there is a cultural variation over what objects exist!

Example 3 We can think of (eminently plausible) fictional examples. Imagine a man from a tribe of people untouched by civilization. Where we see, say, a caravan hooked up to a car – and see two things – he might fail to distinguish between the two. Where we say there are two things – caravan plus car – he might say there is but one thing (for which he would not, as yet, have a name for).

Example 4 Indeed, there are non-fictional examples along the same lines. Take a yam (which is a type of vegetable). For westerners, a yam grows, ripens and then (if it's not eaten) rots away. But not everyone sees things in the same way; in the Trobriander Islands, we find people who won't say that. They live on an island where a big part of the diet is the yam (so much so that the mild contraceptive effects of eating yams means that islanders routinely fell pregnant when they visited nearby islands that didn't have yams growing on them, which led to the islanders forming a myth that there were spirits on those islands that made you pregnant). Their language is very different, and they don't have a word that corresponds to 'yam'. Instead, they have 'taytu' and 'yowanna'. The 'taytu' corresponds to an object that we would think of as an unripened yam. The 'yowanna' corresponds to an object that we would think of as the ripened yam. But the Trobrianders talk as if these two things are very different – so where we see a yam ripening and continuing to exist, they see a 'taytu' ripening which then ceases to exist and is replaced by a totally different object, the 'yowanna'. Again, then, there is cultural variation over what exists. (And it is not so strange for them to talk of objects ceasing to exist and new objects coming into being in this way, for many people think the same thing happens to people, e.g., for a long time a person exists and then, upon death, they cease to exist and where they were we find, instead, a corpse. The 'yowanna' and 'taytu' appear to be very similar.)

Example 5 We can also imagine extending this list with ever more exotic examples. We could imagine, for instance, an alien race coming to earth. Their leader lands and says 'Lo! Take us to the Flergbet, for we have travelled far and it is holy.' When we ask what a 'Flergbet' is, they explain that it's that object composed out of all of the toilets in New York and the cast of *Friends*. The aliens believe in the Flergbet, and we do not.

With this in mind, the **argument from cultural prejudice** goes something like this. If composition was restricted but everyone's intuitions about what existed were more or less in line with one another, perhaps we wouldn't have a problem. But they are not in line with one another, as the examples show, and there's no clear way to resolve who is right and who is wrong. Whilst we can resolve certain disputes about what objects exist, the above disputes are not of that sort. For instance, if we met people who said 'Demons inhabit the mountain over there' or 'There exists a race of space goats that fly through space watching over us,' we could resolve that kind of dispute. Once we go over to the mountainside and show that there are no horned, tailed, red-skinned monsters, or looked through a telescope and saw that space was very much goatless, the disagreement would be resolved in our favour. But the divisions above are nothing like this, for both sides are broadly in agreement over what the world is like (e.g., they agree that a particular region of space has a vegetable in it, they just disagree over whether or not it's a 'taytu' or a yam). And no matter how hard we look, or what device we might use, no empirical resolution appears to be forthcoming. Even if we had the world's most powerful microscope, we won't see a magical particle which appears when some things compose. There is no 'compositron' that latches onto our atoms when they compose us but which fails to latch onto the toilets of New York and the cast of *Friends*. There is nothing we can look at, or test, to see whether composition takes place. So, were composition restricted, there'd be no empirical method to tell which things composed and which didn't. In fact (goes the argument), it'd be sheer prejudice to think that you have got it right and everyone else has got it wrong – that is, it's irrationally prejudicial to believe that there are cars, tables, yams and so on, rather than the objects another culture believes in, like the 'taytu' and the 'yowanna'. Far better to say that composition is unrestricted, such that everything composes. This is called **universalism** (or, sometimes, unrestricted mereological composition):

for any *x*s, those *x*s compose a further object. If universalism were true, then (contrary to your intuitions) all of those things above would exist: every cut of meat; every putative country; the caravan does indeed compose something along with the car; the yam, 'taytu' and 'yowanna' all exist; the Flergbet is indeed there and so on. Now we have resolved the cultural prejudice, for now everyone is in the same boat – no matter what culture you are in, you are right to say that there are such objects and wrong to deny their existence. Further, if composition were restricted, and it was impossible to know exactly which things composed further objects, you'd be taking a risk when you said, say, 'There is a table over there.' For all you know, there isn't a table (perhaps you are in the position we intuitively think the aliens are in – where they say that the toilets and *Friends* cast compose, we think they are wrong, but perhaps *we* are wrong when we think that the putative parts of the table compose a table). But if universalism is true, then the universe kindly obliges us by ensuring that there are always objects there to refer to when we say that some parts compose a further object.

Here's another way of getting to the same conclusion by similar means. You might have read the above examples with some element of incredulity. You may have thought thus: it's not that the French don't believe in the object that is the sirloin; it's just that they don't think that such an object is a particularly good cut of meat (in the same way that we don't think teeth are particularly good cuts of meat, but we still believe they exist). Similarly, it's not that people don't believe in the huge objects that we identify with Israel or Cyprus, for everyone agrees that those lumps of soil and dirt exist. Rather, some people deny that those composite objects count as being legitimate political states. So there is variation over what predicates those objects fall under (e.g., whether they are good cuts of meat or legitimate political entities) but not over whether they *exist* or not. These might be sensible things to say but, if you apply similar thinking to the rest of the examples, we get universalism. If we say the same thing of the aliens turning up and asking to see the Flergbet, then we have to say that we *should* believe the Flergbet exists, and that it's just that we disagree over what it's like. That is, we think the object is pointless and not worth thinking about, whilst the aliens have accidentally misunderstood some TV show broadcast across the galaxy and think it's the most holy of all objects that there is: we vary over the predicates that the Flergbet falls under, not whether it exists or not. As there can, in theory, be a dispute over whether any things compose or not, to say that the dispute is never about what things exist but about what the composite object is like is to effectively sign up to universalism.

The argument from vagueness

This is not the only argument for universalism. Another is the **argument from vagueness**. Imagine we took a teddy bear and fed it through a wood chipper. This obviously destroys the teddy bear. Moreover, as the stuffing and fabric flitter out of the other end, it seems that the pieces of fluff and fabric (call them the 'bear bits') now compose nothing. Not only have we destroyed a teddy bear, but intuitively the pile of detritus that we are left with composes nothing at all. If restricted composition is true, then this (or a story much like it) is true as well.

But at what point *exactly* does the teddy bear cease to exist? It's impossible for you to say. Imagine I set up a camera to take pictures during the process of the teddy bear being destroyed and got it to take one picture every millisecond. I would end up with lots of pictures, each representing the bear bits at some point during the process of the bear's destruction. When you looked at those pictures, you could point at some where the teddy bear clearly did exist. That is, there would be some pictures where the bear bits definitely composed a teddy bear (e.g., just as it was being placed in the chipper and before any part of it touched the chopping blades). You'd also be able to point at some pictures where you were certain that the bear bits definitely did not compose anything (e.g., at the end of the process, when you are left with a pile of fluff, those bits intuitively compose nothing). But at no point in the stuffed toy snuff album would there be two consecutive pictures, each taken a millisecond apart, where you could say that in one picture the bear bits definitely composed something and in another they did not. The changes between the pictures would be far too minute for that – indeed, they'd be imperceptible and you wouldn't be able to even perceive the difference between two photos. If you can't tell the difference, there can be no way to say in which photo the bear was destroyed and the bear bits stopped composing something. We could arbitrarily pick one of the photos, one in which we were not sure whether composition took place or not, and decide that this was the instant that the bear bits stopped composing, but then our decision would seem unjustified. With those two facts in mind, the argument goes that we should escape this problem by saying that there's never an occasion when the bear bits fail to compose. They might not always compose a *bear*, but they always compose *something* (even if it's a gerrymandered object composed of bits of disconnected fluff and stuffing). We thereby deny restricted composition and endorse universalism.

You might, though, be suspicious of this argument. You might want to compare it to a similar scenario: the **sorites paradox**. A man with no hairs is bald, and a man with a trillion hairs is not. But if you imagine removing each hair one by one, there is no point in the process which we can clearly pick out as being the point where the man goes from being not bald to being bald (some people think you have to have literally no hair to be bald, so it is only the final hair which results in the man becoming bald – clearly, though, they do not understand how to use the word. Homer Simpson, and many of my ageing friends, can all tell you that the odd hair does not stop you from being bald. If it really bothers you, come up with an example of your own, such as people being heavy or tall, rather than people being bald).

The sorites paradox seems very similar to the problem above, and you might think that answers to the sorites paradox will help here. But there's a difference between the bear bits and a man's head of hair. In the case of the sorites, a staple response is to say that the man goes from being definitely not bald, to being vaguely bald (or 'kind of bald' or 'indefinitely bald'), to then being definitely bald. Theories vary over exactly how this solves the problem, but there is a general agreement that sharp cut-off points between being bald and not bald are eliminated by introducing a vague territory in between the two that you end up being in at some point or another as you lose your hair. It's unclear that we can do the same with composition. The proponent of the argument from vagueness tends to think that the sorites paradox is resolved by saying it's a problem to do with language: we get vague cases of people being bald because our linguistic community never sat down and specified exactly what it took for a man to be bald. We could have got together and fixed every detail of how the word 'bald' functioned and made precise what the sharp cut-off point was concerning how many hairs you need to have to not be bald, thus eliminating any vague cases. But our linguistic community never did that. So whilst the way we use the term makes clear that Homer Simpson, with his two hairs, is bald, and a man with a full head of hair isn't, because we've never explicitly fixed exactly what makes someone bald, we end up with vague cases. But, it seems, we cannot say the same of objects existing. Imagine that there are just two bear bits in a particular photo (perhaps as the bear is being spliced into two), and we are wondering whether these two bear bits compose a third object: the bear. So we are asking whether or not there are two objects present (and, if not, there are presumably three, for we must include the bear). It seems difficult how an answer to that question could be vague. With baldness, vagueness arises because for some part of the statement 'That man is bald' we haven't set down the exact rules of how it works (in this case, we haven't set down the exact rules about how '__ is bald' works). But the same doesn't apply to 'There are exactly two objects,' as every piece of that sentence appears to be very precise. Express it in logic, where F stands for the predicate '__ is a material object':

> There are exactly two objects. $\exists x \, \exists y \, (x \neq y \, \& \, F x \, \& \, F y \, \& \, [\, \forall z \, (F z \to (x = z \lor y = z)) \,] \,)$

No part of that sentence appears to be vague. We make up the sentence out of logical connectives like &, v and →; the predicate F, i.e., the predicate '__ is a material object'; and quantifiers like ∃ and ∀. If each bit isn't vague, and if vagueness only arises because bits of language are vague, then the overall statement can't be vague either. Therefore, it could never be vague whether there are exactly two things or not. Certainly, the logical connectives aren't vague – we know exactly how they function: 'P & Q' is true if and only if both P and Q are true; 'P v Q' is true if and only if either P or Q is true, etc. Nor does it look like it can be vague whether something can be a material object. If there definitely exists something, it's hard to think you can be unsure which ontological category it fits in. You might find yourself wondering whether some man is bald or not, but how could you wonder whether something was a material object or not? How odd it would be to believe that there definitely existed a something or other, but that you were unsure whether it's an object (a physical thing, located in space and time) or, say, a number (an abstract entity in platonic heaven). How could you end up not being sure which it was? That only leaves the quantifiers and, whilst some have argued that the vagueness might lie in the quantifiers, the standard position is that they are not vague. So it goes, it seems that the destruction of cuddly toys isn't the same as the standard sorites paradox, and the universalist resolutely denies that it can be solved using analogous responses. And with no analogous move to be made, they say to opt for their universalist response.

Restricting quantifiers

Surprisingly, whilst not everyone believes it, universalism is the most popular answer to the SCQ. With the arguments for it in place, turn to look at how it responds to some of its problems. What do the universalists have to say about the fact that, contrary to what we first thought, weird objects like the Flergbet exist? Generally, they say that **quantification is restricted** most of the time. Quantifier restriction is a feature of language that you are already familiar with. If you come back from the supermarket, when I ask where the beer is and you say 'All of the beer is in the fridge,' you would think that would be a true statement (unless you store your beer in a funny place). But imagine I reply 'All of the beer? *All* of the beer? What of the rest of the beer in the supermarket? Is it in your fridge too? What of the beer in the rest of the world? Is it all crammed in there? What about all of the beer from the 1800s – for I'm an eternalist – is *that* all in your fridge?' Clearly, you would be unimpressed. Whilst I would, in a sense, be right that not *all* of the beer was in the fridge, when you said that 'all' of the beer was in the fridge you didn't mean that. You would be restricting the domain you were quantifying over – you didn't mean all of the beer, no matter where or when, but all of the beer that you bought from the supermarket. Further, because of the context of the conversation – you coming home from the supermarket – it is reasonable to think that this is what you are talking about (and it does differ from context to context: in the boardroom of a gigantic beer company, 'all the beer' might mean all of the beer that the company has produced, not the odd bottle or two from the local supermarket). This restriction move is not just common in everyday language, but common in other metaphysical theories. Eternalists can, truly, say that there aren't any dinosaurs, just as long as it's tacitly understood that they are restricting their quantifiers to only cover the presently existing things (for there are no dinosaurs *now*). If a Genuine Modal Realist says it's not the case that there are dogs that can shoot bees from their mouths, that would be a true statement as long as you understand that she is restricting her quantifier (the 'There are . . .' bit) to the actual world and its contents. Unrestrictedly there might be dinosaurs (given eternalism) and unrestrictedly there are dogs that can shoot bees from their mouths (given GMR, for it's logically possible that dogs can shoot bees from their mouths), but in the same way that unrestrictedly not all of the beer is in the fridge, that doesn't prevent those statements from being true. Universalists make the same move to deal with gerrymandered objects. Such weird objects can be safely ignored for, more often than not, we do not find ourselves quantifying over them. They exist, but only unrestrictedly. In the same way that we ignore all of the beer in Canada when asking for a drink (or the past and future beers, or what have you), we generally ignore the gerrymandered objects when we talk about what exists. Only when we find ourselves in certain, unnatural, contexts (such as those we find ourselves in when doing metaphysics) do we end up quantifying over them.

Mereological nihilism

The final answer to the SCQ is **mereological nihilism**: that composition never takes place. That doesn't mean that nothing exists, just that the only things that exist are not composed of anything, i.e., have no proper parts. Usually nihilists take those things to be the smallest subatomic particles that there are. Whilst science has not settled for certain what the smallest particles are, nihilists say that whatever those things turn out to be, they are all that exists. They would be things with no proper parts whatsoever – what are called **mereological simples** (sometimes 'atoms', although don't confuse them with the 'atoms' of physics which do have parts, e.g., a hydrogen atom is composed of a proton and an electron). The nihilist denies that there are composite objects. There are, say, no tables, just lots of simples arranged in a certain way such that, if they had composed, they would've composed a table. We shall call this being arranged 'tablewise'. Similarly, there are no trees, just lots of simples arranged 'treewise', no goats, just simples arranged 'goatwise', and so on. So whenever we think the simples would otherwise compose a further object, the nihilist resists this – in the same way that we tell the alien race that they are mistaken and that the toilets and the cast of *Friends* compose nothing, the nihilist tells us that this is true of everything we normally think of as being composite.

Nihilism has been motivated on various grounds. For starters, universalism isn't the only way out of the problems listed in the previous section. With regard to the argument from cultural prejudice, universalists say that their theory amounts to a non-prejudicial answer, which doesn't favour any culture, for everyone (no matter their culture) is always right to assert that composition takes place and always wrong to deny it. The nihilist simply flips it around the other way: everyone is *wrong* to say that there's an object composed of some things and right to deny it. As with universalism, nihilism isn't prejudiced, in favour of or against, any particular culture, for each culture ends up as right and as wrong as any other (that is, they all end up being very wrong when they say that some composite object exists). The problem of vagueness can receive a similar treatment. We only had a problem with the bear bits composing if we assumed that sometimes they composed and sometimes they didn't, for only then do we have to make an awkward decision as to when, exactly, composition stops happening. The universalist escaped this problem by denying that sometimes they don't compose. The nihilist escapes the problem by denying that sometimes they do – we avoid having to decide when the bear bits go from composing to not composing a bear, for they *never* compose a bear. So nihilism has many of the same motivations as universalism, plus the benefit of being ontologically parsimonious – after all, it ditches all of those objects! (We'll also see, in the next chapter, how nihilism might be motivated on the grounds that it avoids certain paradoxes.) Let's turn instead to some of the problems it faces.

Radical underpopulation

Where universalism includes lots of objects that we don't naturally believe in, nihilism goes the other way around and misses them out – it **underpopulates** our ontology. How can we believe a theory which says that there are no tables or chairs, goats or gazelles, mountains or planets? In reply, the nihilist makes the same moves as anti-realists do about entities from other categories. Where other ontologies miss out things we intuitively think exist, or naturally talk about, we introduced some sort of strategy to account for this. So where we end up talking about properties, numbers, possible worlds, past/future objects and so on, the anti-realist explains why such talk doesn't necessarily lead us into believing that those things exist, and instead tells us a tale about paraphrasing away such talk, or accounting for it in terms of alternative truthmakers and so on. Similarly, the nihilist thinks that we might talk about goats, chairs and mountains (etc.) without ontologically committing to any such thing.

Extant nihilists have offered up a paraphrasing strategy. Where we previously said that there were tables, nihilists offer up a para-phrase that only quantifies over simples: 'There are simples arranged tablewise', or some such. If a car engine is shot by a bullet, we would say instead 'The simples arranged bulletwise intermingled with some simples arranged car-enginewise, causing those simples to be arranged holewise' which quantifies only over simples, and not over composite objects like cars and bullets. Therefore, if you're attracted to anti-realism in other areas of ontology, you should like-wise see nihilism as an open option (so if you've spent this book besmirching the existence of abstracta, and thinking that talking about those things doesn't indicate that they exist, you'll have to work hard to not be a nihilist as well).

There is a special worry, though, in the case of being an anti-realist about objects. Unless you are a substance dualist about the mind (that is, like Descartes, you believe that you are an immaterial soul), then you are a physical object. As you are not a tiny subatomic particle, you can't believe nihilism without believing that you don't exist. But, you might have thought, if you know anything, then you know that you exist! That is the lesson of the Cartesian *cogito*: 'I think, I am'. It is meant to be an incontrovertible belief that you exist, which no theory can rally against. A nihilist might endorse substance dualism (a radical move that is deeply unpopular in the increasingly secularized discipline of metaphysics). Alternatively, they might bite the bullet and agree that they do not exist. They might try and temper this by saying that statements like 'I am think-ing' can be paraphrased away into talk about simples arranged humanwise, collectively thinking. The claim would be that it is enough for us to continue to talk about ourselves even if we don't exist. Most people can't quite stomach this, though. It might be hard for them to put their finger on exactly why but many people deny that we can paraphrase ourselves away! Exactly who is right, and even how we should settle the question, I leave you to decide. One final alternative that nihilists opt for is to weaken their position and become **eliminativists**. They believe that there are *very few* compos-ite objects. There are no tables or chairs, no mountains or galaxies, but there *are* things like you and I. That is, we make an exception for composite objects like human beings. Indeed, Peter van Inwagen is just such an eliminativist and argues that all that exist are simples plus living composite objects (another eliminativist, but for differ-ent reasons, is Trenton Merricks, who believes that there are only certain subatomic particles – some of which might be composite – plus conscious beings).

The problem of gunk

Another problem for nihilism concerns 'atomless gunk'. The term was coined by David Lewis, and is defined as follows:

x is a piece of atomless gunk = $_{df}$ every part of x has a proper part.

So whenever we examine a piece of gunk, or any of its parts, we find that each part has further parts as well, and when we examine *those* parts we see they have even more parts and so on. If there were atomless gunk, we could keep dividing it for ever, finding more and more parts every time we did so.

Gunk is a problem for nihilism because, given nihilism, the only material objects that exist are simples. Gunk, in not being a mereological simple, cannot exist. Worse, the nihilist wants to say that talk about composite objects is paraphrased into talk about the simples that we thought composed those objects. We previously thought there was a table composed of some simples, and the nihilist paraphrases talk about the table into talk about those simples being arranged tablewise. But if it turned out that the table is gunky, then there aren't any simples and so we can no longer paraphrase table talk (or, indeed, talk about anything that is gunky).

So if there is gunk, nihilism must be false. Moreover, if we want nihilism to be a necessary truth (which sounds plausible – it'd be odd if answers to the SCQ varied from world to world), then even the *possibility* of gunk is enough to cause a problem for nihilism. And it looks as if gunk is possible. It is a legitimate scientific hypothesis that there is no smallest thing (and that, as science progresses, we'll keep discovering more and more levels of reality). Certainly, this seems to be an open possibility – it's not as if the nihilist, from an armchair, can dictate to the scientists that there must be a lowest level of subatomic particles. How strange it would be for a mere metaphysician to place such demands on science (not, at least, without some particularly compelling argument). So nihilism, whilst it perhaps offers more benefits than universalism, appears to have more problems as well.

Neo-Carnapianism

Verbal disputes

The debate in mereology allows us to illuminate a particularly interesting theory in metaontology: **Neo-Carnapianism** (so named as it extends some of the deflationary ideas of Quine's sparring partner, Rudolf Carnap). Many readers may think that ontological questions are somehow 'all to do with language', and result from a confusion of how words function. Neo-Carnapianism is one way to cash out such a claim, so counts as a **deflationary** theory (that is, a theory which says that the questions, in this case ontological questions, aren't really serious questions or worthy of study – permissivism, from chapter 1, would be a type of deflationary theory). However, before turning to Neo-Carnapianism, first look at some of the pitfalls there are with deflating questions by saying that they're just linguistic confusions. To deflate a debate by merely saying that it is 'all to do with language' is, by itself, too glib. Lots of interesting questions and issues arise with purely linguistic enquiries (just imagine the reaction you would get if you told a linguist that what they study is 'all to do with language', before snootily refusing to discuss linguistics any further on the grounds that it clearly wasn't a serious discipline!). Moreover, simply saying that something is 'all about language' doesn't tell us where any of the above arguments go wrong. It doesn't tell us why the argument from vagueness doesn't work or get us any closer to finding out what the correct answer to the SCQ is. So a deflationary metaontological theory treating ontological debates as a form of linguistic confusion also has to deliver an explanation of why those arguments are unsound and/or grossly ill-founded. In short, only the naive think that saying a theory (or discipline) is all a verbal confusion is itself enough to end discussion on the matter.

Neo-Carnapianism sets out to remedy these concerns. Neo-Carnapians treat (at least some) ontological debates as being the result of a **verbal disagreement**. A verbal disagreement would be something along the following lines: imagine an American and an Englishman have to decide what the shape of a football is. The American says that footballs are prolate spheroids with pointed ends (that is, that they're shaped like a squished egg). So he would further say that:

'Footballs aren't round'

whilst the Englishman says:

'Footballs are round.'

Thus ensues a huge argument, as they battle back and forth, where each side genuinely believes that they have it right and the other side has it wrong. This is, of course, merely a verbal disagreement, for both are labouring under a confusion about what the other thinks a football is. Once they see that what the American means by 'football' (e.g., a ball used in American football) is different from what the Englishman means by 'football' (e.g., a ball used in soccer), they'll see that they're *both* right, and neither is wrong. We could help highlight the problem by translating those two sentences into first-order predicate logic. The translation of what the American says would be:

$$\forall x\, (F x \rightarrow \sim H x)$$

and the Englishman's would be:

$$\forall x\, (G x \rightarrow H x)$$

where F is the predicate '__ is an American football', G is the predicate '__ is a soccer ball', and H is the predicate '__ is round.' So whilst the word 'football' *sounds* the same coming from the American's and the Englishman's mouths, once represented in logic, we can see that they *mean* totally different things. Most importantly, they do not contradict one another (as the two speakers previously assumed). Notice what has happened here: we haven't just said that the debate is a verbal disagreement; we've also explained *why* this is the case (i.e., they are confused about what 'football' means) and *how* this resolves the apparent difficulties (i.e., it is clear that they are asserting sentences with different logical forms, and are not contradicting one another).

Quantifier variance

Neo-Carnapians, spearheaded by Eli Hirsch, think a somewhat similar verbal dispute is happening in the case of the SCQ (and, also, whether there are temporal parts – see the next chapter). But where the American and the Englishman have a verbal dispute about a predicate (erroneously thinking they are both using the predicate '__ is a football' in the same way) the Neo-Carnapian thinks that the parties debating issues in composition have a verbal dispute about the *quantifiers* being used (i.e., about ∀ and ∃). Just as the American and Englishman both use the same phonetic sounds to express two totally different predicates (i.e., they both say something that sounds the same when they say 'football' but they mean something different), the Neo-Carnapian thinks the same thing is going on when the respective parties involved in a mereological dispute say 'There is'. So where the Trobriander people say there is a 'taytu', and we say that there isn't, the Neo-Carnapian sees this as a verbal dispute because 'There is' functions differently in the mouths of the respective speakers. Each functions as a quantifier, says the Neo-Carnapian, but they're not the *same* quantifier. Where, in classical logic, there's just the one existential quantifier, ∃, the Neo-Carnapian thinks that there can be many different quantifiers. Different cultures unwittingly use these different existential quantifiers, and it is ignorance of this fact which gives rise to the (merely verbal) disagreements apparent in the ontology of material objects. This phenomenon – of there being multiple, different quantifiers – is called **quantifier variance**.

It becomes clear what is going on when we translate into logic what the westerner and Trobriander say. Western society would have its own existential quantifier, $\exists_W$, whilst the Trobriander people have their own, different, quantifier, $\exists_T$. When westerners say there isn't a vegetable that exists only until ripened, i.e., there isn't a 'taytu', that gets represented as:

$$\sim \exists_W x \,(\, x \text{ is a vegetable that exists only until ripened})$$

whilst the Trobriander says that there is such a vegetable:

$$\exists_T x \,(\, x \text{ is a vegetable that exists only until ripened}).$$

As the quantifier used is different, neither party ends up negating what the other says. So, in the same way that the American and Englishman don't end up contradicting one another, nor do the westerner and the islander. Even though, on the surface, our respective assertions about whether or not there is a 'taytu' *sound* the same, the Neo-Carnapian thinks that we are merely talking past one another. Thus, there is no problem of cultural prejudice, and *both* Trobriander Islanders and westerners are right about whether or not 'taytu' exist.

Given Neo-Carnapianism, then, questions about what objects exist turn into questions about how language works. To figure out whether there is some thing or not (be it a 'taytu', a yam, a house or a Flergbet), we first figure out what quantifier we are using when we say 'There is'. If we are using the western quantifier, $\exists_W$, then we just look at how westerners talk. That'll indicate to us whether or not it is correct and true to say that there is a certain thing or not. So as westerners don't believe that the Flergbet exists – or, at least, we don't talk as if there is such a thing – 'There is a Flergbet' is false when uttered in, say, English (i.e., '$\exists_W x$ (x is composed out of all of the toilets of New York and the cast of *Friends*)' is false). But the alien race that has travelled here to find it, equipped with their own quantifier (e.g., $\exists_A$), do talk about the Flergbet – it's acceptable, for them, to refer to such a thing, and their quantifier does quantify over it (i.e., '$\exists_A x$ (x is composed out of all of the toilets of New York and the cast of *Friends*)' turns out to be true).

But it's not all smooth sailing. Whilst it's fairly obvious that people can utter the same noises and yet mean different things (so 'football' might refer to either American footballs or soccer balls; someone saying 'Nine' might mean the number or might, if they're German, mean 'no'; 'bank' might refer to a place where money is taken off normal folk to be squandered by a select few, or it might refer to a place near a riverside), that this is taking place with material objects is a bit more of a stretch. We have to believe that the Trobriander people and westerners are talking past one another whenever they say 'There is' or 'There are'. It seems easier to see how this is with the American and the Englishman, but harder with the Trobriander and the westerner. The American and the Englishman are clearly misunderstanding throughout their discussion, and their ignorance of what the other means might result in them having many false beliefs. For instance, imagine they never get into an argument about the shape of footballs and never realize they're talking past one another; instead, they are just talking about how expensive footballs are or how their daughters enjoy playing with them. Even though they don't notice any disagreement, verbal or otherwise, they've definitely still miscommunicated – after all, the Englishman erroneously thinks the American's daughter enjoys playing soccer, and the American wrongly thinks the Englishman's daughter enjoys playing American football. These false beliefs make it harder for them to navigate the world (for instance, if the Englishman is on *Who Wants to Be a Millionaire?* and phones up the American for a question about soccer balls, he's in for a rude surprise). These facts clue us into the presence of a 'merely verbal disagreement', whether they notice it or not. But is the same thing going on with us and the Trobriander Islanders? Imagine that, like the American and Englishman, a westerner and an islander talk to one another without realizing that their quantifiers vary. 'There is a boulder coming' shouts the Trobriander native, pulling me out of the way to safety, whilst I later say 'There is a spider crawling up your leg' as I brush it off him. (Use some poetic licence here, for obviously what the Trobriander says doesn't even *sound* like English.) Unlike the Englishman's and the American's sentences about footballs, which leads to them having false beliefs, the westerner and the Trobriander Islander appear to communicate effectively and never get led astray. You could even imagine that ten years pass before the islander brings home a yam and a misunderstanding is finally unearthed. Given so many elements of communication are present, it seems hard to believe that, like the American and Englishman, they were talking past one another for an entire decade! In essence, there is a problem with believing that the Trobriander Islander really does mean something totally different by 'There is . . .' to what a westerner does.

Nor is that the only objection. Generally people sign up to a principle, associated with the logician Alfred Tarski, which states that if a singular proposition is true, then the things it refers to must exist. And there's a lot to be said for such a principle. If I say that Barack Obama is president, you would think that this would require me to have successfully referred to Obama and for him, then, to exist. You might be suspicious of this principle, given that throughout this book we've been offering sentences and then explaining how the things they apparently refer to aren't in our ontology, e.g., by offering a Quinean paraphrase or saying what the sentence's truthmakers are (as we might do if we were, say, a presentist – see chapter 7). But the Neo-Carnapian is unlikely to say such a thing as Neo-Carnapianism is intended to deflate ontology, replacing paraphrase theory, truthmaker theory and such like with quantifier variance. So assume the principle is true. Turn back to the westerner and the islander, and imagine that both are convinced Neo-Carnapians looking at a specific vegetable on a table that will be ripe by the end of the day. Call that specific vegetable Veggie. The westerner believes that if he said, in English, 'Veggie will cease to exist at the end of the day', he'd be saying something false, as English recognizes no such entity that ceases to exist merely because it ripens. But, as a Neo-Carnapian, he believes that if the islander says 'Veggie will cease to exist at the end of the day', the islander is saying something true. That is, the westerner can still recognize that the islander has said something true, even though the latter said something in a different language, as that's the Neo-Carnapian insight. But, given the Tarskian principle, the westerner should then agree that the islander has successfully referred to something *and so Veggie must exist*. And that was exactly what the westerner, as a Neo-Carnapian, *didn't* want to say. So there are other problems for the theory. (Something like this objection is discussed by both Matti Eklund and John Hawthorne.)

So, we have introduced another metaontological theory. This one, rather than trying to deliver some clever new theory of ontological commitment, tries to deflate the entire debate and show it to be a verbal dispute. We have also talked of Neo-Carnapianism only with reference to material objects. As with all of the metaontological theories that we examine throughout this book, you should feel free to try and deploy it regarding other ontological categories. (And, notably, not every Neo-Carnapian thinks that the lessons learnt here can be deployed with regard to every other field, e.g., Eli Hirsch believes that we should be Neo-Carnapians about mereological disputes but not, say, disputes about whether numbers exist, for he thinks that such a debate cannot be deflated in a Neo-Carnapian fashion.)

Chapter summary

In this chapter, we have:

- introduced mereology and the special composition question.
- seen the argument from cultural prejudice and the argument from vagueness for universalism.
- seen the motivations and problems for mereological nihilism.
- examined Neo-Carnapianism, which tries to deflate the entire debate.

Further reading

Amie Thomasson (2010b), Ned Markosian (2007), Kris McDaniel (2010) and myself (2009) have all written introductions in this area. The Markosian piece contains a survey of numerous restricted answers to the SCQ. Proponents of middle of the road, restricted composition include Lynne Rudder Baker (2008), Ned Markosian (1998), D. H. Mellor (2008) and Uriah Kriegel (2008). Karen Bennett (2009) discusses whether we can even know what the answer is.

Universalism has been widely defended. The argument from cultural prejudice is discussed in Effingham (2011) and by Daniel Korman (2010a). For the vagueness argument, the best start is Ted Sider's formulation (2001) and Korman has written an extensive introduction to the argument (2010b). Other defences of universalism have been given by John Bigelow and Robert Pargetter (2006), as well as Michael Rea (1998). More attacks on universalism have been provided by Einar Bohn (2009) and Juan Comesaña (2008).

Nihilism has been defended by Cian Dorr (2005), whilst eliminativism has been defended by Peter van Inwagen (1990) and Trenton Merricks (2001) (a symposium about Merricks's book is in *Philosophy and Phenomenological Research* 67). The problem of thinkers existing has rarely been discussed, although Eric Olson (2007) makes a notable contribution. Sider (1993) argues that gunk poses a threat for eliminativism, and the argument applies just as much to nihilism (whilst Robbie Williams (2006) argues against this being a problem).

If you're looking for how some previous metaontological theories we've discussed bear on this problem, Gideon Rosen and Cian Dorr (2002) have developed a fictionalist approach. Neo-Carnapianism with regard to composition is discussed by Eli Hirsch (2005). Matti Eklund's response is in his 2009 chapter and John Hawthorne's in his 2006 essay.

9

Material Constitution

The statue and the lump

Terminology alert: numerical and qualitative identity

In English, the word 'identity' (and, similarly, 'is') is quite a confusing word for it covers (at least) two concepts. To help distinguish between the two, philosophers introduce extra terminology to make up for the defects of the English language. The first is what philosophers call **qualitative identity**. That is when things have all of their qualities and properties in common. Two identical pens, for instance, would be qualitatively identical. The second is **numerical identity**. That is when things are literally one and the same object. So 'Cassius Clay is identical to Mohammad Ali', or 'Superman is identical to Clark Kent', are statements of numerical identity.

This chapter examines a paradox concerning the ontology of material objects. Imagine I awake at 9 am and go into my garden, collecting tiny bits of clay together. At 10 am I go into my house and form those bits into one huge lump. At 11 am, I skilfully shape the clay into the form of a statue. At 1 pm, I become bored of the statue and crush it back into a lump. At 3 pm, I decide I was better where I began, and so put my lump of clay through the wood chipper at

the back of my house, converting it back into numerous, disconnected, bits of clay.

Let's establish some (putative) facts about this scenario. The story
features at least two things – a lump of clay (call it Lump) and a
statue (call it Statue). It appears that:

(1) Lump comes into existence at 10 am and ceases to exist at
    3 pm.
(2) Statue comes into existence at 11 am and ceases to exist at
    1 pm.

Further, most people believe the **indiscernibility of identicals**:
that if two things are identical – that is, numerically identical – then
they have to have the same properties. This principle seems true
enough: if Superman is 6 ft tall, Clark Kent has to be 6 ft tall too
(they can't be one and the same person if Superman is tall and Clark
is short). Given the principle, then, if Lump was numerically identical to Statue – if they were one and the same object – then they
would have to come into, and go out of, existence at the same time.
So it follows that:

(3) Lump is not numerically identical to Statue (from (1), (2)
    and the indiscernibility of identicals).

Now ask where Lump and Statue are at midday. Clearly, they are
in the same place – how odd it would be for Lump to be on one
side of the room and Statue to be on the other. So it appears:

(4) Lump and Statue are in the same place at the same time.

But it also seems true that you can't have two things in the same
place at the same time. Perhaps a ghost can be in the same place at
the same time as some other object (say, a wall that it's passing
through), but of more commonplace objects this is not the case. So
assume:

(5) Two objects cannot be in the same place at the same time.

Clearly, we end up with a contradiction, as given (3) and (4), there
are two objects in the same place at the same time, which is ruled
out by (5). So this very simple tale about Statue and Lump seems
to be not so simple after all, and at least one of the premises has to

go. The rest of this chapter examines how we can set about solving this paradox, and which premise we are most justified in denying.

The standard account

We might think the problem is with (5). Whilst it is impossible for me to walk through walls, or for a table to fall through the solid floor and so on – examples which justify (5) – you might feel hoodwinked when I use it to rule out statues and lumps of clay from being in the same place at the same time. What we need, you might think, is a principle that rules out the former types of interpenetration, whilst permitting the more sensible sounding cases of statues and lumps of clay coexisting at the same spot. For a while, this was the standardly received theory, so it has been called the **standard account** (alternative names include 'coincidentalism'). Proponents say that the lump of clay **constitutes** the statue, where constitution is some sort of intimate relation between two objects, whereby one object (e.g., Statue) depends on the other (e.g., Lump) in a certain way (often times the claim is made that Statue is a part of Lump – just a strange sort of part that is composed of the same atoms as Lump is). And in those cases where one object constitutes the other, it's okay for them to be in the same place at the same time. Statue and Lump both have the same atoms as parts – they share the same basic make-up – and this is why we should say one constitutes the other (and why it's okay for them to be in the same place at the same time). This is quite unlike, say, myself and a wall. I can't walk through walls (and cannot be in the same place at the same time as a wall) because, unlike Statue and Lump, myself and the wall are composed of different atoms. Standard as this response was, it has come under heavy fire in recent years for various reasons. We'll consider only two objections.

First, some worry that the standard account leads us to 'double counting'. If I pointed at Statue and said 'How many objects are there?', it seems natural to reply 'Just one'. But if the standard account is true, then there are, in fact, two. This objection might be relatively straightforward to avoid. As has been discussed in previous chapters, the context one finds oneself in affects what things we quantify over. In some contexts, when we say that there are no dinosaurs, that's a true statement because (even though, say, eternalism is true) we are not quantifying over times that dinosaurs exist at; when we say there is no object composed of toilets and actors, that's true (even though, say, universalism is true) because we are not quantifying over such objects and so on. Similarly, when we count how many objects there are at a given place, we tend to restrict our quantifiers as well. For where Statue is, there are many other objects that you have ignored when you say that there is only one thing. Statue is composed of many atoms, somewhere in the region of 10^{28} atoms. So when I point at the objects over there, you don't count *all* of the objects – you ignore all of the atoms. Nor do you count objects like the arm of the statue, or its legs, or its head and so on. All of those objects are ignored. And rightly so, for the context you are normally in when I ask you how many objects there are is one that excludes counting such things – it'd be *crazy* to routinely count those things when I asked you how many things there were. So when you are asked to count how many objects are where Statue is, and you say one, we can just say that you were restricting your quantifiers such that you ignored Lump (as well as the atoms, and the legs, arms, head, etc.) and only counted Statue. Only in attenuated circumstances – such as when discussing solutions to the paradox of the statue and the clay – do we end up saying that there are two objects, whereas in everyday parlance, there's no need to double-count at all.

The second objection, the **grounding objection**, is more difficult. Say that two objects **mereologically coincide** when they are composed of the same parts. Statue and Lump, being composed of the same subatomic atoms, apparently coincide. But it seems natural to think that the properties of an object **supervene** on the arrangement and properties of its parts. For those not familiar with supervenience: we say that some properties supervene on some other properties if and only if a change in the former demands a change in the latter. For instance, it seems reasonable to think that moral properties supervene on your actions. It's impossible for there to be two people who act exactly the same, but somehow one is good and one is evil (maybe this is false – perhaps intentions are highly relevant to morality – but we can ignore such quibbles for now, as this is just an example). If Jack goes out and kills innocents, and is therefore evil, it's not possible for Jill to do exactly the same and yet be good (supervenience doesn't demand the converse: people can have the same moral properties and yet have different properties concerning what actions they've committed. If Jack selflessly gives billions of euros to charity, and Jill devotes all her spare time to helping the poor, each is engaging in different actions and yet both are morally worthy). When it comes to objects, the properties of an object supervene on the arrangement of its parts (and the properties those parts have). That is, properties like size, shape and colour are such that, for them to change, the arrangement of an object's parts (or the properties those individual parts have) has to alter. For instance, it's impossible for two objects to be composed of (qualitatively) identical parts, arranged in exactly the same way, except one is a 60 ft-tall cube and the other is, say, a 1 ft-tall pyramid! But if Statue and Lump coincide (which we said above that they appear to do), then they have the same parts arranged in the same way. Since the properties of an object supervene on those parts, it follows that Statue and Lump must have the same properties. But they don't! We've already said that some of their properties differ, namely the length of time that they exist for – Statue exists for two hours, Lump for five. (And, in the wider literature, you'll find more examples of properties they supposedly differ over.) So the standard account appears to have difficulties with issues to do with properties supervening.

Perdurantism

A second escape attempt from the puzzle is **perdurantism**. To get a grip on what perdurantists say, it's worthwhile hearing two differ- ent expositions of their theory – one antagonistic to perdurantism and one charitable. The unfriendly explanation of perdurantism is that perdurantists believe in far more objects than we normally would believe in. Wherever there is an object, e.g., Lump, the per- durantist believes that over any period of time there are an infinite number of other objects exactly located where Lump is. But these objects are truly bizarre, for they wink out of existence after but an instant, to be replaced by a totally different, instantaneously exist- ing, object (again, located exactly where Lump is). So, the antagonist says, we have a bizarre situation indeed.

The charitable exposition of perdurantism says this is true, but poorly expressed. The objects which pop in and out of existence are **temporal parts** of the larger whole (e.g., temporal parts of Lump). Temporal parts are a lot like spatial parts (such as your hand or your head) but are the parts of you that are extended throughout time, not just space. The easiest way to get your head around this is to imagine some flatlanders. The flatlander, who would be extended in two dimensions of space, would be stretched in a third dimension as well – the dimension of time. So even though flatlanders lived on a flat surface and didn't know what 'up' and 'down' was, they would be *three*-dimensional entities. And just as regular three-dimensional entities have three-dimensional parts (you, for instance, have your hand as a three-dimensional part), we can imagine the flatlander having three-dimensional parts as well. For instance, a flatlander that existed from 1979 to 2079 would have a part that corresponded to all of her throughout 2008. That part of her, says the perdurantist, would be her 2008-temporal part. That temporal part would, at every moment that it existed, have the same parts that the flatlander had at the various moments that she exists at during 2008 (so both she and her temporal part would, for example, have hands and feet). Nevertheless, the temporal part is distinct from her and would cease to exist at the end of 2008. Nor are there just year-long temporal parts. In the same way that your hand has smaller and smaller parts, the flatlander would have ever smaller temporal parts, like week-long temporal parts, or day-long temporal parts. Usually perdurantists assume that there is a small-est temporal part which exists for only an instant. Our flatlander, then, is composed of an infinite number of these instantaneous temporal parts and (as the antagonistic exposition of perdurantism makes clear) these instantaneous temporal parts would cease to exist after an instant before being replaced by a new one. The per-durantist says that we're just like the flatlander, except where the flatlander is a three-dimensional object extended in two spatial dimensions and one of time, we are four-dimensional objects extended in three spatial dimensions and then one of time (which is why perdurantism is sometimes called **four-dimensionalism**). And we, too, have temporal parts which exist for only a set period of time (sometimes but only an instant) and which have exactly the same parts as we do when they exist. So perdurantists agree with the uncharitable exposition but say that the objects that flicker in and out of existence don't seem so strange once we come to realize that they're the instantaneous temporal parts of the perduring whole.

More technically, we can define perdurantism as follows. We first need the definition of what a temporal part is:

> x is a temporal part of y during period $T =_{df}$ (i) x is a part of y throughout T; (ii) x exists during, and only during, T; and (iii) at every instant during T, x has a part in common with every part of y.

So an instantaneous temporal part is just a temporal part where the period *T* is but a single instant. Perdurantism is then the thesis that, *at every instant that an object exists*, it has an instantaneous temporal part. The opposition, who are generally called **endurantists** (or, sometimes, 'three-dimensionalists'), deny this – they deny that everything has temporal parts, and they deny that there are large quantities of objects that flicker in and out of existence wherever a persisting object is found. Clearly, then, the two sides are debating a question in the ontology of material objects: are there, or are there not, any instantaneous material objects flicking continuously in and out of existence?

Perdurantism and material constitution

With perdurantism made clear, we can see how this is meant to help with the paradox of the statue and the lump. The perdurantist says that Statue and Lump both exist, but that Statue is a (non-instantaneous) temporal part of Lump (see Figure 9.1). Moreover, the region of spacetime that Lump occupies is different from the region of spacetime that Statue occupies (as Lump exists at spacetime regions that Statue does not). So they aren't located at the same place as one another, as the standard account suggests. Further, it solves the standard account's problems with supervenience. Statue and Lump are composed of different temporal parts (even though they might share *some* instantaneous temporal parts). So they don't mereologically coincide and so don't face the problems that the standard account faces.

Figure 9.1 A perdurantist view of Statue and Lump

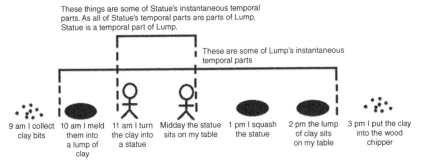

At least, this has been the standard perdurantist line for some years. However, recently a lot of metaphysicians have come to doubt it. Perdurantists, they say, end up in exactly the same boat as the standard account. Start by returning to the three-dimensional flatlander and focus on an example from Ross Cameron. Imagine that the flatlander starts off as a small circle which gets larger over time, and then ceases to exist when she passes away. What shape would she be? It seems obvious that she's a cone (see Figure 9.2).

But, in the same way that it makes sense to ask about a polka-dotted cube what colour it is at different places on the cube (it's black where the black spots are and white at every other point), we can ask what shape our flatlander has at a particular *time*. And, no matter what instant we pick, our flatlander is – not conical – but circular at that time. So the flatlander is a cone, but at (say) 9 am on Tuesday she's a circle – we might say she is a cone *simpliciter* but circular *at certain times*. Notice that the instantaneous temporal part she has at that time is a circle, indeed the temporal part is circular *simpliciter* as well (in the same way that a polka-dotted cube is not black *simpliciter*, only black *at a certain place*, whilst the black dot is simply black – it is black *simpliciter*). Perdurantists usually want to say that every property that an object's instantaneous temporal part has is a property that the persisting object has *at that time*, e.g., if

Figure 9.2 A perduring flatlander as she appears in three-dimensional spacetime

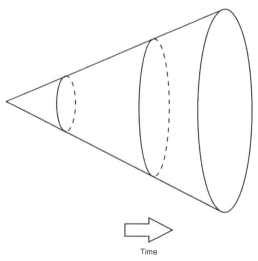

Time

the flatlander is heavy on Tuesday but light on Thursday (after a particularly successful crash diet), that's because her temporal part on Tuesday was heavy, and her temporal part on Thursday was light. And what goes for the flatlander goes for us. So perdurantists standardly endorse:

> The properties a perduring object has at a given time *t* are just those properties that its instantaneous temporal part at *t* has *simpliciter*.

But this now causes problems. Notice what we've done here – we've separated what it is for an object to be a certain way *simpliciter* from what it is for an object to be that way *at a certain time*. Once we introduce this distinction, it seems that perdurantism isn't that dissimilar from the standard account after all. For instance, I said above that perdurantists think that the objects aren't exactly located in the same place. That's no longer true. It is true that where Statue is *simpliciter* is different from where Lump is *simpliciter* – the regions of spacetime that they occupy are different. But at, say, 11 am, where is Statue? Now we've moved from asking where Statue is *simpliciter* and asking where Statue is at a certain time, so we use the above principle. Statue is at 11 am just where Statue's 11 am instantaneous temporal part is. Where is Lump at 11 am? Again, we have to use the same principle and ask where Lump's 11 am instantaneous temporal part is. But every temporal part of Statue is a temporal part of Lump – that's the whole idea behind the perdurantist solution to the paradox – so Statue and Lump's 11 am instantaneous temporal part is just one and the same. So wherever Statue is at 11 am, so is Lump! So whilst they are in different places *simpliciter*, at 11 am they are in the same place. So they *are* in the same place *at the same time*, and perdurantism ends up denying the same principle that the standard account denies.

Moreover, the grounding objection was that if two objects have the same parts (arranged in the same way) at a given time, then their properties should be the same. Perdurantism seems to conflict with that principle as well. Whilst it is true that Statue and Lump have different parts *simpliciter* (for they have different temporal parts), we can again ask what parts they have at a particular time – say 11 am. And it again turns out that, as they have the same instantaneous temporal part at 11 am, they must have the same parts at 11 am. So perdurantism conflicts with the problematic principle just as much as the standard account does!

We might say that, whilst it has the same parts *at that time*, it's enough to escape the grounding objection to say that it has other temporal parts. But if we say that, then the supporter of the standard account can escape the objection as well, for they can say the same thing! Recall that perdurantism isn't the thesis that objects have just *some* temporal parts; instead, it's the thesis that everything has temporal parts at *every* instant that it exists at. The proponents of the standard account don't end up thinking that objects have a temporal part at every instant that they exist at, but – given the above definition of what a temporal part is – they do end up saying that Statue is a temporal part of Lump. Recall the definition:

> x is a temporal part of y during period $T =_{df}$ (i) x is a part of y throughout T; (ii) x exists during, and only during, T; and (iii) at every instant during T, x has a part in common with every part of y.

Let T in the above refer to the period between 11 am and 1 pm. Now we can check to see if Statue is a temporal part of Lump during T (so, in the above, let x stand for Statue, and y stand for Lump). Look at the conjuncts in reverse order. The third conjunct is true for, at every instant during T, Statue and Lump have the same parts. That was meant to be what was causing the problems with the standard account in the first place! So, clearly, every part of Statue overlaps every part of Lump. Next, the second conjunct is clearly true as we've stipulated that Statue exists only during T. So that just leaves the first conjunct, but – as mentioned above – many proponents of the standard account already think that Statue is a part of Lump and that this is crucial to one object constituting another. Statue *is* a temporal part of Lump, even according to the standard account. So if the perdurantist gets to say that Lump has different properties than Statue because of a difference in temporal parts, so too can the proponents of the standard account. It's therefore not clear what benefits perdurantism offers over and above the standard account.

Other motivations for perdurantism

Perdurantism can be motivated on grounds other than that of material constitution. For instance, if you believe that we should endorse universalism because of concerns with cultural prejudice (see chapter 8), you'll likely go on to endorse the existence of temporal parts. Imagine an exotic culture which, like the Trobriander, believes that where a yam is, there is actually an object, a 'yamil', with radically different persistence conditions to those we think a yam normally has. They think that the 'yamil' only exists for a single instant, before being replaced by another 'yamil' (in the same way that the Trobriander people think the 'taytu' gives way to the 'yowanna' upon ripening). If we think we are obliged to believe in the objects that the Trobriander believe in, we should be obliged to believe in the 'yamils'. And the 'yamils' are just what an instantaneous temporal part of a yam would be. As we can run this argument for all kinds of objects, we can imagine a culture that believes that everything has instantaneous temporal parts at every instant a thing exists, and the argument from cultural prejudice would oblige us to believe in them. Ergo, the argument from cultural prejudice seems to entail, not just universalism, but perdurantism.

There are other motivations besides. Imagine that every fact supervenes on the tiny point particle distributions of the world (this principle is called **Humean supervenience**). To illustrate the principle, shift back to the God metaphor. Given Humean supervenience, God only has to fix the properties of the tiniest subatomic particles and how they are arranged in order to fix every fact about the world. So, two worlds that are identical with regard to these local matters of fact are one and the same world. Put like this, you might think (as many do) that Humean supervenience is a compelling thesis. David Lewis believes that the thesis can motivate perdurantism, for the endurantist should think there *could* have been things a lot like instantaneous temporal parts, even if they do not think that any actually exist. For instance, it could be that when I was born an evil demon annihilated me an instant after, before creating a very similar baby in exactly the same place as where I would've been. The demon then allows that baby to exist for a single instant before replacing it with another one, and so on. For every instant of my life, the demon would create a person who is qualitatively identical to me at that instant (and then promptly destroy him). The demon could even do this for everything, not just me. And if the demon did this, then those objects would be just like instantaneous temporal parts. Indeed, it could be that there's no demon at all and it just happens for no apparent reason that the world consists of nothing but instantaneously existing objects, each of which is a qualitative duplicate of how everything at our world is at that time. But then the local matters of fact at that world would be the same as those in our world. That is, if you used the ultimate microscope to zoom down and look at the smallest bits of each world, they'd appear to be the same at that level. Given Humean supervenience, that means that our world and the world where there are just instantaneous objects popping in and out of existence – the temporal parts – are one and the same world. So our world, Lewis says, must be a world of instantaneous objects flitting in and out of existence, which compose big objects stretched across time, i.e., our world is one at which objects perdure.

Another widely discussed argument (again, popularized by David Lewis) is the **argument from temporary intrinsics**. At one time I am short; at another (latter) time I am tall – but does that not entail that I am tall *and* short? And that's a contradiction! We can resolve this by saying that it's true at *one* time that I am tall, and true at *a different* time that I am short, but David Lewis argues that, whilst this might be the case, questions arise as to *how* that comes about (in this vein, you might see this as a request for the metaphysical explanation for how it is that things are short and tall at different times; just as some are sceptical of metaphysical explanation – see chapter 2 – some are sceptical as to whether the argument from temporary intrinsics is actually a problem). Given perdurantism, we can explain this by saying that an object has a short temporal part and then, latter, a tall temporal part – and there's no contradiction for now no single entity is both tall and short, for the properties actually belong to distinct temporal parts.

There are other motivations. We might endorse supersubstantivalism (see chapter 6). As spacetime regions can be split into parts – temporal parts – then if objects are regions, it follows that objects have temporal parts. So they perdure! Ted Sider also thinks that we can extend the argument from vagueness for universalism (see chapter 8) to become an argument for perdurantism. Nor does it stop there. In the same way that there are arguments for eternalism on the grounds of special relativity, we also see such arguments motivating perdurantism. Some (including some earlier temporal parts of myself) have even argued that the possibility of time travel indicates that perdurantism must be true. So there are lots of reasons other than material constitution that the potential perdurantist ought to peruse.

Other endurantist theories

Anti-realism about objects

In other chapters, where we ran into ontological difficulties with regard to certain entities, it was always open to us to deny that they existed. We can do that here too. In the most extreme case, we can deny that neither Lump nor Statue exist, say by endorsing mereological nihilism. If there were no composite objects, then there would be no statues or lumps to cause any problems (there would only be simples arranged statue-wise or lump-of-clay-wise). We've already discussed nihilism, so let's just chalk up another benefit of mereological nihilism – that it avoids the paradox of the statue and the clay – and move on to other alternatives.

Identifying Statue and Lump I: The crude approach

We may deny that there are two objects present by saying that Statue and Lump are identical. There are three ways to do this. The first, crudest, way is to simply say that Statue and Lump are identical such that there's only one object present throughout the whole story, and that Statue did *not* come into existence at 11 am and cease to be when it was squished at 1 pm. Instead, as Statue just is Lump, it came into existence at 9 am and ceased to exist at 3 pm (just like Lump – which is unsurprising as Statue just *is* Lump).

This theory has not proven popular. The main objection is that if Statue is Lump, then it persists for the wrong period of time. Intuitively, Statue *doesn't* come into existence at 9 am but instead comes into existence at 11 am. This theory, though, says the exact opposite. Another example: imagine that you own an expensive television. When you are out of the house, I come in with a large, superpowerful oven, place your television inside it and melt it into a single blob. When you return, you will rightly complain that I have destroyed your television – that is, that it has ceased to be. But on this view, this is false. The television still exists, for it is identical to the lump of matter that composed it, and that lump still exists in the form of the boiling, bubbling blob of plastic I left in your lounge.

This objection has normally been the end of the matter. However, it might strike you as unfair. It has been a running theme throughout this book that what we say, and what the ontological facts are, might not dovetail neatly with one another. So we may talk as if there are holes, or as if there exists a property that things can have in common, or as if there are tables and so on, even though there aren't any such things. Instead, we might introduce paraphrases to account for the prima facie disparity. So one wonders why we should not do the same here. We could talk as if statues are created by moulding clay into a certain shape, but then say that this talk is paraphrased, for example, 'Nikk created a statue at 11 am by making it out of clay' is paraphrased as 'The lump of clay became statue-shaped at 11 am.' In this manner, this sort of theory might be able to progress. Whilst neglected by contemporary philosophy, then, it's possible that this theory might have some life left in it. But, with little more said about it in the literature, let us press on to a more sophisticated twist on identifying Statue with a lump of clay.

Identifying Statue and Lump II: The Burkean approach

To understand Michael Burke's answer to the paradox, we have first to understand what **sortal essentialism** is. Say that an object falls under a sortal predicate just in case it is the kind of thing that the sort says it is. So a human being falls under the sortal '__ is a human being', a panda falls under the sortal '__ is a panda', a statue falls under the sortal '__ is a statue' and so on. Sortal essentialism is, then, the thesis that objects fall under their sortals essentially – that is, a human is essentially a human, a panda is essentially a panda, a lump of clay is essentially a lump of clay, and so on.

Return now to the paradox. At some time, say 10 am, Lump is not a statue, so it follows that it cannot *essentially* be a statue. Given sortal essentialism, it therefore cannot be a statue at any time (for if it's ever a statue, it essentially has to be a statue). So Lump can never become a statue. But Burke also thinks that there is just one object where Statue is so, as Lump can never become a statue, when I sculpt the clay into a statue, Lump must be destroyed. Similarly, as Statue is essentially a statue, it cannot survive being crushed, so must cease to exist at 1 pm. So Burke escapes the paradox by denying that Lump exists from 10 am to 3 pm. Instead there are three objects, one is a misshapen blob of clay (call it $Lump_1$) that exists from 10 am to 11 am; the next is a statue-shaped lump of clay (call it $Lump_2$) that exists from 11 am to 1 pm; and the third object is another squashed lump of clay (call it $Lump_3$), existing from 1 pm to 3 pm. And don't think that Statue doesn't exist – it does! Statue is numerically identical to $Lump_2$ for, in the same way that a human being can fall under multiple sortals (e.g., '__ is a person/ human/mammal/animal'), Statue falls under *both* the sortal '__ is a statue' and the sortal '__ is a lump of clay'.

Note that when Burke says that $Lump_1$ is destroyed and $Lump_2$/ Statue takes its place, he doesn't believe it's magically whisked away and some wizard conjures up a statue to take its place. Far from it. The bits of clay that composed $Lump_1$ – the bits of matter that made $Lump_1$ up – remain exactly where they are; it's just that they now compose Statue/$Lump_2$ instead of $Lump_1$. This is no more mysterious than bits of wood making up a table at one moment but a distinct chair later on after those bits of wood have been rearranged – the table is destroyed and replaced by a chair, but we don't think anything magical has occurred.

Burke's theory does run into some difficulties. The biggest problem is saying what counts as a relevant sortal and what doesn't. For example, '__ is a child' appears to be a sortal, but no one thinks children are essentially children (or else we would not celebrate your eighteenth birthday and would instead hold a more sombre wake the night before – a funeral for your forthcoming demise at the stroke of midnight, whereupon a new 'adult' will appear and take your place). Or another example again plays on the issues to do with cultural prejudice. Imagine a culture that has a sortal for every possible shape that a lump of clay could have – for ease let's call those sortals '__ is a $statue_1$', '__ is a $statue_2$', '__ is a $statue_3$', etc. So each tiny modification to its shape results in it falling under a new sortal. As the smallest atom of clay moves, it ceases to be a $statue_1$ and becomes a $statue_2$. As time passes and gravity ever so slightly drags a tiny atom down towards the earth, it ceases to be a $statue_2$ and becomes a $statue_3$. And so on. But we don't want to say that an object is a $statue_1$ essentially (and a $statue_2$ essentially, etc.), for then even the slightest change to the statue results in it being destroyed and being replaced by a wholly new object – and that doesn't sound right. And the same reasoning applies to other objects – including us! And we don't want to say that we cease to exist given the most minor of changes! So Burke has to say something that rules out sortals like '__ is a child' and these bizarre sortals like '__ is a $statue_1$', '__ is a $statue_2$' and so on from counting as sortals relevant to determining what sortals you fall under essentially (and Burke has, of course, made attempts to do just that, which you should feel free to look at).

Identifying Statue and Lump III: The relative identity approach

Finally, perhaps we want to say that Statue and Lump are the same object but *maintain* that they persist for different periods of time – so affirm that Lump exists from 10 am to 3 pm and Statue exists from 11 am to 1 pm, but insist that they are nonetheless numerically identical. This is a hard sell, but people have attempted such moves by accepting some version of **relative identity** whereby we take a contra-standard view of how the identity relation functions. For instance, we generally think that identity is a two-place relation, for example, that Superman is numerically identical to Clark Kent, or that Mohammad Ali is numerically identical to Cassius Clay. In these cases, there are two terms and it's a two-place relation (that is why in classical logic it's represented as, e.g., $'a = b'$).

But not everyone thinks this, instead taking identity to be, say, a three-place relation – one that is *relativized* to something or other. Sometimes the relativization is made to sortals (whereby it turns out that whilst I can be the same *person* as someone else, and the same *lump of matter* as something else, it makes no sense to say, simply, that I am just identical to something else). However, we'll concentrate on the relativization of identity to times. If identity is relativized to times, then it's simply wrong to say that Superman is Clark Kent or that Statue is Lump – we need to say *at what time* they are these things. You already implicitly do this for a lot of other relations. For instance, when I say that Harrison Ford and Calista Flockhart are married, I implicitly intend that relation to be relativized to a certain time – namely the time at which I speak. I don't think they are married at *every* time. Of course they aren't! They were not married before they were born; they were not married when they were children; they were not married when Ford was instead married to Melissa Mathison (his previous wife) and so on. So even though you often talk about being married as a two place relation, you are always implicitly relativizing it to times. So, the relative identity theorist holds that the same thing is going on with identity: at 11 am, Statue is identical to Lump, but not at, say, 10 am, or at 2 pm when Statue has been destroyed, at which point it is not identical to Lump.

This helps avoid the paradox because relative identity theorists deny the indiscernibility of identicals – they believe that two things can be identical and yet not share all of the same properties. Statue will persist for one length of time, and Lump for another, and yet nevertheless be identical. So the relative identity theorist prevents us from making the move from their having different properties to their being distinct. However, comes the retort, this is why their theory makes no sense. When we say that one thing is numerically identical to another, we are meant to see that they are one and the same – that they are *one* thing. And it seems bizarre to imagine that one thing could have two different sets of conflicting, contradictory properties! Indeed, it's exactly this kind of (supposedly obvious and unimpeachable) intuition that drives us to accept the indiscernibility of identicals in the first place. But even though this sounds like a damning criticism, you will find that a number of people try and defend some form of relative identity (and, of course, think they can reply to these problems!)

Further reading

Further introductions to these issues include those written by Laurie Paul (2010), Katherine Hawley (2010), Ryan Wasserman (2009), Matthew McGrath (2007) and Ted Sider et al. (2007). Collections of papers can be found in compilations edited by Michael Loux (2001) and Michael Rea (1997).

David Wiggins (2001) and E. Jonathan Lowe (2009) are both famous proponents of the standard account, whilst the grounding objection receives its most popular form by Michael Burke (1992). Many people have responded to that objection, including Judith Thomson (1998), Karen Bennett (2004) and E. Jonathan Lowe (1995). Ryan Wasserman (2002) (amongst others) argues that the standard account is on an equal footing with perdurantism.

Monographs arguing for perdurantism include those by Hawley (2001), Mark Heller (1991) and Sider (2001) (there's a symposium on Sider's book in *Philosophy and Phenomenological Research* 68). The argument from Humean supervenience was introduced by David Lewis (1986), and is discussed by Sally Haslanger (1994), Ryan Wasserman, John Hawthorne and Mark Scala (2004), as well as by Harold Noonan (2001). The argument from temporary intrinsics is surveyed by Haslanger (2003) and also discussed by Wasserman (2006) (whilst Thomas Hofweber (2009b) is a good example of someone who argues that it isn't a worry in the first place). How time travel bears on the debate is discussed by myself and Jonathan Robson (Effingham and Robson 2007) as well as Cody Gilmore

(2007) (who has also written a survey of how relativity bears on the debate (2009)). Arguments that the debate between endurantists and perdurantists can be dissolved, a move similar to that which the Neo-Carnapians make, are discussed in McCall and Lowe (2006). I've also written an introduction to the dispute between perdurantists and endurantists (Effingham 2012).

Michael Ayer (1974) argues for the crude identification of Statue and Lump, whilst Burke's theory is introduced in his 1994 article (responses include those by Carter (1997) and Fred Zammiello (2001)). An introduction to relative identity theory is by Harry Deutsch (2007), and famous proponents include André Gallois (1998), George Myro (1997), Nicholas Griffin (1977) and Peter Geach (1967).

10

Works of Music

It is not just properties, numbers, objects, regions and so on which come under the purview of ontological interrogation; we can be inquisitive about the ontological status of anything. We could examine whether football matches (and events in general) exist; whether aid workers talking about food shortages are committed to 'food shortages' existing; whether shadows exist; whether fictional characters exist; whether organizations (such as football teams or banks) exist and so forth. And in each case we could apply the lessons that we have learnt thus far (and, indeed, apply other interesting theories out there that this book does not cover). This final chapter examines just such an application, and the example we shall concentrate on is the ontology of **works of music**.

What is a work of music?

We need to distinguish between a work of music and a **performance** of a work. The existence of performances is relatively uncontentious. Every time an orchestra plays Beethoven's *Piano Sonata No. 14*, or my MP3 player plays Arcade Fire's *My Body is a Cage*, or Bob Dylan performs *Blowin' in the Wind* in a café laced with smoke from a dubious source, we have a musical performance. And every time the song is played again, we have a *different* performance: if an orchestra did a matinée and an evening sitting, then they would give two performances of Beethoven's Sonata every day; if I put the musical track on repeat, my headphones would produce numerous performances of *My Body is a Cage* and so on. The performance, then, is a non-repeatable entity – and appears to have a (albeit vague) location (the performance of the Sonata is where the orchestra is; the performance of Arcade Fire's song is where my headphones are; the performance by Bob Dylan is where he is, etc.). So performances appear to be concrete entities – a type of sound, perhaps identifiable with certain air molecules which are vibrating in a certain way. By the by, most ontologists (except those sceptical about such complex concreta in general, like mereological nihilists) are going to be unfazed by believing in them so won't be worried about ontologically committing to performances. The work, on the other hand, is the thing that those air vibrations (or whatever performances turn out to be) are performances *of*. The works are clearly not the same as the performances.

Example 1 If Bob Dylan gave a concert where he played *Blowin' in the Wind* seventeen times over, then, whilst there would be seventeen different performances, only one song – one work of music – would have been performed.

Example 2 Beethoven created a single work of music when he wrote the score for his sonata, but he clearly *didn't* create every single performance (just go and find someone playing it on a piano and you will see that *they* create the performance, whilst it is Beethoven who created the work of music that they are performing).

Example 3 The *presto agitato* movement of Beethoven's sonata is incredibly difficult to play. Many people will have performed that sonata badly because of this, and their performance won't be aesthetically pleasing. But the work of music is always aesthetically pleasing – Beethoven's sonata is a fabulous work of music, no matter how poorly someone bungles playing it. Similarly for all other aesthetically pleasing works of music – no matter how poorly they are sung in the shower or how terribly the tune is mangled, the aesthetic properties of the work of music itself remain unchanged. The properties of the work are clearly different from those of the performance and so they must be different things.

Clearly, then, works are not performances. And it quickly becomes obvious that their ontological status is far more controversial.

Realism about musical works

Works of music as abstract types

Start by considering a realist theory, where we take works of music to be abstract. One popular identification that ontologists have made is to identify works with **Types** (I'll use capitals to make clear that by 'Type' we are referring to a reified ontological entity). Understanding what a Type is is relatively straightforward, although to understand it properly you need to know what a **token** is as well. Here are some examples to clarify the terms:

- If I own three washing machines, two made by Zanussi and one made by Whirlpool, then I have three tokens of the Type 'Washing Machine'. Each one is also a token of a second Type. In this example the Type 'Zanussi' has two tokens, and the Type 'Whirlpool' has but one.
- In the word 'Cool', there are four letter tokens (one 'c', two 'o's, and a single 'l') but only three letter Types (c, o and l).

Types, then, are somewhat similar to properties, but let's not conflate the two, and let's not get caught up in (admittedly, serious and interesting) questions about whether Types are properties or properties are Types. What is more crucial is that Types are similar to works of music. Just like Types, works of music appear to be abstract in some respects. Whilst performances might be located in space and time, it seems odd to think that works of music might be similarly located. What sense would it make to say that Beethoven's *Piano Sonata No. 14* was in Belgrade or New York? Alaska or Pluto? It seems very odd indeed. (However, below we'll find some reason to think it quite sensible to think they're located in time if not in space). Similarly, just as Types can have many tokens, a work can have many performances. If works were Types, we could account for this by saying that the performances were just their tokens.

But which Types could works be? Julian Dodd argues that they are Types of a very familiar form: Types corresponding to sound structures. So imagine playing C sharp on a piano. That particular sound would be a token of the 'C-sharp sound structure' – a Type corresponding to that particular sound. And whenever anyone produces a C sharp, they produce a token of that Type. Indeed, it could be that there is a valley somewhere such that, when the wind blows just right, it produces a C-sharp sound – that, too, would be a token of that Type. We can imagine more complex Types corresponding to more complex sounds, from chords to the sound that an entire performance of a song makes. It is the latter Types that Julian Dodd thinks works of music are.

There are problems with this, however. Many believe the **creatability thesis**: that works of music can be brought into existence by their composers. That is, prior to 1801, there was no such thing as Beethoven's *Piano Sonata No. 14*, whereas – post-1801, after Beethoven had composed it – that work of music existed. Beethoven *created* that work of music. But if Types are abstract objects, beyond time and space, then they don't come into existence in 1801, any more than the number 4 came into existence at some point (or was created by someone). (Some, including Dodd, argue that Types are in time and space, but are eternal – existing at every time – but we obviously get the same sorts of problems). There are a few responses to this problem.

The first response is Dodd's own. He argues that the Types do indeed have properties that we wouldn't, at first glance, think works of music have. But, says Dodd, this is no great impediment. We should, contrary to prima facie intuitions about works of music, think that works are *discovered* rather than created. There are worries that this somehow downplays the creative role of the composers and that it removes from the likes of Beethoven the mark of genius for coming up with the pieces of work that they compose. We might liken the process to that of exploration. In the same way that an explorer discovers a (already existing) country, the composer discovers the (already existing) work of music. But that doesn't seem to carry the same mark of genius – explorers might have many qualities to be admired, and some amount of common sense is surely one of those qualities, but *creative* genius doesn't seem to be anything involved in exploration. Dodd responds by instead likening musical composition to mathematical cases (note, of course, that by 'composition', we mean something different from what we did in chapter 8 – it is *musical* composition, not *mereological* composition, which interests us now). Whilst one might think that mathematicians are generating the numbers and creating the rules of mathematics as they go along, the (more orthodox) realist theories would rally against that. Mathematicians are not *creating* mathematics; they are discovering more and more about an already existing world of abstract mathematical objects. So when a complicated mathematical proof is given, say the proof of Fermat's Last Theorem by Andrew Wiles (a very complex proof, running to 130 pages, which proves one of the long-standing theories in mathematics), the details of the proof are not being created but discovered. But this is, surely, no slight on the genius of the mathematician! So some discoveries can be indicative of genius, and – so Dodd's counter-argument goes – we should think the same of musical composition.

A second, different, response is to locate the Types in space and time. We've seen moves like this already in connection with properties. Therein the immanent realist believes that properties exist but says that they are located where their instances are. We could do the same for Types and say that Types are located where their tokens are. This move has many of the same pros and cons that it has for properties, as well as other unique issues. For instance, the creatability thesis is not just about when works of music persist, but also about who makes them. So even if locating them in time gets works of music to come into existence at the correct moment, it doesn't follow that it's right to say that the composer created the Type. Imagine we live in a world that, up until now, has no blue objects in it. When I make the first blue object, the (immanent) property *blue* comes into existence at that point in time and space. But it seems stretched to then say that I *made* the property *blue*. I may have made the first blue thing, but that's different from making the property itself. (Indeed, if anything, it's more like discovery!) Similarly for immanently located Types: I may make the first performance (i.e., token) of that Type, but that's different from creating the Type itself.

A third response is to simply set about undermining the claim that abstract objects cannot be created. One worry with our being able to create abstract objects is that there should be no causal interaction between the abstract and the concrete (another problem is that it might seem magical that we can create abstract objects just by talking in a certain fashion; look back at p. 68). Generally speaking, people assume that the concrete world is causally closed, and no abstract object causally interacts with any concrete thing. It would, after all, be very strange if the number 7 caused me to trip over, or the (false) proposition < Chingiz Khan built New York > cornered me down a back alley one evening and mugged me. Abstracta can't cause anything to happen and such claims are absurd. You might think, though, that we can't go from that claim to the claim that there is no causal interaction at all. As Ben Caplan and Carl Matheson have argued, you might think that, in the case of entities like works of music, causation can run in the other direction – that whilst the abstracta might not cause anything to happen in the concrete world, the concrete world can cause things to happen in the abstract world, for example, causing Types to exist. In that case composers would – literally – create works of music, for they create those abstract objects. But in that case we need a theory different from Dodd's, for sound-structure Types exist independently of a composer's intentions. With that in mind, turn to the fourth response.

The final response is Jerrold Levinson's theory. He believes that works of music are Types, but identifies them with *different* Types than those that Dodd does (just to note: Levinson's paper is chronologically earlier than Dodd's). Levinson complicates matters by saying that works of music are not sound structures but what are called **indicated Types**. The idea behind indicated Types is that a composer 'indicates' a sound structure when they compose a work of music, for example, in 1801 Beethoven composed *Piano Sonata No. 14* and, in doing so, indicated the sound structure that Dodd otherwise would say was *Piano Sonata No. 14*. In doing this, composers *create* a new Type. Where a composer x indicates a sound structure s at time t, Levinson says that the new, indicated, Type that comes into existence is 'sound-structure-s-as-indicated-by-x-at-time-t' which is a Type *in addition* to the sound structure, for example, a performance of *Piano Sonata No. 14* would be a token of some given sound structure s^*, but would also be a token of the indicated Type of 'sound-structure-s^*-as-indicated-by-Beethoven-in-1801', for the latter is the Type Levinson identifies with the work. Unlike sound structures, we might think that these Types can only exist given a composer with the correct intentions, so (coupled with the third response) we have a competing solution to Dodd's for the argument from creatability.

Works as concrete

Types are not the only abstract entities that works might be. As with properties, numbers, propositions and possible worlds, we might identify works of music with a kind of mathematical set, for example, the set of all of the work's performances. Or we might say that they are irreducible abstracta and in a category of their own.

But we'll move on, and turn instead to look at whether works are concrete.

Whilst we've already decided that they can't be identical to the concrete performances, we might think they are identical to the fusion of all of the performances: that is, that they are identical to that object (mereologically) composed of every performance that there is. Given the considerations of chapter 8, many people (e.g., universalists) will already believe in, not just the performances of *Piano Sonata No. 14* but also the thing that they compose. Caplan and Matheson identify works of music with that composite. By making them concrete, we avoid all sorts of awkward questions. First, works of music are not eternally existing for they are now like perduring objects. Just as a perdurantist would say that I come into existence alongside my first temporal part, works are now perduring fusions of their performances and come into existence with the first performance. (However, we might still have problems with creatability, for whilst Beethoven is at least partly responsible for the existence of all of the performances, he isn't *solely* responsible for them all, and many orchestras are needed as well. Yet it seems right to say that Beethoven solely created the work of music.) Second, if works are concrete, we can easily explain how we know what their aesthetic features are. For instance, if they are abstract, one might wonder how we can hear them, for how can you hear an abstract thing? But if they are concrete, then this is easily resolved (although we again have a problem since the fusion of all performances is, in most cases, going to outlast you; you will never hear all of that fusion, even though we tend to think we *can* hear all of a work of music).

It also gels with other popular ontological theories. If you believe perdurantism, then you already believe some things have temporal parts and perdure. If you believe unrestricted mereological composition, then you will further already believe in the fusion of performances that Caplan and Matheson want to identify with the work of music. As believing the combination of perdurantism and mereological universalism is a popular combination, this fits well with those theories (although perdurantists, as previously noted, often say that the properties an object has at a particular time are just those properties its temporal part has at that time. But during a badly played performance of Beethoven, it seems odd to say of the work of music – as we should of the fusion of performances – that it sounds quite bad at that point in time; the work always sounds good and should never sound bad. So, again, we might have problems with this theory).

Anti-realism about musical works

Turn next to attempts to rid our ontology of musical works. Once again, try the anti-realist strategy of paraphrasing. Some sentences seem to have workable paraphrases. For instance:

'Beethoven's *Piano Sonata No. 14* is a sonata'

is easily paraphrased into:

All performances of *Piano Sonata No. 14* are composed of a succession of three movements

which, in first-order logic, becomes something like:

$\forall x$ (x is a performance of *Piano Sonata No. 14* $\rightarrow$ x is composed of a succession of three movements)

And that only quantifies over performances, not works (although I leave to you to decide how legitimate it is to lay claim to the predicate '__ is a performance of *Piano Sonata No. 14*', given that you don't believe in works and so don't believe there is anything that it is a performance *of*).

But similar paraphrases run into difficulties. Nine Inch Nails perform a song called *March of the Pigs* which features a seven-second silence. But if we said:

'*March of the Pigs* features a seven-second silence'

then this seems to translate into:

All performances of *March of the Pigs* feature a seven-second silence.

which might well be false. Perhaps during one performance they only incorporated a five-second silence, or in another they had a minute's silence as a joke, or in another the electrical equipment shorted out for five seconds or so, giving them a 12-second silence, and so on. We might change it to say that *most* performances of the work feature a seven-second silence (exactly what counts as 'most' is vague, which might be a problem, but let's ignore that here).

However, similar paraphrases don't work elsewhere. Take songs featuring swear words, which are then subject to radio edits. A good example is Beautiful South's *Don't Marry Her* which features the phrase 'sweaty bollocks'. Unsurprisingly, that couldn't be played on the radio and was replaced by the phrase 'Sandra Bullocks'. But now imagine that the radio-edit version was played more often than the non-edited version (indeed, in this case, that's not hard to imagine as it was a very popular song – certainly, every karaoke bar I have stepped into offers only the radio-edit version rather than the original). Now, it seems that most *performances* of the song feature the inoffensive phrase (well, depending upon how offensive one finds Sandra Bullock), even though it seems true to say that the *work of music* – that thing originally created by the Beautiful South before it was edited for decency – features swear words.

There are more problems besides just this. Recall holes. There was a specific difficulty with creating paraphrases when we are counting those things that we are meant to be an anti-realist about. Dodd offers the following sentences that are problematic to paraphrase:

'Mozart composed more than thirty symphonies.'

Or

'Exactly one of Bruckner's symphonies is unfinished.'

Paraphrasing them will prove a non-trivial task. So paraphrasing away commitment to works will have its issues (as it seems paraphrasing has with everything else!). Of course, we have introduced metaontological theories other than paraphrasing, so you might want to consider Meinongian, Neo-Carnapian or truthmaking approaches to works of music. With alternative metaontological principles now in mind, turn to the final metaontological theory that this book will consider: that of fundamentality.

Fundamentality

A crash course in fundamentality

Throughout this book, we have concerned ourselves only with asking what exists. But not every philosopher thinks that ontology is about what exists. They instead think that what exists is obvious, but that what **fundamentally exists** is not. Call these ontologists **fundamentalists**. Fundamentalists say a lot of connected things about these fundamental entities, for example: they are the things which form the bedrock of reality; they are the entities which explain everything about the world we live in or – alternatively – entail everything that is true about it; these things are such that it is in virtue of them that every other fact holds; or they are the entities upon which everything else depends. Concentrate on the last formulation, which relies upon the notion of **ontological dependence**. In the same way that there are many different kinds of explanation (look back at chapter 3), there are many different types of dependence. For instance, amongst others, there is causal dependence (the kettle boiling depends on it being plugged in; the universe and everything in it depends upon the Big Bang, etc.), emotional dependence (I depend on my friends and family), modal dependence (such as the varieties of supervenience) or economic dependence (the success of the banks depends upon the size of their bailouts, etc.). And in the same way that some metaphysicians want to add metaphysical explanation to the list of types of explanation, the fundamentalist says that there is a notion of ontological dependence that sometimes holds between a thing and some other thing. With that notion of ontological dependence in place, they set about defining a host of other terms, including what it is for something to be fundamental:

x is fundamental $=_{df}$ There is no thing that x ontologically depends upon.

(For other terms, see the box.)

Terminology alert! (Probably) synonymous expressions

A lot of different terms get used for very similar ideas when talking about fundamental existence. Here is a list, and some definitions, to give you an idea of what such terms might mean. They should all, however, be taken with a pinch of salt. Remember, every metaphysician may take a different slant on exactly what their terms mean (and, indeed, some might think there are genuine debates to be had about whether the definitions I've given here are right or not). But, as a working model, the following should help you. So, taking ontological dependence as primitive, we can define terms like:

x really exists = $_{\text{df}}$ x is fundamental.

x is derivative = $_{\text{df}}$ there is some thing that x depends upon.

x merely exists = $_{\text{df}}$ x exists and is not fundamental.

x is ontologically prior to y = $_{\text{df}}$ x depends upon y (alternatively some people say 'prior in nature')

x is grounded by y = $_{\text{df}}$ x depends upon y

x is nothing over and above y = $_{\text{df}}$ x ontologically depends upon y.

There are also some other terms that get bandied around. For example, you might come across the phrase 'Turtles all the way down'. This refers to situations where one thing depends on another thing, which in turn depends on another, and so on, such that nothing in the chain is fundamental (the phrase is attributed in urban myth to a funny exchange between either William James or Bertrand Russell and an old lady who insisted that the world is held aloft on a giant turtle; when the myth-mouthpiece of James/Russell asks who holds aloft the turtle, the old lady replies: 'Why, it's turtles all the way down!'). Generally, those who buy into talk of ontological dependence deny that there can be such situations, arguing that everything that is non-fundamental must ultimately depend upon something fundamental.

Fundamentalists believe that ontology should be less about what exists and more about what fundamentally exists. There are many reasons for this (and some fundamentalists do leave open that questions about mere existence are just as pressing), but here are just two motivations to help maintain focus. First, as the fundamental entities are the entities that are, ultimately, responsible for everything, it is clear that ontologists should be primarily interested in them. After all, surely isn't discovering the ultimate explanation of reality exactly the sort of thing that metaphysics is meant to be doing? So ontology should be mainly concerned with that ultimate explanation and the entities that play a role in it, that is, interested, if not exclusively then almost entirely, with the fundamental existents. Second, fundamentalists usually take a deflationary stance towards mere existential questions like those this book has been concerned with thus far. Just like the permissivist from chapter 1, they think it is uncontroversial which entities exist: numbers clearly exist as 'There is a prime number between 5 and 11' is a true statement; fictional characters clearly exist as 'Sherlock Holmes is a detective' entails that there's at least one fictional character etc. But they distinguish themselves from the permissivist by saying that questions about what fundamentally exists are nowhere near as easy to answer – ontology has a serious and non-trivial task in determining what things count as the fundamental existents that explain everything else. For whilst a fundamentalist might think numbers exist, they are far more concerned with whether they fundamentally exist – which they very well may not, for their existence may be explained by facts that have nothing to do with the numbers themselves existing. In this sense, you may find them saying that they have ontologically reduced the derivative entities down to the entities that they depend upon. There is, then, (at least) one other way to carry out ontological reductions besides *identifying* the entities to be reduced with other entities in your ontology (which is how we've been using the term since chapter 2); we could instead say that one entity is reduced to another if the former ontologically depends upon the latter.

If we agreed with the fundamentalist over these issues, no longer would we need to concern ourselves with whether there were abstract objects (for of course there are!); or whether there were regions of spacetime (for there are clearly many!); or whether there are statues and lumps of clay (for denying such a thing would be absurd!). Indeed, this entire book instead should have dwelled on whether or not these things were fundamental. So we might think that we can explain the existence of numbers and other abstracta solely in terms of concrete entities, or that no regions really exist for their existence is explained by the (fundamental) state of affairs of entities being spatiotemporally related to one another, or that no statues or lumps fundamentally exist and instead the only fundamental existents are, for example, tiny subatomic particles with no parts. So how a fundamentalist practises ontology is substantially different from what we've seen thus far.

Is fundamentality intelligible?

Before we move on to an example of fundamentalism in action, look at a detractor of fundamentalism. Not everyone agrees with the fundamentalist that ontology should be exclusively about what fundamentally exists as opposed to what merely exists. Many say that they just don't understand what ontological dependence is meant to be. Indeed, as the various terms such as '__ is fundamental', '__ exists in virtue of __ existing', 'entity __ grounds the existence of entity __' can (to varying extents) be inter-defined, those opposed to fundamentalism have to not just fail to understand ontological dependence but also to fail to understand those cognate terms as well (e.g., if you understand what it is for one thing to exist in virtue of another, you understand ontological dependence, for x depends on $y =_{df} x$ exists (at least) partly in virtue of y). As with metaphysical explanation, there are worries that all of these terms are made-up nonsense words which have no place in a serious discipline. The fundamentalist, they say, has to make more of an effort to demonstrate what ontological dependence (or some cognate notion) is, and why we should think that items in the world all depend on some fundamental entities.

Fundamentalists are not shy on this matter. The main tactic they use to help explicate what ontological dependence is (or what fundamentality is, or what it is for one thing to exist in virtue of another thing, etc.) is to give various examples which they think you should understand and which already rely upon the relation. Some cite historical precedent: if you have been fortunate enough to study the works of philosophers like Descartes, Spinoza or Aristotle, they seem to make use freely of such terms. So, the late and great philosophers certainly understood, and were interested in, fundamentality. But, unless you already hold the views of the long-dead 'late and greats' in particularly high esteem, this probably won't convince you that these things make sense. So sometimes fundamentalists instead rely on specific cases, such as Plato's **Euthyphro Dilemma**, which you might well be familiar with already. The Euthyphro Dilemma assumes that the gods exist (later Christian philosophers instead assumed a single, monotheistic, deity) and then points to the moral facts and asks whether the gods believe that the moral facts are true because those facts hold independent of what the gods believe or desire, or whether the moral facts are what they are because the gods ordained them to be that way (in the same way that one might imagine the gods ordaining that the earth is round, or that we need oxygen to respire, etc.). Even if you are a gung-ho atheist, the idea is that the scenario, even if it isn't an actual scenario, makes sense. And if this scenario makes sense, then it demonstrates that we can make sense of the fundamentalist's terms, for in the Euthyphro Dilemma we are being asked whether the moral facts hold in virtue of (or depend upon, or are more fundamental than, etc.) the opinions of the gods, or whether the opinions of the gods hold in virtue of (or depend upon, or are more fundamental than, etc.) the moral facts. So if you even *comprehend* the situation, then you must comprehend the relations involved. So, says the fundamentalist, you *do* know what it is for one thing to be more fundamental than another, and what it is for one thing to depend upon another, and what it is for one thing to exist in virtue of another, and so on. Similarly, fundamentalists often cite other examples where those relations hold. Isn't it obvious, they say, that the statue depends upon its atoms, or a set (e.g., {Brad Pitt}) depends upon its members (e.g., Brad Pitt)? Or they might talk about truthmaking, for if you believe in truthmaking, then you believe that some things – the truthmakers – are the fundamental entities of the universe that make true all of the propositions. So if you understand any of these things, it follows that you understand what it is for there to be fundamental truths and what it is for there to be derivative truths. Just as clearly, the fundamentalist thinks you should then see that these entities are the true focus of ontology.

Are there really any musical works?

So set aside worries about the enterprise making sense and instead turn to seeing it in action. We can see a good example of how the introduction of fundamentality might be thought to work in ontology by referring to the ontology of works of music. Ross Cameron, for instance, offers such a theory. Take a sentence like:

'Beethoven created *Piano Sonata No. 14* in 1801.'

Cameron says that, clearly, this sentence is true. It also entails that musical works exist (for there is at least one: that work created by Beethoven). However, Cameron doesn't think that we need to go as

far as including any musical works in our ontology. Cameron thinks
that we are only ontologically committed to those things which it
would take to make the above sentence true, and he doesn't think
that includes works of music. Rather, Cameron considers an ontology of abstract sound structures and says that all it takes for a
sentence, like the above, to be true is for a composer to indicate the
work during the process of composition. When the composer brings
our attention to that musical work, by laying down the musical
score, that is the truthmaker for the sentence. We don't need,
in addition, for there to exist a fundamental entity that is the
musical work.

Note three things. First, note the difference between Cameron's
theory and both Dodd's and Levinson's. Cameron has an ontology
of abstract sound structures. This is like Dodd's theory. But, unlike
Dodd, these abstract sound structures aren't musical works (for
there aren't any in his ontology!). Cameron's theory has composers
indicating certain sound structures. This is like Levinson's theory.
But, unlike Levinson's theory, this act of indication doesn't bring
about the existence of a new Type (nor is there any Type which is
identical to a musical work). Whilst, like Dodd's and Levinson's
theory, talk of sound structures and indication features in Cameron's theory, neither a sound structure Type, nor some special indicated Type, ends up being a musical work. Far from it. It is merely
that a composer's act of indicating a sound structure is the truthmaker for the (true) sentences in English about there being musical
works and Beethoven having made a particular work of music back
in 1801.

Second, Cameron makes a distinction between what exists and
what we're ontologically committed to. For Cameron, what exists
is a trivial matter – clearly works of music (and numbers, and properties, and regions, and statues, etc.) exist. But what matters in
ontology – what we should be worried about when we discuss
ontological commitment – are just those fundamental items of our
ontology. And we figure out what those fundamental entities are by
identifying them with the truthmakers of the English sentences. So
Cameron thinks that we can capture both the common-sense intuition that musical works come to exist (for the sentence about
Beethoven creating *Piano Sonata No. 14* is true), as well as the metaphysician's intuition that we should not ontologically commit to
abstract entities that pop into existence (for there are no musical
works at all in Cameron's ontology).

Third, in a sense, Cameron believes *both* that there are musical works and that there aren't. You might smell a contradiction in this, but Cameron believes that there is none. Cameron certainly believes the English sentence 'There are musical works' is true, but when he says that there aren't any musical works, he believes he's uttering that sentence in a different language. Indeed, it's a common theme in recent ontology that metaphysicians are speaking a special, attenuated language when they discuss matters metaphysical. Call this language, as many do, **Ontologese**. Ontologese, unlike English, is stipulated to be the language that better captures the fundamental nature of reality. This is unlike English for, the fundamentalist will say, English is quite bad at picking out the fundamental entities, for English has many sentences that quantify over mere, non-fundamental, existents (like works of music!). Ontologese, on the other hand, specifically aims at only picking out the fundamental facts. In the same way that the technical vocabulary of, say, physics only picks out natural, physical properties and relations (so talks about particles being charged or spinning up), and does not include other properties (so does not mention romantic relations or the property of being a rock star), Ontologese is that language which features only talk about fundamental entities, properties and relations. And, as it is not a fundamental fact that 'There are works of music', then, in Ontologese, that sentence is false. So there's no contradiction in what Cameron says, any more than there's a contradiction in an American insisting that a food bowl at a party contains chips and a British native insisting that it doesn't. It turns out that the same phonetic sounds (e.g., 'That bowl has chips in it') means something different in American English than it does in British English. Cameron means the same here: 'There are musical works' means one thing in English (American, or British) and a totally different thing in Ontologese. Contradiction averted.

Thus, Cameron's theory seeks to reconcile competing intuitions about musical works existing and not existing (they *merely* exist, but they don't *fundamentally* exist). But notice how this is not a trite approach to ontology – even as we introduce fundamentality, we don't get out of providing any metaphysical theory for, as Cameron's theory shows, we are obliged to provide a metaphysical theory about what the fundamental entities are and how their existing explains the sentences about musical works being true.

Ontologese

You might find the idea of ontologists all speaking a special language, one that is not English but is better at picking out the salient metaphysical facts, to be somewhat bizarre. After all, you should hopefully – having got this far through the book – class yourself as an ontologist and yet you probably don't feel like you've sat through a French class or otherwise become bilingual. Some metaphysicians implicitly recognize this worry and have something to say about Ontologese and how it is that you end up speaking it. We'll look at an explanation of Ontologese by Ted Sider. It's somewhat more complicated than most of the ideas we've looked at, so I've put it in this boxed text – you can ignore it if you want!

Start by talking about **naturalness**. We might think that some predicates are better at 'carving nature at the joints' – that is, they are better at picking out natural facts about the world. So the predicate '__ is charged', which applies to charged electrons, is a very natural predicate – one well aligned with the joints in the world. Whereas the predicate '__ is a rock star' is not. Indeed, we can make up predicates. I might say that '__ is a *schmergan*' applies to anything that is a cat or that is currently within five metres of Brad Pitt. So many people have *schmergans* as pets, and there are also lots and lots of *schmergans*, which aren't feline in nature, near Brad Pitt. It would be a bizarre predicate to use, but there are no constraints on what pieces of language we can coin the meaning of. At best, we might say, *schmergan*ing is just a very unnatural predicate. So the naturalness of predicates can be ranked, and some predicates are more natural than others. Moreover, it seems intuitive that the natural facts about the world explain the unnatural ones. Take a cat – that it is a cat explains why it is a *schmergan*, not the other way around!

Some fundamentalists have taken this idea further. They think that not only predicates come in orders of naturalness, but that quantifiers do too! So, as with Neo-Carnapianism, there are lots of different quantifiers. But, unlike Neo-Carnapianism, Sider argues that one of those quantifiers is special: it is the most natural quantifier. So whilst Neo-Carnapians think that there being lots of different quantifiers means that metaphysics is basically a damp squib, the fundamentalist thinks that the different quantifiers allow him to explain what Ontologese is: it is that language that exclusively uses the most natural quantifier (and most natural predicates and relations, etc.). So, in English, when we assert that there are statues or numbers, we use one quantifier (use $\exists_E$ to represent the English quantifier) and assert the following, true, proposition:

$$\exists_E x \ (x \text{ is a statue}).$$

But there's the most natural quantifier, which Ontologese uses (use $\exists_o$), where it's true to assert:

$$\sim \exists_o x \ (x \text{ is a statue}).$$

And, as the natural facts explain all of the unnatural ones, whilst it is a fact that, in English, there are statues, this is explained by (the exceedingly natural) facts expressed in Ontologese, e.g., that there are lots of subatomic mereological simples arranged statue-wise (where 'There are' is Ontologese's '$\exists_o$'). No wonder, then, that it seems natural to think that we should be interested in what facts are captured in Ontologese, for it is the facts that this language expresses which – in being the most natural facts – explain every other fact that there is. Moreover, it's now clear how we end up managing to speak Ontologese without having to sit through the equivalent of a French lesson. All we need to do is stipulate that, rather than using the English quantifier, we are explicitly aiming at using the most natural existential quantifier. So whilst we *sound* as if we're speaking English (after all, we seem to be saying things that use English words), we're now speaking a different language using the quantifier of Ontologese.

Priority monism and other alternative theories

Nor is Cameron the only fundamentalist. We can easily imagine alternatives along the same lines. For instance, we might imagine a similar theory but where the truthmaker for the English sentences about musical works are totally different and make no mention of sound structures. If we imagine the state of affairs of Beethoven acting in a certain way, having certain mental states and being situated in a certain cultural context, and so on, that single, enormous, complex state of affairs could be the truthmaker for the sentence about Beethoven creating *Piano Sonata No. 14*, that is, be the fundamental entity that grounds the mere existence of the work of music. So we could, perhaps, live without fundamental sound structures.

Indeed, some fundamentalists consider even more radical truthmakers. We've previously discussed the idea of ontological parsimony: that we should have as few entities (or kinds of entity) in our ontology as possible. For a fundamentalist, this translates into a demand that we should have as few as possible *fundamental* entities (or fundamental kinds of entity) in our ontology. One way to meet this demand would be for there to be only one fundamental entity, that is, the universe itself. Jonathan Schaffer (amongst others) has argued for this thesis, which he calls **priority monism**. Where we normally think that the parts of an object are more fundamental than the whole, Schaffer argues that we should think the reverse. Rather than thinking that, say, you and I (and mountains and galaxies, etc.) ontologically depend upon our atoms, and in turn that the universe depends upon things like you and I (and mountains and galaxies and all of the other things that are a part of the universe), we should think that the parts depend upon the whole: my atoms depend upon me; your atoms depend upon you; and we both further depend upon the universe (for we are both parts of the universe). And there are reasons for believing priority monism besides considerations of mere ontological parsimony. For instance, return to the possibility of atomless gunk (see chapter 8). The fundamentalist intuition that the tiniest subatomic particles are the fundamental entities breaks down in a world containing atomless gunk (which, recall from chapter 8, might well be our world!). In such a world, there are no tiniest things, and so no fundamental entities – but there *have* to be fundamental entities in order to explain the rest of the universe (i.e., it cannot be 'turtles all the way down'). Schaffer argues that, as the possibility of gunk is eminently plausible, we should instead give up on the intuition that the tiny things are fundamental. Instead, we should say that the entire universe is fundamental and that parts depend upon their wholes, rather than vice versa. Now there's no problem: gunk can exist, for it all ontologically depends on the fundamental universe (which explains the existence and nature of everything). Priority monists have other arguments as well (e.g., Schaffer pulls in quantum physics to help defend his position, an argument too complex to detail here) but this gives some idea of how priority monism might be defended.

Moreover, with priority monism in place, we can see how we might account for the existence of things like musical works. To see how, first imagine a flatland universe that was nothing but a flat, black polka-dotted plane. If we pointed at a certain region of that plane, r, where r lay within one of the polka dots, and asked why r was black, what would the fundamentalist say? Regular, non-priority monists would say that this is explained by a certain part of the plane being black. But the priority monist cannot say this. The explanatory burden has to be shouldered by the fundamental entities – that's what they're there for! – so, as only the universe is fundamental, a *part* of that universe can't be the ultimate explanation of r being black. Here, priority monists tend to rely upon distributional properties (recall they were deployed in chapter 7 to help with concerns to do with presentism). The universe instantiates some fundamental distributional property of it having a certain variation of colour. And that distributional property is such that anything instantiating it is black at region r. Similarly, we can see how to extend this to more complex situations. In our world, we might ask what is the (metaphysical) explanation for the Eiffel Tower existing. The priority monist will reply that the world instantiating a certain distributional property, such that the world is 'Eiffel Towerly' in a certain place (in a similar way that you can have a polka-dotted distributional property that makes you black in certain places and white in others), is what explains this. So now turn to musical works. Where Cameron has argued that acts of indicating sound structures are truthmakers for musical works existing, priority monists can say that a world that has the distributional property that our world has (e.g., that is distributed such that Beethoven is doing what he's doing back in 1801; that is distributed such that pieces of paper have certain musical notes scrawled upon them; that is distributed such that the audience of a performance of the sonata is doing what it is doing, etc.) must be a world where it's true that musical works like *Piano Sonata No. 14* exist. So the world instantiating the distributional property it instantiates is the explanation of why musical works exist. That is, the explanation of works of music existing at our world is analogous to the case of the flatland universe instantiating the polka-dotted distributional property being an explanation of why a particular region is black (except that, rather than the universe instantiating the distributional property explaining the existence of a black polka dot, it explains the existence of a musical work). So there are more varieties of fundamentalism out there, and more variety over exactly what entities and facts end up being fundamental.

Further reading

A good introduction to the ontology of music is by Julian Dodd (2008), and you might also want to look at chapter 4 of Peter Kivy's 2004 and chapter 8 of Jerrold Levinson's 2003. Dodd's own theory is given in his 2007. Ben Caplan and Carl Matheson argue for musical perdurantism in numerous articles in the *British Journal of Aesthetics*, starting with their 2004 article (in which they also argue against the creatability thesis). Levinson gives his defence of his classic theory in his 1980 article. Alternative ontologies include work by Andrew Kania (2006), Peter Lamarque (2002) and Guy Rohrbaugh (2003). Chris Tillman concentrates on works as material objects in his 2011 article. Anti-realist approaches include fictionalist attempts (e.g., Kania (2008)) and attacks on the enterprise as a whole (such as that by Aaron Ridley (2003)).

Cian Dorr introduces 'Ontologese' in his 2005 chapter, and fundamentality is further discussed by the likes of Kit Fine (2001), Ross Cameron (2010), Jonathan Schaffer (2009a) and Ted Sider (2009) (who gives a similar, but substantially different, theory in his 2011 book). Sceptics about fundamentality include Thomas Hofweber (2009a) whilst Stefano Predelli (2009) is sceptical about it with particular reference to Cameron's deployment of it to musical works. Cameron argues for his theory about musical works in his 2008 paper, although you might find reading others of his works fruitful as well (particularly as what he says in other papers heavily modifies the theory described in this chapter). Schaffer's priority monism is defended in his 2010 paper.

Finally, any self-respecting ontologist (which, having finished this book, you should hopefully count yourself) should listen to everything that the *The 21st Century Monads* ever composed (http://the21stcenturymonads.net/).

References

Armstrong, D. (1989a). *Universals: An Opinionated Introduction*, Boulder: Westview Press.

Armstrong, D. (1989b). *A Combinatorial Theory of Possibility*, Cambridge: Cambridge University Press.

Armstrong, D. (1997). *A World of States of Affairs*, Cambridge: Cambridge University Press.

Armstrong, D. (2004). *Truth and Truthmakers*, Cambridge: Cambridge University Press.

Aune, B. (1985). *Metaphysics: The Elements*, Minneapolis: University of Minnesota Press.

Ayer, M. (1974). Individuals without Sortals, *Canadian Journal of Philosophy* 4: 113–48.

Baker, L. (2008). A Metaphysics of Ordinary Things and Why We Need Them, *Philosophy* 83: 5–24.

Belot, G. (1999). Rehabilitating Relationism, *International Studies in the Philosophy of Science* 13: 35–52.

Benacerraf, P. (1965). What Numbers Could Not Be, *Philosophical Review* 74: 47–73.

Bennett, K. (2004). Spatio-Temporal Coincidence and the Grounding Problem, *Philosophical Studies* 118: 339–71.

Bennett, K. (2009). Composition, Colocation, and Metaontology, in D. Chalmers, D. Manley and R. Wasserman (eds), *Metametaphysics*, Oxford: Oxford University Press.

Bergmann, M. and Brower, J. (2006). A Theistic Argument against Platonism (and in Support of Truthmakers and Divine Simplicity), *Oxford Studies in Metaphysics* 2: 357–86.

Bigelow, J. (1988). *The Reality of Numbers*, Oxford: Clarendon Press.

Bigelow, J. and Pargetter, R. (2006). Real Work for Aggregates, *dialectica* 60: 485–503.

Black, M. (1971). The Elusiveness of Sets, *Review of Metaphysics* 24: 614–36.

Bohn, E. (2009). An Argument against the Necessity of Unrestricted Composition, *Analysis* 69: 27–31.

Bourne, C. (2006). *A Future for Presentism*, Oxford: Oxford University Press.

Bricker, P. (2001). Island Universes and the Analysis of Modality, in G. Preyer and F. Siebelt (eds), *Reality and Humean Supervenience*, Lanham: Rowman and Littlefield.

Bricker, P. (2006). Absolute Actuality and the Plurality of Worlds, *Philosophical Perspectives* 20: 41–76.

Burke, M. (1992). Copper Statues and Pieces of Copper: A Challenge to the Standard Account, *Analysis* 52: 12–17.

Burke, M. (1994). Preserving the Principle of One Object to a Place: A Novel Account of the Relations among Objects, Sorts, Sortals, and Persistence Conditions, *Philosophy and Phenomenological Research* 54: 591–624.

Cameron, R. (2008). There are No Things that are Musical Works, *British Journal of Aesthetics* 48: 295–314.

Cameron, R. (2010). Quantification, Naturalness and Ontology, in A. Hazlett (ed.), *New Waves in Metaphysics*, New York: Palgrave-Macmillan.

Cameron, R. (2011). Truthmaking for Presentists, *Oxford Studies in Metaphysics* 6: 55–100.

Campbell, K. (1990). *Abstract Particulars*, Oxford: Blackwell.

Caplan, B. and Matheson, C. (2004). Can a Musical Work be Created? *British Journal of Aesthetics* 44: 113–34.

Carter, W. (1997). Dion's Left Foot (and the Price of Burkean Economy), *Philosophy and Phenomenological Research* 57: 371–9.

Casati, R. (2009). Minor Entities: Surfaces, Holes and Shadows, in R. Le Poidevin et al. (eds), *The Routledge Companion to Metaphysics*, London: Routledge.

Casati, R. and Varzi, A. (1994). *Holes and Other Superficialities*, London: MIT Press.

Chihara, C. (1990). *Constructability and Mathematical Existence*, Oxford: Oxford University Press.

Chihara, C. (2007). *A Structural Account of Mathematics*, Oxford: Oxford University Press.

Chisholm, R. (1973). Beyond Being and Nonbeing, *Philosophical Studies* 24: 245–57.

Comesaña, J. (2008). Could There Be Exactly Two Things? *Synthese* 162: 31–5.

Craig, W. (2001). *Time and the Metaphysics of Relativity*, London: Kluwer.

Crisp, T. (2003). Presentism, in M. J. Loux and D. W. Zimmerman (eds), *The Oxford Handbook of Metaphysics*, Oxford: Oxford University Press.

Dainton, B. (2010). *Time and Space*, Chesham: Acumen.

DeRosset, L. (2009a). Possible Worlds I: Modal Realism, *Philosophy Compass* 4/6: 998–1008.

DeRosset, L. (2009b). Possible Worlds II: Non-Reductive Theories of Possible Worlds, *Philosophy Compass* 4(6): 1009–21.

Deutsch, H. (2007). Relative Identity, *Stanford Encyclopedia of Philosophy*, at http://plato.stanford.edu/archives/win2008/entries/identity-relative, accessed 5 November 2012.

Divers, J. (2002). *Possible Worlds*, London: Routledge.

Divers, J. (2004). Agnosticism about Other Worlds: A New Antirealist Programme in Modality, *Philosophy and Phenomenological Research* 69: 660–85.

Divers, J. (2006). Possible World Semantics without Possible Worlds: The Agnostic Approach, *Mind* 115: 187–226.

Divers, J. and Melia, J. (2002). The Analytic Limit of Genuine Modal Realism, *Mind* 111: 15–36.

Dodd, J. (2007). *Works of Music*, Oxford: Oxford University Press.

Dodd, J. (2008). Musical Works: Ontology and Meta-Ontology, *Philosophy Compass*, 3(6): 1113–34.

Dorr, C. (2005). What We Disagree about When We Disagree about Ontology, in M. E. Kalderon (ed.), *Fictionalism in Metaphysics*, Oxford: Oxford University Press.

Earman, J. (1989). *World Enough and Space-Time*, MA: MIT Press.

Effingham, N. (2009). Composition, Persistence and Identity, in R. Le Poidevin et al. (eds), *The Routledge Companion to Metaphysics*, London: Routledge.

Effingham, N. (2011). Undermining Motivations for Universalism, *Noûs* 45: 696–713.

Effingham, N. (2012). Endurantism and Perdurantism, in N. Manson and R. W. Barnard (eds), *The Continuum Companion to Metaphysics*, London: Continuum.

Effingham, N. and Robson, J. (2007). A Mereological Challenge to Endurantism, *Australasian Journal of Philosophy* 85: 633–40.

Efird, D. and Stoneham, T. (2005). Genuine Modal Realism and the Empty Worlds, *European Journal of Analytic Philosophy* 1: 21–37.

Eklund, M. (2006). Neo-Fregean Ontology, *Philosophical Perspectives* 20: 95–121.

Eklund, M. (2009). Carnap and Ontological Pluralism, in D. Chalmers, D. Manley and R. Wasserman (eds), *Metametaphysics*, Oxford: Oxford University Press.

Field, H. (1980). *Science without Numbers*, Oxford: Blackwell.

Fine, K. (2001). The Question of Realism, *Philosopher's Imprint* 1: 1–30.

Friend, M. (2007). *Introducing Philosophy of Mathematics*, Chesham: Acumen.

Gallois, A. (1998). *Occasions of Identity*, Oxford: Oxford University Press.

Geach, P. (1967). Identity, *The Review of Metaphysics* 21: 3–12.

George, A. and Velleman, D. (2002). *Philosophies of Mathematics*, Oxford: Blackwell.

Gilmore, C. (2007). Time Travel, Coinciding Objects and Persistence, *Oxford Studies in Metaphysics* 3: 177–200.

Gilmore, C. (2009). Persistence and Location in Relativistic Spacetime, *Philosophy Compass* 3(6): 1224–54.

Girle, R. (2003). *Possible Worlds*, Chesham: Acumen.

Goodman, N. and Quine, W. (1947) Steps Towards a Constructive Nominalism, *Journal of Symbolic Logic* 12(4): 105–22.

Griffin, N. (1977). *Relative Identity*, Oxford: Oxford University Press.

Hart, W. (1996). *The Philosophy of Mathematics*, Oxford: Oxford University Press.

Haslanger, S. (1994). Humean Supervenience and Enduring Things, *Australasian Journal of Philosophy* 72: 339–59.

Haslanger, S. (2003). Persistence through Time, in M.J. Loux and D.W. Zimmerman (eds), *Oxford Handbook of Metaphysics*, Oxford: Oxford University Press.

Hawley, K. (2001). *How Things Persist*, Oxford: Clarendon.

Hawley, K. (2009). Metaphysics and Relativity, in R. Le Poidevin et al. (eds), *The Routledge Companion to Metaphysics*, London: Routledge.

Hawley, K. (2010). Temporal Parts, *Stanford Encyclopedia of Philosophy*, at http://plato.stanford.edu/archives/win2010/entries/temporal-parts, accessed 5 November 2012.

Hawthorne, J. (2006). Plenitude, Convention, and Ontology, in J. Hawthorne, *Metaphysical Essays*, Oxford: Oxford University Press.

Heller, M. (1991). *The Ontology of Physical Objects: Four-Dimensional Hunks of Matter*, Cambridge: Cambridge University Press.

Heller, M. (2003). The Immorality of Modal Realism, or: How I Learnt to Stop Worrying and Let the Children Drown, *Philosophical Studies* 114: 1–22.

Hirsch, E. (2005). Physical-Object Ontology, Verbal Disputes, and Common Sense, *Philosophy and Phenomenological Research* 70: 67–97.

Hofweber, T. (2005). A Puzzle about Ontology, *Noûs* 39: 256–83.

Hofweber, T. (2009a). Ambitious, yet Modest, Metaphysics, in D. Chalmers, D. Manley and R. Wasserman (eds), *Metametaphysics*, Oxford: Oxford University Press.

Hofweber, T. (2009b). The Meta-Problem of Change, *Noûs*, 43: 286–314.

Hooker, C. (1971). The Relational Doctrines of Space and Time, *British Journal of Philosophy of Science* 22: 97–130.

Huemer, M. (2009). When is Parsimony a Virtue? *Philosophical Quarterly* 59: 216–36.

Huggett, N. (1999). *Space from Zeno to Einstein*, Cambridge, MA: MIT Press.

Jackson, F. (1977a). *Perception: A Representative Theory*, Cambridge: Cambridge University Press.

Jackson, F. (1977b). Statements about Universals, *Mind* 86: 427–9.

Jackson, F. and Priest, G. (eds) (2004). *Lewisian Themes*, Oxford: Oxford University Press.

Jubien, M. (2007). Analysing Modality, *Oxford Studies in Metaphysics* 3: 99–139.

Kania, A. (2006). Making Tracks: The Ontology of Rock Music, *The Journal of Aesthetics and Art Criticism* 64: 401–14.

Kania, A. (2008). Piece for the End of Time: In Defense of Musical Ontology, *British Journal of Aesthetics* 48: 65–79.

Keller, S. (2004). Presentism and Truthmaking, *Oxford Studies in Metaphysics* 1: 83–104.

Kivy, P. (ed.) (2004). *The Blackwell Guide to Aesthetics*, Oxford: Blackwell.

Korman, D. (2010a). Strange Kinds, Familiar Kinds, and the Charge of Arbitrariness, *Oxford Studies in Metaphysics* 5: 119–44.

Korman, D. (2010b). The Argument from Vagueness, *Philosophy Compass* 5(10): 891–901.

Kriegel, U. (2008). Composition as a Secondary Quality, *Pacific Philosophical Quarterly* 89: 359–83.

Lamarque, P. (2002). Work and Object, *Proceedings of the Aristotelian Society* 102: 141–62.

Laurence, S. and Macdonald, C. (eds) (1998). *Contemporary Readings in the Foundations of Metaphysics*, Oxford: Blackwell.

Leftow, B. (2006). God and the Problem of Universals, *Oxford Studies in Metaphysics* 2: 325–56

Levinson, J. (1980). What a Musical Work Is, *Journal of Philosophy* 77: 5–28.

Levinson, J. (ed.) (2003). *The Oxford Handbook of Aesthetics*, Oxford: Oxford University Press.

Lewis, D. (1983). New Work for a Theory of Universals, *Australasian Journal of Philosophy* 61: 343–77.

Lewis, D. (1986). *On the Plurality of Worlds*, Oxford: Blackwell.

Lewis, D. (1990a). *Parts of Classes*, Oxford: Blackwell.

Lewis, D. (1990b). Noeism or Allism? *Mind* 99: 23–31.

Lewis, D. and Lewis, S. (1970). Holes, *Australasian Journal of Philosophy* 48: 206–12.

Lewis, D. and Lewis, S. (1996). Review of Holes and Other Superficialities, *Philosophical Review* 105: 77–9.

Loux, M. (1979). *The Possible and the Actual: Readings in the Metaphysics of Modality*, London: Cornell University Press.

Loux, M. (1998). *Metaphysics: A Contemporary Introduction*, London: Routledge.

Loux, M. (ed.) (2001). *Metaphysics: Contemporary Readings*, London: Routledge.

Loux, M. and Zimmerman, D. (eds) (2003). *The Oxford Handbook of Metaphysics*, Oxford: Oxford University Press.

Lowe, E. Jonathan (1995). Coinciding Objects: In Defence of the 'Standard Account', *Analysis* 55: 171–8.

Lowe, E. Jonathan (2002). *A Survey of Metaphysics*, Oxford: Oxford University Press.

Lowe, E. Jonathan (2009). *More Kinds of Being*, Oxford: Blackwell.

MacBride, F. (1998). Where are Particulars and Universals? *dialectica* 52: 203–2.

MacBride, F. (2009). Universals: The Contemporary Debate, in R. Le Poidevin et al. (eds), *The Routledge Companion to Metaphysics*, London: Routledge.

Macdonald, C. (2005). *Varieties of Things: Foundations of Contemporary Metaphysics*, Oxford: Blackwell.

Maddy, P. (1990). *Realism in Mathematics*, Oxford: Clarendon Press.

Markosian, N. (1998). Brutal Composition, *Philosophical Studies* 92: 211–49.

Markosian, N. (2004). A Defense of Presentism, *Oxford Studies in Metaphysics* 1: 47–82.

Markosian, N. (2007). Restricted Composition, in T. Sider, J. Hawthorne and D.W. Zimmerman (eds), *Contemporary Debates in Metaphysics*, Oxford: Blackwell.

Maudlin, T. (1993). Buckets of Water and Waves of Space: Why Spacetime is Probably a Substance, *Philosophy of Science* 60: 183–203.

Maudlin, T. (2009). Space, Absolute and Relational, in R. Le Poidevin et al. (eds), *The Routledge Companion to Metaphysics*, London: Routledge.

McCall, S. and Lowe, E. (2006). The 3D/4D Controversy: A Storm in a Teacup, *Noûs* 40: 570–8.

McDaniel, K. (2010). Parts and Wholes, *Philosophy Compass* 5(5): 412–25.

McGinn, C. (2000). *Logical Properties*, Oxford: Oxford University Press.

McGrath, M. (2007). Temporal Parts, *Philosophy Compass* 2: 730–48.

Melia, J. (1995). On What There's Not, *Analysis* 55: 223–29.

Melia, J. (2003). *Modality*, Chesham: Acumen.

Mellor, D. (2008). Micro-Composition, *Philosophy* 83: 65–80.

Mellor, D. and Oliver, A. (eds) (1997). *Properties*, Oxford: Oxford University Press.

Merricks, T. (2001). *Objects and Persons*, Oxford: Oxford University Press.

Merricks, T. (2007). *Truth and Ontology*, Oxford: Oxford University Press.

Miller, K. (2007). Immaterial Beings, *Monist* 90: 349–71.

Monton, B. (2011). Prolegomena to Any Future Physics-based Metaphysics, *Oxford Studies in Philosophy of Religion* 3: 142–65.

Moreland, J. (2001). *Universals*, Chesham: Acumen.

Myro, G. (1997). Identity and Time, in Michael Rea (ed.), *Material Constitution: A Reader*, Rowman and Littlefield Publishers: Oxford.

Nerlich, G. (1976). *The Shape of Space*, Cambridge: Cambridge University Press.

Nerlich, G. (1994). *What Spacetime Explains*, Cambridge: Cambridge University Press.

Nerlich, G. (2003). Space-time Substantivalism, in M.J. Loux and D.W. Zimmerman (eds), *The Oxford Handbook of Metaphysics*, Oxford: Oxford University Press.

Nolan, D. (1997). Quantitative Parsimony, *British Journal for the Philosophy of Science* 48: 329–43.

Nolan, D. (2011). Modal Fictionalism, *Stanford Encyclopedia of Philosophy*, at http://plato.stanford.edu/archives/sum2011/entries/fictionalism-modal, accessed 5 November 2012.

Noonan, H. (2001). The Case for Perdurance, in G. Preyer and F. Siebelt (eds), *Reality and Humean Supervenience*, Lanham: Rowman and Littlefield.

Oliver, A. (1996). The Metaphysics of Properties, *Mind* 105: 1–80.

Olson, E. (2007). *What are We? A Study in Personal Ontology*, Oxford: Oxford University Press.

Parsons, J. (2004). Distributional Properties, in F. Jackson and G. Priest (eds), *Lewisian Themes*, Oxford: Oxford University Press.

Parsons, J. (2007). The Location of Properties, *Oxford Studies in Metaphysics* 3: 201–32.

Paul, L. (2010). The Puzzles of Material Constitution, *Philosophy Compass* 5(7): 579–90.

Predelli, S. (2009). Ontologese and Musical Nihilism: A Reply to Cameron, *British Journal of Aesthetics* 49: 179–83.

Priest, G. (2005). *Towards Non-Being: The Logic and Metaphysics of Intentionality*, Oxford: Oxford University Press.

Quine, W. (1948). On What There Is, *Review of Metaphysics* 2: 21–38; reprinted in Loux (ed.), *Metaphysics: Contemporary Readings*, London: Routledge.

Rayo, A. (2007). Ontological Commitment, *Philosophy Compass* 2(3): 428–44.

Rea, M. (ed.) (1997). *Material Constitution*, Lanham: Rowman and Littlefield.

Rea, M. (1998). In Defence of Mereological Universalism, *Philosophy and Phenomenological Research* 63: 347–60.

Rea, M. (2003). Four-Dimensionalism, in M. J. Loux and D. W. Zimmerman (eds), *The Oxford Handbook of Metaphysics*, Oxford: Oxford University Press.

Resnik, M. (1997). *Mathematics as a Science of Patterns*, Oxford: Oxford University Press.

Ridley, A. (2003). Against Musical Ontology, *The Journal of Philosophy* 100: 203–20.

Rodriguez-Pereyra, G. (2002). *Resemblance Nominalism*, Oxford: Clarendon Press.

Rodriguez-Pereyra, G. (2004). Modal Realism and Metaphysical Nihilism, *Mind* 113: 683–704.

Rodriguez-Pereya, G. (2006). Truthmakers, *Philosophy Compass* 1: 186–200.

Rohrbaugh, G. (2003). Artworks as Historical Individuals, *European Journal of Philosophy* 11: 177–205.

Rosen, G. (1990). Modal Fictionalism, *Mind* 99: 327–54.

Rosen, G. and Dorr, C. (2002). Composition as Fiction, in Gale (ed.), *The Blackwell Guide to Metaphysics*, Oxford: Blackwell.

Schaffer, J. (2009a). On What Grounds What, in D. Chalmers, D. Manley and R. Wasserman (eds), *Metametaphysics*, Oxford: Oxford University Press.

Schaffer, J. (2009b). Spacetime the One Substance, *Philosophical Studies* 145: 131–48.

Schaffer, J. (2010). Monism: The Priority of the Whole, *Philosophical Review* 119: 31–76.

Shapiro, S. (2000). *Thinking about Mathematics: The Philosophy of Mathematics*, Oxford: Oxford University Press.

Sheehy, P. (2006). Theism and Modal Realism, *Religious Studies* 42: 315–28.

Sider, T. (1993). Van Inwagen and the Possibility of Gunk, *Analysis* 53: 285–89.

Sider, T. (2001). *Four-Dimensionalism: An Ontology of Persistence and Time*, Oxford: Oxford University Press.

Sider, T. (2009). Ontological Realism, in D. Chalmers, D. Manley and R. Wasserman (eds), *Metametaphysics*, Oxford: Oxford University Press.

Sider, T. (2011). *Writing the Book of the World*, Oxford: Oxford University Press.

Sider, T., Hawthorne, J. and Zimmerman, D. W. (eds) (2007). *Contemporary Debates in Metaphysics*, Malden: Blackwell.

Sklar, L. (1992). *Philosophy of Physics*, Oxford: Oxford University Press.

Sober, E. (1981) The Principle of Parsimony, *The British Journal for the Philosophy of Science* 32: 145–56.

Swoyer, C. (2008). Abstract Entities, in T. Sider, J. Hawthorne and D. Zimmerman (eds), *Contemporary Debates in Metaphysics*, Oxford: Blackwell.

Tallant, J. (2011). *Metaphysics: An Introduction*, London: Continuum.

Teller, P. (1991). Substance, Relations and Arguments about the Nature of Space-Time, *The Philosophical Review* 100: 363–97.

Thomasson, A. (2010a). *Ordinary Objects*, Oxford: Oxford University Press.

Thomasson, A. (2010b). The Controversy over the Existence of Ordinary Objects, *Philosophy Compass* 5(7): 591–601.

Thomson, J. (1998). The Statue and the Clay, *Noûs* 32(2): 149–73.

Tillman, C. (2011). Musical materialism, *British Journal of Aesthetics* 51: 13–29.

Tooley, M. (1997). *Time, Tense and Causation*, Oxford: Oxford University Press.

van Cleve, J. (1994). Predication without Universals? A Fling with Ostrich Nominalism, *Philosophy and Phenomenological Research* 54: 577–90.

van Inwagen, P. (1990). *Material Beings*, Ithaca: Cornell University Press.

van Inwagen, P. (1998). Meta-Ontology, *Erkenntnis* 48: 233–50.

Vetter, B. (2011). Recent Work: Modality without Possible Worlds, *Analysis* 71: 742–54.

Wake, A., Spencer, J. and Fowler, G. (2007). Holes as Regions of Spacetime, *Monist* 90: 372–78.

Wasserman, R. (2002). The Standard Objection to the Standard Account, *Philosophical Studies* 111: 197–216.

Wasserman, R. (2006). The Problem of Change, *Philosophy Compass* 1(1): 48–57.

Wasserman, R. (2009). Material Constitution, *Stanford Encyclopedia of Philosophy*, at http://plato.stanford.edu/archives/sum2012/entries/material-constitution, accessed 5 November 2012.

Wasserman, R., Hawthorne, J. and Scala, M. (2004). Recombination, Causal Constraints and Humean Supervenience: An Argument for Temporal Parts? *Oxford Studies in Metaphysics* 1: 301–18.

Wiggins, D. (2001). *Sameness and Substance Renewed*, Cambridge: Cambridge University Press.

Williams, R. (2006). Illusions of Gunk, *Philosophical Perspectives* 20: 494–513.

Zammiello, F. (2001). The Logic of Burke's Sortal Essentialism, *Pacific Philosophical Quarterly* 82: 71–86.

Zimmerman, D. (2008). The Privileged Present: Defending an 'A-Theory' of Time, in T. Sider, J. Hawthorne and D. W. Zimmerman (eds), *Contemporary Debates in Metaphysics*, Oxford: Blackwell.

Index

Made in the USA
Monee, IL
10 February 2023

27460435R10131